She Searches For Monsters To Destroy

AMERICA AND THE ETERNAL
RECURRENCE OF UNNECESSARY WARS

Richard Morchoe

Copyright © 2021 by Richard Morchoe.

All rights reserved. No part of this publication may be reproduced, distributed or transmitted in any form or by any means, including photocopying, recording, or other electronic or mechanical methods, without the prior written permission of the publisher, except in the case of brief quotations embodied in critical reviews and certain other noncommercial uses permitted by copyright law.

Published in the United States by
Mora Press
PO Box 691
West Brookfield, MA 01585
Morapress.com

Contents

Introduction	1
King Philip's War	4
The American Revolution or One Becomes Two	7
The Quasi-War	12
The Barbary Wars	19
The War of 1812	28
John Quincy Adams and the Monroe Doctrine	38
Fifty-four Forty or Fight –The Oregon Boundary Dispute	43
The Mexican War	46
The Civil War	56
Foreign Policy After the Civil War 1865 to 1895	57
Hawaii	61
The Spanish-American War or Imperialism Really Takes Wing	64
The Panama Canal	69
World War I	73
The Interwar Years	82
World War II	90
The Cold War Arrives	107
Korea	109
The 1950s	113
Cuba Heats Up	121
The Berlin Crisis of 1961	125
The Vietnam War	128
Post-Vietnam	141
The Reagan Revolution	146
The Elder Bush Presidency	159
The Clinton Administration	172
George W. Bush and The Beginning of The Eternal War	183
The Second Iraq War	190
Libya	204
Syria	213
Iran	224
Russia	235
China	263

Africom	278
Venezuela	283
NATO	287
The Press and the Punditocracy	294
Finance, Sanctions, Bankruptcy	318
Force Structure	326
In Conclusion	337
Addendum, August 29, 2021	352
Acknowledgments	353
About the Author	354
Bibliography	356

Introduction

Even before our country became a country we were involved in wars. As it turns out, on reflection, not all wars were necessary. In fact, most could have been avoided. The problem was and is plain: reflection rarely happens before the fact.

The title of this volume, *She Searches For Monsters To Destroy*, refers to the words of President John Quincy Adams where he averred that our republic does not do that. It's no surprise that when we look to problems in foreign parts, we must rationalize fiendishness in any opponent.

A war slogan that suggested the banks will love this war, or the arms manufacturers will do well, is not the stuff to bring the young and fit to the colors. Demonizing the Hun or making out the Spaniard as dastardly murderers of sailors might get things moving.

It happens again and again.

The subtitle, *America and the Eternal Recurrence of Unnecessary Wars*, isn't intended as a reference to Nietzsche's thought, but if past is prologue, we shall keep finding conflicts that do nothing for the nation or the people as long as the republic endures—unless we change.

She Goes Abroad in Search of Monsters To Destroy looks at America's record of war. For the most part, the conflicts with foreign nations were avoidable and not to our benefit. That is not to say no one did well out of them, rather that the nation and people were, for the most part, ill served. The kindest thing one can say of those who promoted them is they were guilty of bad judgment at best and self-serving at worst.

Much of the long sweep of American foreign policy has been one of a mistake and then a mistake to correct the first mistake. The compounding of errors has not yet been fatal, if only because our enemies have been unable to match us in firepower and resources or have surpassed our incompetence.

There has been much made of "American Exceptionalism" in the early years of the twenty-first century. Somehow we are a special country and different, and by inference better than others. Loving my land as I do, I do believe it is special, at least to me. There is nowhere else I would rather live. Does that mean there's a qualitative difference between the United States of America and the rest of the world?

Yes, at least in the sense that there's a difference in quality between any two nations. In the sense of a specialness that makes us better, a citizen should hope so. The question of this book comes down to this: Does this mean our nation is not subject to historical forces that have beset other countries? Does a foreign policy of interference in other nations run chance of eventual disaster?

Yet, we continue to have troops in numerous other countries. In Afghanistan, the nation's longest war, there was not rhyme or reason left, but we stayed on.

Can this go on forever? Maybe, but we should look at where we have been and think about where we are and where we are going.

Briefly, during Vietnam and shortly after, there was a questioning of the American military industrial complex by liberals. Today, there is almost no reflection by the neoliberal and neoconservative combine of the war machine.

Someone should have written this book a long time ago. Maybe they have. Still, I have looked and haven't come across anything that has examined the foreign wars we have fought since becoming a republic as a whole. Someone could've done it better, and one would wish they had.

It is past time.

This is not a work of a famous historian, or a historian at all. The reputations of Thucydides, Herodotus, Flavius Josephus, Gibbon, William H. Prescott, Crane Brinton and others are not in danger. Instead, this book is an assertion of a truth that stands on its own.

1

King Philip's War

America's first wars occurred before we were even a nation. The English settlers pursued foreign policy as an interest of the Crown, at least nominally. As a New Englander, we will look at the conflicts that happened between the native populations that were already here, and the colonists.

In 1620, when the Pilgrims arrived at Plymouth, they were not opposed by the most important native chieftain, Massasoit, because he needed them. His tribe, the Wampanoag, and its allies had been devastated by outbreaks of smallpox. The "greatest commander of the country" was hard pressed by neighboring Narragansett and was happy for a treaty with allies who could make his position less precarious. If ever there was a Faustian bargain, this was it.

As the English prospered, Massasoit's position was secure against other tribes, but the colonies' power versus the Wampanoag waxed more and more. On the lower Connecticut River, the powerful Pequot tribe had been brutally destroyed by the allied English colonists. It was a lesson in English power that didn't go unnoticed by the various tribes though it did not lead to unity.

If any factor made war between the colonists and native tribes inevitable, it was English land hunger. Growth in population, due both to immigration and a baby boom, could only exacerbate a desire for more settler *Lebensraum*. The land hunger was described by Roger Williams as a "depraved appetite after... great portions of land... This was one of the great gods of New England."

The English observed all the legalistic forms of land acquisition. Deeds were signed and amounts were paid. However, an agreement between willing buyers and sellers was not always the case—and this became apparent even more as time went on and as the consequences of loss of territory became more obvious to the tribes. Pressure and trickery were resorted to by the English to achieve the territorial imperative that demography required.

In 1675, the consequences of the years of settlement upon the natives and pressure from the English led to a drift to war. The colonial governments probably didn't realize how potent the remaining powers of resistance the Indians possessed were. The fractious tribes, understanding their peril, attained a sense of unity, albeit imperfect. The Wampanoag, who had welcomed the English to resist the Narragansett, would now ally with the latter. For the first period of the war, Indian tactics were devastating. The militia trainband system of the mother country was of little use in forest warfare.

The colonies began to understand the deficiencies of their forces and altered methods. Leaders such as Benjamin Church, who caught on to the Indian style of war, changed tactics, spreading out instead of bunching up as easy targets. It was the English strategy that was more important. They enlisted the Indians they had been abusing to fight the enemy. This would prove decisive.

Could the Indians have won? Possibly with a few more victories and a little luck, or at least a temporary peace might have been attained. At Brookfield, early in the war, they had ambushed a colonial detachment that was saved by its accompanying ill-treated Indians. Had that force been annihilated on the field and the garrison captured, the colonial government might have opened negotiations. Or they might have woken up to their deficiencies sooner.

By the end of the war, southern New England had been ethnically cleansed of its indigenous population. They had been killed, or had fled, or had been sold into slavery by the devout Calvinists.

It was, however, no victory. The alacrity with which the colonial authorities went to war had led to a struggle, though fatal to Indian society, was catastrophically costly to the English.

According to Eric B. Schultz, and Michael J. Tougias in their history of King Philip's war, "Between six hundred and eight hundred English died in battle during King Philip's War. Measured against a European population in New England of perhaps fifty-two thousand, this death rate was nearly twice that of the Civil War and more than seven times that of World War II. The English Crown sent Edmund Randolph to assess damages shortly after the war and he reported that twelve hundred homes were burned, eight thousand head of cattle lost, and vast stores of foodstuffs destroyed."

Would a people or leaders, given a vision of the devastation of their wars beforehand, have chosen a different path? Given clairvoyance in the later 1920s of the devastation of Germany after the war, it is doubtful the people would have given the National Socialist many votes. Would the Calvinists leaders have sought conciliation with the tribes if they knew how much would have been lost in their "triumph?" Was there even any possibility of enough common ground to come to an accommodation? We can never know, and any real attempt was never made. The Indians, other than remnants, were gone, and the English ruled supreme, but the people had been defeated.

2

The American Revolution or One Becomes Two

After King Philip's war, New England's foreign policy was, in the main, merged with the mother country's, as were the other colonies. England would pursue its colonial and mercantile wars with the other European powers and America would participate as part of the team. This generally worked to the benefit of the colonies, as more Indian land was opened for settlement.

The last war, known in the colonies as the French and Indian War and in Britain as the Seven Years' War, ended with France no longer a power in North America. The motherland had large debts as a result of the imperial adventures. Not without reason, Great Britain wanted the colonies to share in the burden.

The colonies were no longer faced with the French threat. The Indians might be bothersome, but were now distant from the major population centers and unable to threaten them. The colonial provinces may have seen some obligation to share some of the burden, but they were not without a conviction that they had already shared in the war's cost.

There was also the fact that British North America was not represented in Parliament. This would be a rallying cry for resistance. Whether the desire for representation or avoiding postwar costs was the major cause of the rupture may be important, but it is not the main point to be discussed. Foreign policy was now to be divided into that of the colonies and the mother country. As our first civil war led to separation it would never again be one united foreign policy. Well before the end of the conflict, there would be United States foreign policy and that of the United Kingdom.

The humorist P.J. O'Rourke wrote a short volume called *On the Wealth of Nations*, part of a "Books That Changed the World" series published by Atlantic Books. It is a discussion of the thoughts of Adam Smith who wrote *An Inquiry Into the Nature and Causes of the Wealth of Nations*. O'Rourke may not approve of it being made use of as part of a book supporting a neutral foreign policy, as he has in the main been a supporter of our overseas adventures.

Part of O'Rourke's book deals with Smith's thoughts on the contretemps between mommy country and wayward kiddie nation. Smith was not all that enthusiastic about the colonial project to begin with. He wasn't in favor of British government actions that led up to the war. He did not see Adams, Jefferson, Franklin, et al. in the same light as we do either.

O'Rourke notes that the British government consulted with Smith about the war of separation. Smith complied in a letter to Alexander Wedderburn that Wedderburn referred to as "Smiths Thoughts on the State of the Contest with America, February 1778."

Though there was probably no such thing in his day as a think tank, there was no lack of learned men who could be called on for their thoughts. It is doubtful that all the cabinet saw or read the memorandum. It's even less likely they had a moment where they agreed that Smith had set out the problem for them and they should be guided by his thoughts. The loss of an army at Saratoga had certainly concentrated their minds but not enough to see that continuation of the effort would lead to no good outcome. Surely, individuals saw futility, but it would take more defeats and a wider war with associated expenses to bring that to the collective consciousness, so to speak, of the government.

Smith would set out four possible outcomes for the war. They are listed below and the eventual result is known to any American elementary school student who stayed awake in history class.

"First, it may be conceived to end in the complete submission of America; all the different colonies, not only acknowledging, as formerly, the supremacy of the mother country; but contributing their proper proportion towards defraying the expence expense of the general Government and defence of the Empire.

Secondly, it may be conceived to end in the complete emancipation of America; not a single acre of land, from the enterance into Hudson's Straits to the mouth of the Mississipi, thereby acknowledging the supremacy of Great Britain.

Thirdly, it may be conceived to end in the restoration, or something near to the restoration, of the old system; the colonies acknowledging the supremacy of the mother country, allowing the Crown to appoint the Governors, the Lieutenant-Governors, the secretaries and a few other officers in the greater part of them, and submitting to certain regulations of trade; but contributing little or nothing towards defraying the expence of the general Government and defence of the empire.

Fourthly, and lastly, it may be conceived to end in the submission of a part, but of a part only, of America; Great Britain, after a long, expensive and ruinous war, being obliged to acknowledge the independency of the rest."

The fourth possibility mentioned by Smith was, as we all know, the outcome. In hindsight, it is probably the only possible outcome. As Wales became the British Celtic refuge after the Saxon invasion, Canada could be a Loyalist refuge and the "part only" to maintain political ties with the Crown."

To bring the rest of the Thirteen Colonies into submission would have taken an officer of genius that the faraway government would have enough confidence to place trust in and support. In the event, there was no Scipio Africanus available to His Majesty. Subjugating the rebellious Americans would be only half the task. As Smith pointed out:

> *If the complete submission of America was brought about altogether by Conquest, a military government would naturally be established there; and the continuance of that submission would be supposed to depend altogether upon the continuance of the force which had originally established it. But a military government is what, of all others, the Americans hate and dread the most. While they are able to keep the field they never will submit to it; and if, in spite of their utmost resistance, it should be established, they will, for more than a century to come, be at all times ready to take arms in order to overturn it. The necessary violence of such a government would render them less able, than they otherwise would be, to contribute towards the general expence of the empire. Their dislike to it would render them less willing. Whatever could be extorted from them, and probably much more than could be extorted from them, would be spent in maintaining that military force which would be requisite to command their obedience. By our dominion over a country, which submitted so unwillingly to our authority, we could gain scarce anything but the disgrace of being supposed to oppress a people whom we have long talked of, not only as of our fellow subjects, but as of our brethren and even as of our children.*

The Scipio, or a successor proconsul, would have had the unenviable task of making a defeated people a happy citizenry of the restored order. Needless to say, that level of both military and political genius is rare in any government.

Smith's memorandum was elicited by someone in government. He was probably one of many who were asked for opinions. If there had been a near unanimous call for a quick end to hostilities on as favorable terms as possible, the war might not have dragged on. Maybe too many of the suggestions were for a change of strategy and tactics.

It is easy to insult hindsight, but it is far more reliable than foresight. Still, it would have been better for London to have accepted Smith's clairvoyance and to seek as amiable a peace as possible. As it turned out, continuing a near hopeless struggle would lead to an unpleasant rupture. Relations in the nineteenth century would be more unpleasant than necessary.

As long as there was anything such as Anglo-America, that is, an English-speaking nation that would take most of its culture, if not its people, from the mother country, then there would be a natural affinity—and perhaps, an alliance. Bismarck called the English colonization of North America "the decisive fact of the modern world." Wisdom in government would have led to recognizing the harm of not ending the conflict.

3

The Quasi-War

Without the assistance of Royal France, the path of the American war of Independence would have been different. It is hard to see that any good outcome would have eventuated without the French alliance. Had they not intervened at all, a military suppression might have occurred. Smith's belief that the Americans would not accept it is probably true. It could be speculated that the American situation would have devolved into something like Ireland with a long period of suppressed rebellion—hardly a foreign policy success for the mother country.

The French did intervene and had a measure of revenge for the 1763 Treaty of Paris and its territorial losses. Little good did that do the Gallic monarchy, as the country was moving toward revolution and the king would lose the throne (and his head) and a republic would be established. The course of events changed our nation's relationship with France.

There isn't an abundance of material discussing the contretemps between newly independent America and its first ally. This appears to be a grand oversight, as The Quasi-War, as the conflict was known, was the first large-scale foreign policy problem faced by the nation. Gardner Weld Allen, a naval historian and author of *Our Naval War With France*, indicated that making an alliance solves an immediate problem. The present is not the future and complications unseen oft arise. Mr. Allen puts the problem thusly:

> *In their desperate strait the Americans gladly assumed obligations imposed by these treaties, which in after years proved embarrassing. Without the French alliance and the liberal loans of the king the fortunate outcome of the war must surely have been impossible; and gratitude to France was a universal sentiment in America. Some of the provisions of a consular convention, concluded between the two nations in 1788, also caused complications a few years later.*

Republican France found itself at war with much of Europe. Our alliance was made with the royal government. Yet it seemed no one at the time saw this as abrogating Franco-American treaties. Washington's cabinet agreed they were still in force. There was the sticky point that we were obligated to aid France militarily, but that was not on, as Weld pointed out "to have embarked in another great war would have been suicidal." The United States recognized the revolutionary government and would receive a French minister. Also, we proclaimed with all nations, friendly relations. The proclamation setting out the policy omitted the word neutrality.

The French sent a minister who arrived on April 8, 1793. This was before the proclamation. Edmond-Charles Genêt, rarely referred to as anything but, Citizen Genêt, would be a diplomatic trial for the American government. According to Allen, "his behavior indicates a misapprehension of the rights and powers of the American executive under the Constitution as well as of the duties and limitations of his own office." To digress, it could be argued that the same goes for some U.S. presidents and not a few who have held cabinet and legislative offices.

Genêt carried 250 blank commissions with him. Many were issued to privateers. Ships were fitted out and went to sea with crews, part French and part American. They began to take in English prizes, some in American waters. Needless to say, His Majesty's representatives were not amused. It did not cause Secretary of State Jefferson, predisposed to the sister republic, to be pleased either. Clearly, Le Citoyen was no Dale Carnegie.

Genêt, being received warmly by the American people, expected more support from our government. That it did not come was a disappointment. The American republic could not be seen to be supporting a campaign of naval privateering against a powerful nation that she was at peace with. A more diplomatic emissary might have worked within such parameters to greater effect. The French minister was a hothead and did not.

The American debt to France was also a subject within the remit of Genêt. The agreement had been one of installment payments over a number of years. The French government wanted it paid at once with the funds spent in the United States for provisions and naval stores needed by the French. America's fiscal situation made that impossible.

Our alliance with France called for us to assist in case of war. This would have meant naval support of the French in the West Indies. Genêt and his government did not insist on this provision. The thought is that the French saw the Americans more useful as neutral shippers than as belligerents with a near non-existent navy.

Genêt continued to send privateers to cruise, despite the American government's displeasure. On occasion the British objected as well to the protests of Secretary of State and an outraged Citizen Genêt.

The American government eventually asked for the recall of the Citizen. The French government complied and new commissioners arrived in February 1794. It was the Committee of Public Safety that disavowed the actions of Genêt and told his replacements to send him home. The committee instigated the terror. Maybe it was thoughts of his neck, but Le Citoyen did not express homesickness, rather the opposite. He requested asylum, married well–twice, and died an American in 1834.

As the Committee of Public Safety had disavowed Genêt's actions and sent replacements, it would seem auspicious for negotiations. Unfortunately, the new minister, Fauchet, may not have been a firebrand, but neither was he a pushover.

> *The administration, while relieved from the embarrassments brought upon it by Genêt, was nevertheless for the next four years subjected to the annoyance of incessant complaints on the part of the French department of foreign affairs and its ministers, Fauchet and his successor, Adet. These complaints were made a pretext for hostile acts which bore heavily upon American commerce.*

So, begins the second chapter of Allen's book. This is how it was, a slow descent into conflict. The chapter title is "Negotiations." There was that, but everyone could have been saved time if they just started fighting. Every American high school student, of at least a few decades ago, knows of the XYZ affair. The attempt by the French minister Talleyrand to extort a "douceur" was unsuccessful. The young republic was not trying to be obstinate, but it didn't see why a bribe to the even younger republic was necessary.

The French government of the time, the Directory, was corrupt, but not unsuccessful. French armies had pushed the European powers out and were on the move. They saw no reason that if the United States wanted friendship with France, they should not grease some palms and loan some cash. Short of buying peace, there was little the United States could do.

The conclusion that if Republican France could not squeeze a few dollars of a loan out of the United States, maybe they could steal some on the high seas is not unwarranted. France's navy may not have been as effective as Britain's, but it had fleets and privateers were available. We possessed neither. The last ships of the revolution had been sold off and no naval department existed. Other than revenue cutters, there was nothing. American merchant shipping would be an easy target.

Attacks began. As it was not a declared war, France made up some rules. For example, part of a decree of March 2, 1797, specified, an American ship not having a "role d'equipage or list of the crew in proper form, should be a lawful prize." Such a rule appeared to be a contrivance to seize the ships without announcing hostilities.

The United States had no choice but to react. A navy would be in order. Any country with our coastline needs a seagoing force. As Allen noted, "No sooner had the old navy disappeared than the need of such a force began to be appreciated." In 1785, Barbary pirates took merchantmen. Though the stirrings came because of Algerians, the French were the true stimulation, and a force of frigates was built and sent to sea after some procrastination. A few hundred private armed vessels were commissioned as well. These were not privateers per se, as they could only attack armed ships. On May 21, 1798, the capable Benjamin Stoddert became secretary of the new Department of the Navy.

On May 24, the purchased *Ganges* was the first to sail. More were to come including the famous *Constellation* and *Constitution*. (As an aside, though a museum ship now, the Constitution can be toured at the Charlestown Navy Yard in Boston. She was one of our first frigates and is the oldest commissioned naval vessel in the world.)

They began patrolling and defending against the French seizure of ships. Almost immediately, the situation changed for the better. Allen notes:

> *The effect of these defensive measures of the government was very considerable. After the appearance of American armed vessels on the sea, the rate of marine insurance to foreign ports fell in a marked degree. It was estimated that more than eight and a half million dollars was saved in insurance during this first year. The whole cost of the navy from 1794 to the end of 1798 was about two and a half million dollars. The saving in insurance was of course only part of the gain. The commerce of the country, which without naval protection would have been nearly ruined, was soon in a flourishing condition. Confidence was restored, and people felt that the honor of the country was redeemed.*

The record of 1799 would be even more impressive. In perhaps the most celebrated engagement of the Quasi-War, the Constellation, under Commodore Thomas Truxton took on *L'Insurgente* and captured the French frigate in February. American tactics of aiming at the gun ports proved superior to the French practice of trying to undo the masts and rigging.

The French howled at the injustice. Desfourneaux, the governor of Guadeloupe, protested that there was no declaration of war. So, there wasn't. Though constitutionally one may argue his point, French depredations invited defense and even retaliation.

So, it would go, with the American forces acquitting themselves well and making it so that commerce could go unhindered, or at least less hindered. Private armed vessels also were involved, but the Navy had the major part. What is impressive is how a navy came into being out of nothing. The main credit must be given to Secretary Stoddert.

The drift to war and subsequent hostilities would then be followed by a drift to peace. It began in mid 1798 when an American and a French diplomat in Holland conversed on the relations between the two nations. When Talleyrand was apprised of the discussion he made an effort to begin negotiations. No more douceurs. William Vans Murray, the American diplomat mentioned above who reported the French intentions, was sent to Paris along with Oliver Ellsworth, Chief Justice of the Supreme Court, and the governor of North Carolina, William R. Davie. They would be negotiating with the new French government, the Consulate. Bonaparte was the power in that entity.

The negotiations commenced and adjustments were made. The main thing is that peace was restored on relative terms, with neither side getting everything it wanted. Nevertheless, the fledgling nation had come off well enough seeing it was a war she had not sought. America had to build a navy from scratch. The force was proportionate to the emergency and was reduced after peace. There would be some more spoliation during the Napoleonic wars. Other disputes over settlement would continue after the demise of Bonaparte. Nevertheless, we continue our longstanding peace with our sister.

4

The Barbary Wars

The Barbary Wars, taken as a whole, is the second American War to be fought. Actually, they started before the Quasi-War but ended long after. The wars were an involvement with four states as opposed to our situation with France. It can be said they were not wars of choice, as we had an option other than war, but it is true that the enemy made unprovoked attacks on shipping.

The naval conflict with France saw the United States resolutely contest the sea-lanes with the French once it was clear that it had to be done. "Millions for defence but not a cent for tribute" was the reply to Talleyrand's demand for a douceur. The Barbary States were much less powerful than France. Frank Lambert in his book, *The Barbary Wars*, says of our original response to the North African raiders that "not a cent [was spent] for defence, but millions for tribute in the Mediterranean."

The American Republic in its early days was not ready for the fight with the states of the Maghreb, or the region of Northwest Africa, west of Egypt. During the era of the Articles of Confederation, a response was near impossible due to the lack of a central government that could fund and build a navy.

America would get its first treaty, with the Sultan of Morocco, on the cheap. That sovereign had been well disposed to the new nation to begin with, being the first head of state to recognize the new nation. The new republic had been diffident in responding to his overtures. To make his point, he had his raiders take a prize. As soon as it got our attention, he let it go. Negotiations, begun in earnest, were quickly concluded. It would be the only easy compact.

There were three other states that were not as easy to deal with. Treaties are nice, but booty was the goal for Algiers, Tripoli, and Tunis. Raiding was their stock in trade.

It is important to look at these states in context. They had no doubt as to the legitimacy of the pirate business. Americans, of course, disagreed. We conveniently forgot how much Indian land was appropriated by conquest. Men and women served against their will on plantations. Were not the Barbary States raiding just as legitimate, or no more illegitimate?

St. Augustine told of a pirate captured by Alexander the Great, who said to him "how dare he molest the sea." "How dare you molest the whole world" the pirate replied. "Because I do it with a little ship only, I am called a thief; you, doing it with a great navy, are called an emperor."

Though it is unknown if the argument was ever made, one could consider it analogous to a tribute required by a Northern European state. The king of Denmark would charge a toll on ships passing through straits that separated his territories. He did nothing to facilitate the passage of shipping, but taxed it anyway. The Sound Toll only stopped in 1857 when the straits were declared international waterways by treaty.

Of course, the Danish Crown, at worst, would seize the cargo. The Barbary raiders took the ship as a prize in their sea and enslaved the crew. The Americans were outraged as countrymen languished in servitude awaiting ransom.

We must consider the institution of slavery. It has been practiced among all peoples over time. Our era is but a tiny blip in history, and even today there are places where slaves still toil. Sudanese Janjaweed raiders have taken people in Darfur and pressed them into service. There is an occasional news story of a foreign resident in the United States who keeps someone as a slave and when caught is tried and sentenced. They have no thought that they have done something wrong.

The plantations of cotton in our south and sugar in the West Indies were built and run on unfree labor. The slaves were Africans, often sold by fellow Africans who, as far as it's known, did not suffer sleepless nights for trading in people of the same hue.

It probably would not do to boast about our era. It is true we do recognize slavery as nothing but the theft of labor. Our enlightenment is made easier because the slave is not as valuable in an age of "cheap" energy and machine technology. If every bit of fossil fuel or nuclear energy disappeared tomorrow, would a portion of the population wonder how to utilize the work of others by force?

It was in that milieu that the Barbary States held European and American seamen.

As the Algerines, as they were referred to, continued to hold American sailors and seize U.S. ships, the United States, under its now working constitution, started to act. In 1794 six frigates were authorized. The Portuguese went back to war against the pirates effectively as our ally. The government also sought to negotiate for peace.

Negotiations began before the navy was built. We agreed to buy peace from the Dey of Algiers for $600,000 plus annual tribute in gold and/or U.S.-made ships and supplies. Humiliating, but it was peace and free passage. Oh, and there was another $200,000 to free the captives. Considering that the ships of the new navy would not be ready for another two years, it could've been considered making the best of a bad bargain.

With a treaty in hand, it was time to forget about the navy. The bill authorizing the navy had a clause calling for suspension of the program if peace was agreed to. Three of the ships were built due to pork barrel politics, but this was hardly a force to scare an enemy.

The monies due and payable with the treaty were not paid in a timely manner. Thus, the Dey of Algiers threatened resumption of his war. The treaty was salvaged by paying the Dey with an American-made frigate. So ironically, we were not building ourselves a navy but augmenting our tormentor's fleet.

Tripoli and Tunis had to be treated with as well. In 1796, the Tripolitan Navy captured the Betsey. Like the Europeans, the United States opted to negotiate and pay. Again, it was cash and naval stores.

Next and last was Tunis. In 1796, the Tunisians offered a six-month truce to negotiate payment. The Bey of Tunis signed the truce as "commander ... of the frontier post of the Holy War." The implication being that he represented "the full might of the Islamic world." Again, the deal included naval stores. Congressional ratification emphasized trade reciprocity more than tribute details. The senators thought they were paying more for trading rights. The Tunisians saw it differently. It was an investment in a navy.

So, peace had been bought—or so the Americans thought. Unfortunately, it was not smooth sailing, so to speak, for America in the Mediterranean or in the Atlantic for that matter. The Dey of Algiers made more demands and threats despite a treaty and Tripoli and Tunis looked for excuses to raid. It was also the period of the Quasi-War with France.

The ships built against the Barbary States would be augmented, not to counter the North Africans but to resist

France. Indeed, compared to the 300 ships the French had taken, the less than 30 seized by the pirates seemed small beer.

Yet the demands from the Maghreb kept increasing and the Republic was rethinking the appeasement option. In early 1799 Secretary of State Pickering communicated to the chairman of Ways and Means the amount of the money needed to satisfy the increasing demands of the pirates. The amounts provoked second thoughts. They may not have been blond, blue-eyed Scandinavians, but the demand for Danegeld would not stop.

The last straw was when the indignant Bashaw of Tripoli declared war on the Americans for being in arrears on the tribute. He was also incensed that he did not do as well as the other plunderers. The long-suffering Yankees decided it was time to fight back. The new president, Thomas Jefferson, sent a squadron left over from the Quasi-War to the Mediterranean. In May of 1801, after agonizing over constitutional questions, the strict constructionist Jefferson ordered the ships to cruise as defensively as possible.

Conciliatory notes were sent to Yusuf Karamanli, the ruler, hoping for peace. Joe K was having none of it. His attitude was, as the line went from a popular movie, "Show me the money."

Commodore Richard Dale led three frigates and a schooner. The first encounter on August 1, 1801, saw the defeat of the enemy ship, *Tripoli*. The enemy ship was taken after suffering dreadful carnage and loss of life. There were no American casualties. The adventure had begun seemingly well.

The constitutional question had not been answered. The American commander released the ship and remaining crew after deep-sixing the guns. Without a congressional declaration of war, he felt he had no choice.

Jefferson sought congressional sanction and came under attack from the Federalists. Finally, on February 6, 1802, Congress gave approval to do what needed to be done. In passing the law—"An act for the protection of the Commerce and Seamen of the United Sates against the Tripolitan Cruisers"—Congress gave the president broad powers to deal with the pirates and recognized the state of war.

Unfortunately, all did not go according to plan. A blockade was set up. Because small shallow draft gunboats were not included in the flotilla, the cordon was easily circumvented and the corsairs continued to attack American shipping.

The Dale squadron was replaced by a larger, more powerful group under Captain Richard Morris. Without the appropriate small craft, it was just as ineffectual. The commander thought it better to do convoys. Tripolitans augmented their fleet with vessels from European tributaries. Other Barbary States, seeing the situation, started on the warpath. The campaign was hemorrhaging money with no results.

The fiscal loss was so bad that when Jefferson asked of his cabinet, "Shall we buy peace of Tripoli?" the yes vote was unanimous.

Bad as it was, another squadron was sent to the Maghreb. Commodore Edward Preble replaced Morris. Preble knew the small boats were needed and he would have them. He was a competent sailor with a good plan.

Unfortunately, before he had a chance to affect his plan, the worst debacle of the war occurred. The American frigate, *Philadelphia*, ran aground while chasing a Tripolitan cruiser. The captain and crew were prisoners and Joe K had a new and valuable asset.

Preble could not get the ship back, but he could neutralize it. In an operation as daring as it was brilliant, he sent Lieutenant Stephen Decatur to enter the harbor where the captured ship was anchored. Under the guns of the enemy, the detachment led by Decatur boarded the ship, burned and sank it and withdrew unscathed. It was so daring an exploit that Admiral Nelson considered it without parallel.

The game had changed again and the Americans had the advantage. Karamanli had been spooked. He offered a five-year truce with no money required. Preble, however, intended to continue the campaign. He planned attacks on the coast with small boats.

Circumstances changed. Yusuf had a brother, Hamet. Hamet claimed Yusuf was a murderer and usurper. Yusuf played hardball. He had shot his brother Hassan. Hassan had been the designated successor to the throne. Hamet had been exiled. He wrote to Jefferson promising peace if he were helped in his quest to replace his brother as legitimate ruler.

Spring 1804 saw Preble continuing the blockade, using the gunboats near shore and supporting Hamet's insurgency. More ships and some Marines were sent to support the big push. It was getting expensive for the young republic and Jefferson again polled the cabinet. The result, if the offensive worked, demand the old treaty with no tribute and the prisoners release. If not, ransom for the prisoners and tribute.

The small force of eight Marines, two midshipmen, and a few hundred Arab mercenaries marched from Egypt to the Eastern Libyan town of Derne. With naval support, they took the town. Upon that success, Consul General in Algiers, Tobias Lear, negotiated terms with Yusuf that paid $60,000 for ransom and hanged Hamet out to dry.

The peace treaty was controversial at home with the Federalists excoriating it and the Republican administration defending. William Eaton, the commander, thought it a disgrace and was more than vocal.

One could dwell on the subject at length, but to be brief, in hindsight it was the wrong decision. A cost benefit analysis would suggest that Eaton's force, if as he wanted, had marched to and taken Tripoli, the Barbary wars would have been summarily ended.

By agreeing to the treaty, there was some peace, but Yusuf was not to be deterred for long. The United States would again have to send forces to the Maghreb.

A romanticized version of the events can be found in Kenneth Roberts's historical novel, *Lydia Bailey*. Roberts seems to have felt it as much of a disgrace as Eaton did.

In the wake of the war and treaty, things settled down, but not for long. The pirates would again attack American shipping. Jefferson had planned a naval presence in the Mediterranean, but it was not to be. The United States would be distracted by Britain's heavy-handed maritime policy and French trade restrictions. This would eventually lead to the War of 1812, which will be discussed in the next section.

At the climax of that war, President Madison could give far more foreign policy attention to the Maghreb. As a result of the war with Britain, there was a far more formidable navy to work with. It was hardly able to defeat His Majesty's fleet-sized combat units, but it had acquitted itself well in many single-ship contests. It was more than adequate to deal with the Barbary Coast.

The pirates from Algiers had been the most aggressive, and Madison asked for a declaration of war from Congress and got it. A fleet under the naval hero Steven Decatur was sent and was followed with another one.

Soon after he passed through the Strait of Gibraltar, Decatur engaged the Algerians. In his first contest, he captured their flagship and admiral. Two days later he took a brig. With two ships taken and nearly 500 prisoners, he had the upper hand.

Decatur was able to sail into Algiers harbor and dictate terms as instructed by his government. The other states folded quickly, even paying damages, thus turning the tables as no European power had been able to do.

As much as it was a fine naval campaign, it would not have been possible without the general, post-Napoleon European peace. The Old World noticed it little in the aftermath of the continental wars.

Yet it was a fine accomplishment, and it was a war that America had to fight. It took a while to get right, but it ended the depredations of the corsairs. Once it was over, the forces were done and did not stay and tell the natives how to run their affairs. Today, that in and of itself appears a triumph.

5

The War of 1812

As a child, back in the day, my grammar school teachers spoke of how our new republic stood up to the British Empire in the War of 1812. The old mother country stopped our ships and took American sailors to forcibly serve in the Royal Navy. Our stand was heroic and righteous.

The USS *Constitution* easily triumphed over British ships of war as did other valiant American vessels.

The upper grades did let on that there was a species of congressmen known as War Hawks who were anxious for battle and might have had thoughts about an accretion of territory to the young nation. Other than a small note in texts, there wasn't much notice given to the War of 1812. What was its import?

It was, as a fully independent country, our first war of choice. On June 18, 1812, the United States declared war on Great Britain. The conflict kind of ended when the Treaty of Ghent was signed in Belgium on December 24, 1814. The Americans under Andrew Jackson overwhelmingly defeated the British at New Orleans after the treaty had been negotiated. As the pact ended the war on the basis that nothing changed, the victory changed nothing.

So, how did we get to fight what was ultimately a meaningless war? Well, the British Navy was stopping

American ships at sea and taking men off to serve aboard their vessels.

The Brits ruled the waves through what was, at least in part, a slave navy. Their law "permitted any able-bodied male subject to be drafted into immediate service anytime, anywhere." Being a sailor was no Carnival Cruise. The food was bad, and if it didn't kill you, there were always cannonballs, storms, etc. Enlisting in the Royal Navy was not a popular career path.

His Majesty's Navy needed the men, as they had been at war with Napoleon beginning in 1803. Though generally victorious against main enemy fleets, they would never suppress privateers and blockade-runners. The need for new blood was constant.

When the English stopped an American ship, they were looking for the king's subjects. This was the problem. No government would give another country the right to search its vessels on the high seas unless they had no choice, nor would they happily give up crewmembers.

The British claimed they were only taking subjects and not American citizens. They did not, however, concede the naturalized American who had been a subject but was no longer so. Unlike a sailor on HMS *Pinafore*, not all Anglo-Saxons felt as good about remaining an Englishman, but their former government saw it as once a Brit, always a Brit. If we didn't think the predators of the Maghreb had a right to stop our ships, how could we be wrong in opposing the British?

There were a number of incidents such as the boarding of the *Chesapeake* by the HMS *Leopard* that nearly started a war in 1807.

That the Royal Navy was stopping ships and searching for tars was an insult but hardly the only one. There was an economic *casus belli* as well.

His Majesty's government, being at war with Napoleonic France, wished to restrict trade with the enemy. The cabinet issued Orders-in-Council to effect this starting in 1807. America under President Jefferson responded with laws to counter this. One law, the Embargo Act of 1807, had a huge effect on Americans. The act forbade exports. Whether it taught the Brits anything is debatable, but it certainly taught the American business class a lot and none of it good. Though the Nonintercourse Act of 1809 replaced the Embargo Act, there was no resolution and it would be an aggravation that would be part of the eventual declaration of war. Unknown to the United States at the time of that declaration, the British had rescinded the objectionable rules.

There was another cause maybe even more important than the others. In his *1812: The War That Forged a Nation*, Walter R. Borneman wrote that "Thoughts of quelling Indian influence for good and ousting Great Britain from Canada became the rallying cry for Henry Clay and his close-knit cadre of political compatriots known as the 'war hawks.'"

The desire to be rid of the Indians was deep, especially after the Battle of Tippecanoe, but the lust for Canada as the main motive was probable in the American West of the time. Canada had a lot of land and not a lot of people. Clay had said of the place:

> *The conquest of Canada is in your power. I trust I shall not be thought to be bold when I state that I truly believe that the militia of Kentucky are alone competent to place Montreal and Upper Canada at your feet. Is it nothing to the pride of the King, to have the last of the immense North American possessions held by him in the beginning of his reign taken from him? Is it nothing to us to put out the torch that lights up Indian warfare? Is it nothing to gain the entire fur trade connected with Canada?*

Clay was to be found wrong on all counts and within a short time span. He was not the only war hawk. John Calhoun, as famous in our history as Clay, was in the camp. Clay and Calhoun had presidential aspirations that would never be fulfilled. The war, despite, its course, would not harm their long and influential careers.

It was a drift to war, not without opponents. John Randolph of Roanoke being maybe the foremost. A man of no party, he would lose his seat due to his stand.

Randolph said it was a "war not of defense but of conquest, of aggrandizement, of ambition; a war foreign to the interests of this country, to the interests of humanity itself." He further noted the Constitution "was not calculated to wage offensive foreign war—it was instituted for the common defense and the general welfare."

He was right on both counts though some might disagree on the second. There is a school of thought that has the Constitution as a living document. The idea is that interpretation can change due to changing time and thought. So maybe Randolph had it wrong and a war of choice can be determined as an aspect of common defense.

On June 1, 1812, President James Madison sent a war message to Congress detailing the case for a declaration of war. The restraint of trade and impressment of seamen were given extended treatment.

The word *Canada* was noticeable for its absence. In our nation today, the correct terminology must be observed at all times lest one be accused of some unspeakable attribute. So, the people here at the time of European arrival must be written or spoken of with delicacy. There was none of that in Madison's missive where the English referred to the indigenous people as savages urged to attack. No mention was made of the ongoing displacement of said aborigines who might have found this plan objectionable, a plan that was certainly contemplated by at least some of the war hawks.

On the 18th of June, Congress voted for war. It was not accompanied by the foot stomping and applause that happened on December 8, 1941. It would not be unanimous, but it was now declared.

Thus, hostilities began. General Hull invaded Canada but soon disinvaded. He would surrender Detroit to the competent English general Brock and his Indian ally, Tecumseh. The two worked well together, but were both ill fated.

The war on the Canadian frontier went back and forth. The big action for the Americans was Oliver Hazard Perry's smashing victory on Lake Erie and William Henry Harrison's subsequent campaign culminating in the Battle of the Thames. That battle saw the death of Tecumseh and much of the hope for the native peoples.

There would be more battles to the north and it would be muddled.

At Sea

At the beginning of the war, the American Navy, miniscule in size, would take on the Royal Navy and score some stunning victories over the overconfident British.

The USS *Constitution* took on HMS *Guerriere* in the Atlantic and defeated the enemy ship. The news was stunning, and the nation, even the war shy New Englanders, loved it. October would see the USS *Wasp* capture the HMS *Frolic*. Also in October, the great American naval officer, Steven Decatur, famous for taking on the Barbary pirates, would defeat the enemy in combat.

It was great work on the part of the Americans but short-lived. Eventually, the larger naval resources of the Empire were brought to bear and the American naval forces were for the most part bottled up in harbor.

Back North

The northern frontier continued on as essentially a stalemate, as no one would gain the upper hand despite the Harrison/Perry success. The British commander, General Prévost, was not up to the task, and neither side had enough men or arms for the knockout punch.

The British would get their chance. Their success on the peninsula as well as their allies invading France led Napoleon to surrender, and now troops would be available to punish the former colonials. Finally, Prévost would have the men he needed and could invade through New York. His 14,000-man army would be huge considering the theater and troops facing him.

One has to wonder at the American delusion that would start a war with a tiny, if professional, navy against a power with a huge fleet and maritime tradition. Clay's insane belief in a quick Canadian conquest clouded many minds.

Things looked grim, but though the ocean-going squadrons might be prisoners of the blockade, naval power was going to score dividends for the American war effort elsewhere.

Neither side started the war with a lake navy and both would have to build one. Perry did it at Erie and now another assault would have to be constructed one from scratch on the fresh water of Lake Champlain, which the enemy would have to secure to successfully invade to the south.

Commandant Thomas MacDonough was the man for the job. He arrived at Lake Champlain in October of 1812, still early in the war, and set to work constructing a flotilla.

Prévost would need to take the lake harbor of Plattsburgh to continue his march south. The American general, Macomb, had some regulars and militia, but was heavily outnumbered.

Still, he artfully fortified the harbor and was ready to at least hold Prévost off, if he could, until McDonough secured the lake.

The British would build ships as well. Their overall naval commander in Canada, Captain James Yeo, switched leaders three times, such that when he settled on Captain George Downie, it was almost on the eve of battle. This did not augur well for the Royal Navy.

The signal was given on September 11, 1814, by the firing of Downie's guns for Prévost to attack Macomb. The advance was made in such a desultory way that the battle was lost on the water by the time the troops got moving. Prévost headed back to Canada and a court martial. He would die before he could be disgraced. For the most part, there was not too much more happening in the north.

Britannia may have had the oceans, but we had glory on the lakes.

On to Washington

During the border war, the U.S. forces managed to set fire to the Canadian capital of York. Though it wasn't all that much of a capital, it was still bad form. General Prévost would write to the British admiral enforcing the blockade along the Atlantic suggesting some devastation.

Admiral Alexander Cochrane, the naval supremo, needed no prompting. He was raiding up and down the coast. Soon he would have bigger fish to fry.

The British had been pillaging on the Chesapeake in 1813 with little opposition. Now they would take it a bit farther. Our capital would burn for theirs.

Admiral Cochrane's man for the job, Admiral George Cockburn, would carry soldiers fresh from Napoleonic service and work with their general, Robert Ross, to sail up the Chesapeake and disembark his army.

The forces that could oppose the British were not at all organized under the command of political appointee, Brigadier General William Winder. He did what he could, but it wasn't much.

The British landed on the Patuxent River at Benedict and started marching toward Washington. The Americans met them at Bladensburg and were soundly defeated leaving little to deter the invaders. The seat of government was taken and burned.

Just about everyone had got out while the getting was good, or at least not horribly bad. The president and Dolley Madison had taken off, as had the rest of the government.

Ross and his staff dined at the already set White House table and then burned it and much of the city. On August 26, the British left. Ross was anticipating the regrouping of the militia and understood his vulnerability in enemy territory.

One would think that taking your enemy's capital city at the end of a war would be first and foremost or a paramount decision. The truth is Washington was not as important in those days as it is now. The states were more powerful versus the federal government then. A small bureaucracy could be rebuilt faster, as there was less to be rebuilt. Once the British moved out, Madison et al. returned and picked up the pieces.

What could His Majesty's Forces on the Bay do for an encore? They could head on up to Baltimore and raid a real place, a port with great wealth on the dock to plunder. It was the commercial hub of the Mid-Atlantic States.

So up the troops went and disembarked to march into town. Baltimore, however, was not D.C. Preparations had been made, earthworks dug, and a militia was in place. Also, there were forts with batteries.

General Ross may not have thought it all that wise to continue the campaign. For himself, he was correct and ultimately, for the expedition. Running into the Americans, he was shot from the trees and mortally wounded.

Still, the advance continued with more and better resistance from the Yanks who fell back in good order, as opposed to the previous debacle. Admiral Cochrane could see this was going be different and he wanted to outflank the defenders. To do that, he brought up mortar boats and the rocket vessel, *Erebus*, to pulverize the fort in his way.

A huge flag flew over the fort, but there was little the batteries could do, as they were outranged by the mortars and rockets. A brutal bombardment went on day and night and the flag still waved—but it never wavered.

A British attempt to end run was thwarted by the fortress as the small boats came in range and American guns opened up.

When morning came, a Washington lawyer saw the flag still waving over Fort McHenry. Baltimore would not be another Washington and eventually his poem would become our anthem.

Prévost, up north, thought better of advancing against entrenchments at about the same time; the invaders at Baltimore had come to the same conclusion with better reason.

The campaign was over and the troops set sail, but the war was not done.

Peace in Ghent

The peace commissioners filtered in to Ghent in 1814 though the United States seemed more interested at first. As time went on and political, economic, and military events led the enemy to come around, and so the negotiations proceeded.

Our most prominent commissioners were Henry Clay and John Quincy Adams. Clay, who as much as anyone had started the conflict now had to get as good a deal as possible. Adams was already a seasoned negotiator. They would skillfully get... nothing. They would not give anything up either.

The true losers were the indigenous tribes. The treaty had a provision that they would be restored to their rights, but no one in the English government was going to watch out for that. The inexorable march westward of the American nation would not be impeded.

The other losers were the corpses on both sides of combatants and collaterals and those who lost property. As Canadian author Pierre Berton wrote of the treaty:

> *It was as if no war had been fought, or to put it more bluntly, as if the war that was fought was fought for no good reason. For nothing has changed; everything is as it was in the beginning save for the graves of those who, it now appears, have fought for a trifle:...Lake Erie and Fort McHenry will go into the American history books, Queenston Heights into the Canadian, but without the gore, the stench, the disease, the terror, the conniving, and the imbecilities that march with every army.*

Was it worth it in any sense? Walter R. Borneman, writing in 1812: *The War That Forged A Nation*, contends it did exactly as the title says. There is some sense in that: having passed the shoals, the nation had reached a harbor of strong nationhood.

War is often a question of luck. If Brock had lived and come south, Champlain might have worked out differently and the Hartford Convention might have gone for secession. The oven of the forge may not have heated hot enough.

Had the repeal of the orders-in-council happened earlier or information arrived earlier and the declaration withdrawn, would we have just dissolved as a people without some military annealing?

The nation was fortunate that an ill-thought-out adventure ended so well.

6

John Quincy Adams and the Monroe Doctrine

America settled down after the War of 1812 and the end of the Barbary threat for a period of no wars. That does not mean nothing happened. One of the commissioners from the war just ended would play a significant role in her foreign policy for something that would not bear his name.

After being one of the peace commissioners at Ghent, John Quincy Adams was sent by President Madison to be Minister to the Court of Saint James, serving as our representative to the English king until 1817.

When James Monroe became president, Adams became Secretary of State until 1825. He would negotiate our accession of Florida from Spain. As it was inevitable, it was a minor if maybe uneven affair.

The great event of his tenure was the question of power in the new world. Napoleon had come across the ocean to reassert French rule in Haiti. Would it become a springboard to other conquests? Fortunately, the former slaves in arms put a stop to that.

After the Napoleonic wars had ended and peace was made again with the mother country, there was a question of the old colonial power. Mostly that meant Spain. Her restored monarchy wanted to regain her colonies.

America saw it not in the national interest to see the colonialists reassert authority. Britain concurred from a trade standpoint. Both would not want to see another Napoleon send an invasion fleet as remote as that might be. The Monroe Doctrine would inform the world where we stood.

Adams would be the chief author of the document and on December 2, 1823, in his annual message to congress, Monroe presented it. Most importantly it states:

> The occasion has been judged proper for asserting, as a principle in which the rights and interests of the United States are involved, that the American continents, by the free and independent condition which they have assumed and maintain, are henceforth not to be considered as subjects for future colonization by any European powers.

> This didn't mean we were going to send a huge force to clear everybody out:

> We owe it, therefore, to candor and to the amicable relations existing between the United States and those powers to declare that we should consider any attempt on their part to extend their system to any portion of this hemisphere as dangerous to our peace and safety. With the existing colonies or dependencies of any European power we have not interfered and shall not interfere. But with the Governments who have declared their independence and maintained it, and whose independence we have, on great consideration and on just principles, acknowledged, we could not view any interposition for the purpose of oppressing them, or controlling in any other manner their destiny, by any European power in any other light than as the

manifestation of an unfriendly disposition toward the United States.

So, Cuba could stay Spanish until we got around to it. The Bolivarian countries were not to be reconquered.

In truth, the document had little behind it in light of the relative military weakness of the United States. Great Britain, however, agreed with the general spirit of the doctrine and they would be the muscle. The British had even suggested it be a joint statement.

It was hardly out of a sense of fair play that the United Kingdom took its position. Trade with many independent states would be more profitable than if a returning power asserted control.

Even though the United States lacked the substance to put teeth in the document, it was still a statement of true republican principles. One hopes that John Quincy Adams had learned the lesson of the War of 1812. Our nation had gone into the war following a policy opposite that called for by Theodore Roosevelt. Adams had seen that talking loudly while carrying a small stick lacked effectiveness.

One might hope that Adams believed this to be not only the smart policy, which it was, but the moral one as well.

Indeed, he would give voice to it in a speech before Congress on July 4, 1821, well before the doctrine's issuance. He began by reading completely the Declaration of Independence and then speaking of its meaning.

Eventually, he got down to how we would go about in the world:

> *Wherever the standard of freedom and independence has been or shall be unfurled, there will her heart, her benedictions and her prayers be. But she goes not abroad in search of monsters to destroy. She is the well-wisher to the freedom and independence of all. She is the*

champion and vindicator only of her own. She will recommend the general cause, by the countenance of her voice, and the benignant sympathy of her example.

She well knows that by once enlisting under other banners than her own, were they even the banners of foreign independence, she would involve herself, beyond the power of extrication, in all the wars of interest and intrigue, of individual avarice, envy, and ambition, which assume the colors and usurp the standard of freedom. The fundamental maxims of her policy would insensibly change from liberty to force. The frontlet upon her brows would no longer beam with the ineffable splendor of freedom and independence; but in its stead would soon be substituted an imperial diadem, flashing in false and tarnished lustre the murky radiance of dominion and power. She might become the dictatress of the world: she would be no longer the ruler of her own spirit.

Adams's address was a measured statement about what we couldn't do and how that was the right thing. Would we keep to the spirit? As long as we had to.

In 1842, President Tyler suggested to the British that Hawaii was covered by the Monroe Doctrine. The Crossroads of the Pacific was some ways off from the Western Hemisphere. It could have been nothing other than a desire to extend influence. American settlers were rushing in.

During our Civil War, France invaded Mexico and installed an emperor. While the conflict raged, there was not much we could do. With the Confederacy vanquished, we had a large army here and Napoleon III took the hint and said au revoir. The doctrine was enforced.

Also during the Civil War, Britain asserted control over a bit of Central America calling it British Honduras. We could do little to object and it would be theirs until it became Belize.

During the Grant presidency, the Doctrine was re-asserted. The administration also wanted to annex the Dominican Republic. It did not happen, as some legislators pointed out that it looked like a big business subsidy and that the statelet had a history of instability.

The Doctrine would next be invoked as part of the Venezuelan Crisis of 1895. This was essentially a border dispute between an American Republic and the colony of British Guiana. Britain would give over and submit to arbitration as President Cleveland asserted the Doctrine included an interest in whatever happened on this side of the whole pond. It was accomplished smoothly to the satisfaction of Venezuela, but was an advance of America interest both for and against hemispheric neighbors.

The Big Brother Policy was developed in the 1880s by Secretary of State James to assert American leadership and rally the other countries of the New World behind us. It was not an idea of *primus inter pares*.

And so it went, the big neighbor to the north always interpreting the Doctrine in its own favor. There is nothing wrong with that in the sense that all nations have a duty to look after their own interests. The question is, was it really in the nation's interest?

One might say that by favoring United Fruit the American public benefited by having bananas cheaper than they might have otherwise. Do we consider only that and not the exploitation of the people who grew them? Was a contrived coup worthy of us?

Clearly, the Monroe Doctrine has not always been pursued in the spirit John Quincy Adams presented it to the world.

7

Fifty-four Forty or Fight — The Oregon Boundary Dispute

In 1803, the Jefferson Administration acquired all the land possessed by Napoleon's France in North America. It included the Mississippi River's western shore and the great port of New Orleans as well as the trading city of Saint Louis.

The Louisiana Purchase also included a vast tract of land from the river to the Pacific. Its exact size was in question, as the acquired land was bordered by two other entities.

The first, Spain, was to the south of the territory. Spain claimed that the purchase included only the west bank and New Orleans and Saint Louis. Spain was a declining power and would come to an agreement in the Adams-Onís Treaty acquiescing to most of the American claims.

The United Kingdom was not declining and held all the territory to the north of the new American land. Both the U.S. and the Canadian territories were going to extend from sea to sea. Who would get what was going to be contested, and it would be important to establish a presence on the ground.

To that end, President Jefferson dispatched the Lewis and Clark Expedition. It would also include scientific and economic objectives, but getting across the land and obtaining an idea of what we had and establishing a presence would be foremost.

The expedition was a success. The Corps of Discovery, as it was also known, reached the Pacific Ocean in November of 1805. It returned in 1806 mission accomplished. Trans-Mississippi settlement soon began, but was slower out to the Pacific.

The main interest at first was the fur trade. The British had been active in its establishment. In 1807, the North West Company set up trading posts in the region. The German-American entrepreneur, John Jacob Astor entered into the fur trade at times in cooperation with and sometimes in competition.

Though not a pressing issue then, the two nations began to negotiate in 1818. They did not come to an agreement at the time, but in the Anglo-American Convention of 1818, settling residual issues from the War of 1812, the two parties consented to joint administration for ten years.

In anticipation of the end of the joint administration, negotiations began again. As the sides were still far apart, they eventually agreed to disagree for the time being and renewed the joint occupancy agreement in 1827. A requirement for a year's notice of abrogation was inserted.

Up until that time, the non-indigenous residents had been mostly Hudson's Bay Company employees. Starting in the 1830s American settlement picked up. Missionaries, cattlemen and a few others were joined by newcomers who arrived via the Oregon Trail in the Great Migration of 1843. A provisional government was established in the Willamette Valley, limited to Americans and a few others of course.

With a population living in the territory, Oregon became more important to the country, and became a topic of domestic political concern when Texas had been taken up. Still, in the 1844 election of James K. Polk, it was not overly important. The slogan, "Fifty-four Forty or Fight!" had not been in use if even coined at the time.

Polk's inaugural address claimed he was willing to negotiate and not interested in a war. Still, it was possible that it could've happened. There were senators who were ready to fight if we didn't go our way. Lewis Cass would call for war. There were cooler heads like Daniel Webster who did not think a war winnable.

In the end, there was no real reason for two intertwined trading partners to go ballistic. Disaster, such as loss of Eastern Canada or another brutal blockade or a combination of bad outcomes, would suit no one. The situation was negotiated and the border shared today was agreed.

There would be some small contretemps on occasion, but the neighbors have got on well enough. The two nations might do stupid things internationally, but they would go to some lengths to avoid stepping on each other's toes too badly.

8

The Mexican War

With a soldier the flag is paramount . . . I know the struggle with my conscience during the Mexican War. I have never altogether forgiven myself for going into that. I had very strong opinions on the subject. I do not think there was ever a more wicked war than that waged by the United States on Mexico. I thought so at the time, when I was a youngster, only I had not moral courage enough to resign. I had taken an oath to serve eight years, unless sooner discharged, and I considered my supreme duty was to my flag. I had a horror of the Mexican War, and I have always believed that it was on our part most unjust. The wickedness was not in the way our soldiers conducted it, but in the conduct of our government in declaring war. The troops behaved well in Mexico, and the government acted handsomely about the peace. We had no claim on Mexico. Texas had no claim beyond the Nueces River, and yet we pushed on to the Rio Grande and crossed it. I am always ashamed of my country when I think of that invasion. – Ulysses S. Grant to journalist John Russell Young (1879), quoted by Young in Around the World with General Grant (Baltimore: John Hopkins University Press, 2002), 376–377.

Grant was right. It was not a just war. In real terms, when we boil it all down, it was nothing but a land grab. Right or wrong, most Americans are glad that the land gained in the conflict became part of the United States.

Certainly, the Mexican Nation, recently independent from Spain, was no moral paragon. It was a place of coups and counter-coups. There was a peasantry who had little feeling of nationhood and who were lorded over by a landlord class. Still, there was one area of policy where the southern neighbor had gone beyond the country to the north. Mexico had abolished slavery in 1829.

Mexico invited Americans to settle in underpopulated Texas. Most immigrants did not abide by the requirements to become Catholics and learn Spanish. Also, they brought in slaves. Trouble was probably inevitable.

The question could be asked that if slavery had been allowed and a plantation society came into legal existence in Texas, would there have been a revolt? That is for others to pursue.

Right or wrong, the Texans revolted and won. This was not the end of it. The treaties made by the defeated General Santa Anna were not ratified by the central government and its independence not recognized. It was considered a province in rebellion.

In 1837, the United States recognized Texas independence and sent an envoy.

Politically, Texas had two factions. The nationalists liked Texas being independent. They were opposed by Sam Houston and his followers who desired annexation by the United States. Annexation won out and Texas, by agreement with the U.S. government, became the only state not to have had a territorial phase.

Annexation was one heck of a deal for Texas as they had been notably inept in managing their finances. The latter-day

Texas Republic movement should have all the fun of the struggle, but unless they are better than the previous attempt, victory is the last thing they should want. Of course, if they did run up debts, they could apply for readmission and get the feds to assume all liabilities. It worked before.

Now, if your neighbor to the south has never recognized your independence and another country annexes you, that could be considered a casus belli. So, the Mexicans thought, and the drift to war began.

As the dispute was not only about who owned Texas, but the boundary thereof, it was not going to be hard for a clash to occur on disputed land. It happened and war began in late April 1846.

From the beginning, it did not go well for Mexico. The American army commanded by Zachary Taylor steadily pushed south. Battles were won at Palo Alto, Resaca de la Palma, and Monterey by September. No more big battles were fought in the Northern Mexican front until the New Year. When that battle came, it would be a big one.

Antonio Lopez de Santa Anna was a Mexican general and sometimes president and dictator. He was the man who lost Mexico; he was taking a siesta when the Texans attacked at San Jacinto. Despite that, he managed to restore his fortunes and return to power only to be exiled to Cuba. From exile, he offered his services to his country in its hour of need. Despite his past, the country was in desperate enough straits to accept the offer.

Santa Anna had, at the same time, been in touch with the Americans. If allowed to pass through the naval blockade, he would work to settle the conflict on terms decided by the United States. Both the northerners and those who had invited him back were to be disappointed. Once home, the man on horseback got back up on the horse as president and prosecuted the war.

The commanding general/president trained his army and moved north to face Taylor. He had intercepted a letter and knew of the American general's strength. The larger forces should yield victory. The march north would be arduous and his army would be depleted by sickness and desertion, but he got there.

The Mexican leader's forces slammed into the Americans. It was their best chance for a big victory and it could've happened with some luck. It didn't. Taylor's army held and it was a drawn battle.

The always-interesting New York history writer, William Bryk, wrote of the outcome:

> His attack enveloped Taylor's left and shattered three American regiments. Taylor fell back on Monterrey, where he remained for the rest of the war.
>
> Having effectively neutralized Taylor, Santa Anna turned to face Winfield Scott...

Mr. Bryk almost makes it sound like a strategic success. Taylor, having been bled of a lot troops to increase Scott's army, may not have been going anywhere anyway. Santa Anna was.

Scott had landed at Vera Cruz and "the Napoleon of the West" needed to head south.

The big battles would all take place where we think of Mexico today. Mexico back then, however, was larger. Spain had claimed much more land to the west of Texas. California, New Mexico, and just about everything else were included in the Spanish kingdom's empire.

There were settlements in California and New Mexico, but the Spanish and later Mexicans were hardly thick on the ground.

The Americans sent an expedition west under Colonel Stephen Kearney in May of 1846. Though a short-lived uprising would occur later, Kearney experienced no real opposition. After pacifying New Mexico, he would then take part of his small force to California.

California was not as easy as New Mexico, but it wasn't Stalingrad either. The U.S. Navy was active on the west coast and landed a force of men. An expedition under John C. Fremont arrived and rebel American settlers were in action against the Mexicans. Kearney eventually appeared.

The war in the future Golden State was essentially several hundred men against a few hundred. The Mexican general, José Maria Flores, put up a good resistance, not without success. In the end, it was to no avail.

Peace was made via the Treaty of Cahuenga in January of 1847 that was on fair terms, and though informal, would be essentially affirmed by the treaty that ended the war.

A small force would secure a territory that can arguably be considered the greatest prize of the conflict.

When Santa Anna left to fight Taylor, he believed that the fortress at Veracruz could hold out for a time against the impending invasion by the forces under General Winfield Scott. In this he was wrong.

Recognizing that Mexico was in no mood to give up, Scott had been sent to invade the country's heartland. He made an amphibious landing south of Veracruz and then proceeded to invest the port. Mexican defense was feeble, and on March 29, 1847, the Americans entered the surrendered city.

Before the final surrender, Santa Anna was back south. He dealt with opposition in the capital city and then went to meet Scott's army.

That would be at Cerro Gordo on the road west from Veracruz. Santa Anna had was fortified well with a natural defensive position. Scott would flank and win.

It was a well-fought victory, but Scott's troubles were beginning. Advancing, he settled down in Puebla and spent ten unhappy weeks surrounded and in hostile country. Volunteers, whose enlistments were uphad ended, left thereby leaving the general in the lurch.

Reinforcements arrived, morale improved, and the army was on its march toward Mexico City.

When his army was being defeated at Cerro Gordo, Santa Anna had to flee to avoid capture. This did not help his popularity in Mexico City. No matter, as he was able to retain power with some fancy footwork as the Americans were approaching.

The advancing Gringo army continuously outflanked Santa Anna and his subordinates. Finally, at Churubusco, the Mexicans and Americans would have a straight-up fight. Santa Anna's troops fought well, but in the end, it was the same. Though outnumbering Scott and in a good position, the Mexicans lost.

The battle was costly for Scott. His army had paid for it with more than a thousand casualties and was now in need of rest, which Scott realized. Santa Anna needed respite as much and probably more so. He thus proposed an armistice, and it was accepted by Scott.

Peace negotiations began, but they were only pursued by the Mexican leader to stall for time. It worked, and when it became obvious they were going nowhere, the truce ended.

The Americans approached the city at the southwestern defenses of Molino del Rey and the castle of Chapultepec. Scott hit Molina del Rey first. This turned out to be a bloody fracas that ended with a lot of Mexican casualties, as usual, but Scott's men suffered more than 700. It turned out that the supposed cannon works held little. It was a waste.

Now it was time to move on to Chapultepec, which was the location of the Mexican military academy. It was another hard fought but victorious effort. Resistance was stiffening and the

American casualties were more than 1,200 for the entire day, but the way was open to the capital.

Quickly, Scott's men pushed on and with some struggle took two of the gates. Could they take Mexico City?

It looked like the Duke of Wellington's observation was going to prove correct: "Scott is lost—he cannot capture the city and he cannot fall back on his base."

The army was depleted by casualties and was low on ammunition and supplies. All the Mexicans needed to do was to keep fighting and let the Americans run out of steam.

Fortunately, the enemy was Santa Anna, and though he could pull some clever stunts and outmaneuver Scott diplomatically, he could also be counted on to make a crucial mistake now and again.

Santa Anna despaired of holding the city and left with his army. Maybe he was right and his military situation more desperate than Scott's.

On the 14th of September 1847, the capital of Mexico surrendered.

Upon hearing of the capitulation, the same Wellington called Scott the greatest general of the age. Was that true? Certainly, a better defense should have seen a small force living off the country destroyed or sent packing, as Bonaparte could not hold Russia.

Having Santa Anna as an opponent was not the worst thing to happen to him. Even so, all war has some luck and Scott's victories all were attended by good generalship. At worst, "greatest of the age" is at least arguable.

Interesting as well is the American success in light of all the dissension in officer ranks. Scott had problems with Taylor and vice versa. Taylor suffered verbal sniping from subordinates. Scott also had to endure the slings and arrows of his officers.

Regulars and volunteers did not get along and there were inter-service controversies with the navy.

Both Scott and Taylor entertained political aspirations and that was not going to cause undo harmony with President Polk.

Needless to say, all was not sweetness and light in enemy ranks. Maybe a completely united Mexico would have done better. Whatever disputes occurred among Americans, they did not seem to keep the army from fighting well and winning.

US forces had won all the big battles and possessed the enemy capital city. That did not mean a settlement would be easy.

From the beginning, President Polk had had a willingness to discuss peace, but only on American terms. Those terms were mostly the Rio Grande as a Texas boundary and the desire to annex California.

Undefeated Mexico would not have found the terms as proffered all too interesting. Sooner or later, the situation would at least allow the national leadership to see the necessity of negotiating even the unpalatable.

While the war was in the north, Mexico showed no signs of budging. Thus, the Veracruz expedition. With Scott went Nicholas Trist with powers to negotiate. He possessed a draft treaty and had authority for funds and a letter for the Mexican government.

Not unexpectedly, Scott and Trist didn't get along. Most unexpectedly, they overcame the disharmony and worked together as friends. If he could make peace with Scott, he was the man to do it with the Mexicans.

Trist had a letter from Secretary of State Buchanan to the Mexican government that authorized him to treat. A representative of the British embassy delivered it. No one really wanted to touch it, as Mexico had a law stating that listening to terms made one a traitor.

The hot potato was tossed around. Santa Anna always the opportunist, saw one. He opened secret negotiations. The Mexican general demanded a douceur of $10,000 for his good offices. Scott and Trist took the bait and Santa Anna got some dinero and time to strengthen defenses.

Trist and Scott were not put off by the failure. After Churubusco, Santa Anna made another approach to gain time. The general and the diplomat again bit. The Americans presented the terms on offer, which had not really changed. The Mexicans presented their demands, which showed some movement, but were not acceptable. Talks collapsed, but the Mexican Houdini had again gained some time.

After marching into Mexico City, peace didn't happen. The Mexicans didn't come to Scott and Trist to sue for peace. They had reasons not to. The U.S. Army was a small force among a hostile population and might have problems. The Mexicans knew the war was losing popularity at home. Add to all that, the political instability in Mexico and there was a question of whom to deal with.

Back in Washington, Trist's lack of progress led the administration to recall him. In the days before instant communication, it would take six weeks for word to reach the American representative. During that time, the situation for peace had improved and Trist wanted to exploit that.

When the dismissal arrived, Trist was disappointed but readied himself to leave. Mexico, however, under a new government appointed peace commissioners.

Trist decided to stay and negotiate. For once, he was not chasing a Santa Anna-induced mirage. He sent a justification of his without portfolio activities to President Polk and went to work.

On February 2, 1848, the Treaty of Guadalupe Hidalgo was agreed. You can see its essential nature by looking at a contemporary map of North America. Fifteen million dollars changed hands in a bargain of the century, and the U.S. government assumed any claims against Mexico.

From a moral standpoint, the quote of Grant above says it all. The press of a growing American population on Mexican territory to the north probably made it inevitable that all of it would eventually be part of the US. Mexico had taken the land from its indigenous population where it could and we took it from them.

Breathes there an American with a soul so dead who is not glad that the destiny manifested the way it did.

9

The Civil War

The Civil War was not a foreign war, but it had foreign aspects. While the Confederate States existed, there was little diplomatic interaction between the south and the Union.

The foreign policy of the Confederacy involved the attempt to attain foreign recognition, if not assistance, and to procure supplies and return them through an increasingly effective naval blockade.

The Union, needless to say, pursued the opposite agenda. Whether or not there was a possibility of the rebels attaining recognition or assistance is a question not to be discussed here.

Once Lincoln issued the Emancipation Proclamation, there was no question of France or Britain aiding the South. The decree may have been constitutionally questionable, but that is at this point irrelevant.

10

Foreign Policy After the Civil War 1865 to 1895

The war over, the nation needed time to recover. Fortunately, there were no major wars other than a few minor expeditions not worth noting but probably not worth the effort either.

Militarily, there was much activity in suppressing the Indian tribes.

Immediately after the Civil War, there were a couple of loose ends to tie up. The first was France's expedition to Mexico. We of course had a conflict with our southern neighbor already covered. Understandably, we would not be happy with a major European power fishing in our waters.

France had sent a large army to put the Hapsburg Maximilian on a Mexican throne after an international debt collection with Britain and Spain. They left and Max was made imperator. Though Benito Juarez, the Mexican president, never gave up, the French got effective control and the reins of power.

During the Civil War, the Union wisely followed a one war at a time policy. Our government merely registered its displeasure. Union victory became possible, then probable and then inevitable. American displeasure would turn more insistent.

In 1864, the lower house of Congress resolved that France had to go. General Sheridan missed the grand review at the end of the war, as he was sent with a veteran force of 50,000 to the Mexican border as a very potent and unmistakable threat. President Johnson imposed a blockade.

Napoleon III didn't read every signal correctly or he would not have rushed into his last war in 1870. This one was, however, unmistakable.

Grant wanted war, but Johnson and Secretary of State William H. Seward were restrained. Seward let Napoleon know that it might be in his best interest to leave. It was not overtly a threat, but was real. The French were in no position to carry on a Trans-Atlantic war.

The Gauls left, the "Empire" collapsed, and Maximilian was hung out to die, literally. Seward was deft and even though France was in no position for hostilities, we didn't need a war either.

The Alabama Claims

The other matter was with the mommy country. Britain would naturally want to see its offspring weakened. The United States, now continental in shape, could only be a rival in trade and militarily if it wanted to. Taking Canada, impossible in the bungling of 1812, would now just be a march north, if inclined.

During the Civil War, the British seemed to favor the Confederacy. Their declared neutrality was a victory for the South diplomatically. Britain proposed mediation in 1862. Shipyards in Britain turned out commerce raiders until 1863, the most notorious being Alabama.

The raiding was not as brutal to the Union as the blockade was to the South, but it was costly.

Pushback was inevitable and it started even before the war ended. In 1866, the House passed a neutrality act that would allow for the United States to build Alabamas for belligerents that could only harm the UK.

Senator Charles Sumner claimed the British owed $15 million in direct damages back when a million was really worth a million, but that was not all. $110 million was also owed for lost registrations and increased insurance fees and other damages. That was only a fraction of what the fanatical Sumner wanted. The Western Republic might play hardball.

A lot of politicians were baying for blood and President Grant would not have disliked the idea of Sheridan taking the cavalry up to Quebec. Hamilton Fish, appointed Secretary of State in 1869, was a cooler head.

Though he would have not been unhappy with all the bombastic rhetoric scaring the Brits into giving up Canada, he was willing for a settlement. Britain had started out defiant, but was coming around. They had other fish to fry rather than a replay of their last North American war. With that sun never setting on the empire, who knows what could happen when the eyes have to be taken off possessions to deal with a former colony.

In 1872, the claims were settled for a little more than $15 million. Everyone may not have lived happily ever after, but they got along.

Our Civil War is constantly refought here, but for the rest of the world, it was over.

The Alaska Purchase

America could expand without war. In 1867, the United States purchased Alaska from the Russian Empire. For a little more than $7 million, greater than a half million square miles of territory were gained. One of the reasons Russia sold was they feared that in a war the British would seize it. At least they could get something for a sale.

Whether or not it would have been better to let the UK and then Canada have it is a question that can be taken up elsewhere. The resources alone make the acquisition worth it. Other than a small diversionary landing on a couple of small islands by the Japanese in World War II, we have never had to defend it. So far so good.

U.S. Grant and the Dominican Republic

That we did not engage in foreign wars after the "War Between the States" does not mean our country was not expansionist as noted in our ready grasp of Alaska. President Grant wanted to acquire what was then a Caribbean problem child, the Dominican Republic. He even had an agreement that was submitted to Congress.

That would fail under opposition. His attempted grab also saw resistance from an anti-imperialist faction. The Dominicans would have to do without the tutelage of the US. On balance this should be considered a good thing, as there has been little benefit from our Caribbean forays. Our ownership of and semi-self-government of Puerto Rico has led to de facto bankruptcy, which should lead to jettisoning the possession but will end up with a bailout. Pretending to assist Cuba to gain freedom has led to ongoing problems.

The era from the 1860s to the 1890s was not uneventful, but there was no need to pay attention to foreign matters. We kept out of Europe and Europe didn't bother us for the most part.

The defense budget was for the most part tiny. As to how much that contributed to the explosive economic growth, we can leave that discussion to the economists. Suffice it to say, after World War II our former enemies had economic miracles when we were managing their defenses.

The last part of the century would see the country start to move on the world stage in bigger ways. Columbia was going sailing.

11

Hawaii

Hawaii is as American as the hula and the grass skirt. The average mainlander, when he thinks of those islands of paradise, muses about a vacation. The more outré of our countrymen and women consider Maui Wowie, or at least my contemporaries did.

Our youngest state didn't just apply to be part of the Union on August 21, 1959. It was a long and not really glorious process.

Polynesians, arguably history's greatest navigators, arrived on the archipelago. The population grew and the people coalesced around chiefs. The chiefs engaged in wars to extend influence.

When Europeans first visited is open to debate, but they did and Captain Cook showed up in 1778 and was killed by Hawaiians in a dispute.

House of Kamehameha

One chief, Kamehameha was successful in his battles and brought all of the islands under his rule, became king, and began a dynasty in 1810. The monarchy established itself with a government that included an army and a navy.

Like many non-European or non-African peoples, the Polynesians of Hawaii were susceptible to diseases that would devastate their population. It would not make things easy to maintain national independence.

Hawaii appeared on American radar in 1842 when President Tyler declared that a takeover by a European power of Hawaii, already a stopover on the way to China, could not be tolerated.

A few gestures were made regarding annexation between 1850 and 1870 toward the islands that were a missionary field and whaling station.

As time passed, the United States put the squeeze on. In 1875, a trade treaty allowed Hawaiian sugar into the United States without tariffs. This stimulated sugar growing and tied the islands economy to the American. The pact also required Hawaii to not sell land to other countries.

In 1887, the treaty was renewed with a provision granting Pearl Harbor to the United States. In 1890, a duty was laid on sugar that hurt the American planter economy of Hawaii. The growers would thus wish to be within the American orbit and not having to pay the tariff.

Planters had been agitating and taking over for years and they were going to put the final nail in the kingdom's coffin in 1893.

The planters and allies fomented an uprising and it was supported by the American minister Stevens, who provided some armed support to overthrow the queen, Liliuokalani.

To his everlasting credit, President Grover Cleveland repudiated the action and tried to restore the queen. In the end, without congressional support, the "Republic" stood.

In 1898 Hawaii was annexed by joint resolution after a treaty failed in the Senate.

So, it was all tidily done with just a few men at arms involved and force majeure quickly doing its work. If moralists of this nation have opposed other countries' actions against smaller nations, the swallowing of Hawaii was no less wrong.

Oh well, General Powell's pottery barn has a corollary: if you take land you have to defend it as we found out in December of 1941.

12

The Spanish-American War or Imperialism Really Takes Wing

The United States had been watching Cuba and Spain's attempts to pacify her colony for decades. Offers had been made to purchase the island before the Civil War.

In the island known as the Pearl of the Antilles, the Spanish king was not beloved of all his subjects. The Ten Years War was a rebellion begun by Cuban planters against Spain in 1868. It grew to include people of all social classes but hardly united the nation.

After the Third Carlist War in the mother country ended, Spain sent in a large army. The rebels had many divisions among them, but eventually Spain gained the upper hand and prevailed.

During the long and bloody conflict, the United States remained on the sidelines and didn't participate in any meaningful way.

After the end of the Ten Years' War, Cuba had an era known as the Rewarding Truce. Who it rewarded can be debated. That it was called a truce means that peace did not reign.

Hostilities resumed in August of 1879 in what was called the Little War. It was not terribly well supported and ended in defeat in September of 1880. Reforms were not enough, however, to gain the loyalty of the Cubans.

Cuba's last war against Spain began in February of 1895. Though slavery had ended, the island's people were suffering a depressed economy. Rebellion would surprise no one. The insurrectionists were able to control much of the country.

The United States was going to view this war differently from the two others. The Cuban economy was more and more under American ownership and the rebellion was not good for that property.

The guerilla war that the insurgents waged against regular Spanish forces was successful enough that the government had to respond with harsh tactics. General Valeriano Weyler, the governor, embarked on a campaign of separating the people from the guerillas.

No matter how effective a system it might have been, it caused suffering among the population, as their removal was not adequately supplied with necessities. American yellow journalists such as William Randolph Hearst and Joseph Pulitzer sicced their newspapers on the Spanish with vehemence.

What little biographical information can be garnered about "Butcher" Weyler does not make him out to be a monster. Nevertheless, civilian suffering was great and not all of the soldiers under him could have been saints. The American papers were not shy in exaggeration.

On the 15th of February 1898, the USS *Maine* was in Havana Harbor. She had been sent to protect American interests. At 9:40 p.m., the ship suffered an explosion that would sink her and take the lives of 258 sailors.

Many investigations of the cause of the sinking have occurred. Though a naval inquiry suggested an external explosion, there was no evidence the Spanish had sabotaged the American ship. Indeed, the Spanish had the most to lose and would have been least likely to set a device.

In all probability, the explosion was due to bad design in a class of ships.

The yellow press went wild demanding war. The McKinley administration attempted negotiations, but the drift, with the public demand for action, would be overwhelming. A congressional resolution demanding a Spanish withdrawal and pledging no intention to annex the island was passed on April 20, 1898. Severed relations and a declaration of war followed.

The results were a foregone conclusion. Through superior resources, the U.S. Navy would see that resupply and reinforcements could not get through to the enemy. The Spanish fleet in Cuba was destroyed in an uneven battle.

The land campaign was also an inevitable American victory, and the island conflict ended with Americans in charge.

Most American troops were quickly withdrawn as soldiers became sick with tropical diseases at an alarming rate. That was probably fortunate for Cuba. Who knows how long we would have kept the island if the army had stayed healthy.

The War in Asia

Even though the war was caused by events in Cuba, the first battle took place in the Far East. At Manila, Admiral Dewey destroyed the Spanish fleet. The enemy sailed bravely with a force overmatched to say the least.

The Americans and insurgent Filipinos took over most of the islands. In August, the Americans took Manila to the disadvantage of the local forces.

Spain and America signed the Treaty of Paris. Spain had lost, and America had the Philippines and other Pacific island properties.

The natives of the Philippines were not happy with the arrangement. They had been struggling for independence and didn't want to switch one set of masters for another. Uncle Sam certainly felt they were enlightening the world, but as a byproduct of building an empire.

The Philippines declared for independence, thus beginning the Philippine-American War.

The Philippine forces of resistance were not up to the task of defeating the American military. Nevertheless, they made a brave show of it. Aguinaldo, the president of the declared Philippine Republic, retreated with his army against superior forces and turned the struggle into a guerilla war. Eventually, superior equipment and force led to the resistance ceasing.

In the south of the archipelago, the Moros (Muslims) were under the effective rule of the Sultan of Sulu. Though they did not oppose the American invasion by agreement, they eventually resisted American encroachment and a war was fought against them. The Americans, using force and diplomacy, came to a modus vivendi with the Moros.

Pacified did not mean quiescent. The Philippines never completely accepted the arrangement. To our credit, a free press was respected and pro-Philippine publications were published.

No matter what may have lurked in elite American hearts, the islands would never become the American Raj. Despite attempts at economic exploitation and the luxurious lives of the occupying forces, the colony was not the success we had hoped, and the locals were not the easily gulled rubes we thought. Consequently, Congress passed a bill in 1934 telling them to get lost in 1946. After a three-and-a-half-year occupation by the Japanese, independence was established. As is our national wont, we attached numerous strings, kept some bases, and provided aid.

Since then, our relationship has become even more contentious, there is the possibility of a complete rupture and the Philippines favoring a relationship with China, or not.

One problem with colonialism is that if you invade and take over a place, you may have to defend it—or lose it. In the case of the Philippines, we were unable to provide a defense against the Japanese, and would have to reinvade and reconquer the place.

We can put down the Philippines as a mistake.

Was the war a complete error?

A result of the war was that Spain was expunged from the Western Hemisphere. We legislatively pledged not to keep Cuba, and we did see to that (other than maintaining Guantanamo, which the United States still does). The Cubans never established a stable government until 1959 with the communist takeover under Castro. Before Fidel, Cuba could be a nuisance, but was not too much more.

With Castro, we had a country allied with the Communist Bloc until its break up. The regime was openly an enemy and we, with the embargo, were theirs.

Without our war with Spain, our history with Cuba could not have been the same. Had we not been involved, Spain would have had to be conciliatory toward the Cubans, brutally suppress the people, or leave.

One thing is probable: a Spanish Cuba may not have been our best friend, but it would not be a great threat to us (certainly no more than Soviet allied Cuba was).

In truth, the big winner, even though they didn't realize it then and may not now, was Spain. They lost the albatross around their neck.

We still have Puerto Rico, which has probably been a net financial loss all along. Today they are a fiscal basket case. They are Detroit with bases.

It was a war, small though it was, that we did not need.

13

The Panama Canal

Among the nations involved, thoughts of a Panama Canal anticipated a huge cake and no one wanted to go without a piece of that rich gateau. Excising thousands of miles from a trip from one U.S. coast to another or the trip from Europe to Asia would be worth untold treasure, and who would not want their snout in that trough?

In the events leading up to the building of the "ditch," no nation or individual did much to cover themselves with honor.

The Isthmus of Panama is a narrow waist between the two American continents. For anyone north of it, a waterway between the Atlantic and Pacific Oceans would be a time- and money-saving benefit. Nature didn't provide one, so human ingenuity would be needed. Once it became feasible to dig, it would be inevitable.

Though home to some Indigenes, for Europeans, it was discovered in 1501 and came under Spanish control later. The explorer, Balboa, crossed the isthmus and discovered the Pacific. It was thus of supreme importance to Spain, as it was the shortest route for transshipment of Peruvian treasure.

In the nineteenth century, Spain's colonies sought to be free of her rule. Panama also had an independence movement that, with little trouble, allowed it to separate from Spain. In 1821, with no real struggle, she became a separate country.

Soon afterward, Panama voluntarily became part of Bolivar's Gran Colombia. When that fell apart, she was not too happily stuck attached to Columbia.

Not being satisfied with the union, the country made attempts to separate without success from her neighbor to the south.

Before the idea of a canal could be considered practical, a railroad would itself be of no little benefit. There were proposals and studies, one Colombian, one American, and one French that all foundered.

With West Coast territory gained in war with Mexico as well as the Pacific Northwest, American interest in a Panama railroad increased. In 1846, the Mallarino-Bidlack Treaty was signed giving the United States the right to build a railroad or canal and guaranteed Columbian sovereignty.

The Panama Railway was completed in 1855 and was an engineering feat, not as huge as the eventual canal but big in its own right. It ran as one of the most profitable railroads in the world.

During the latter part of the nineteenth century, the Colombians indulged in their national sport of civil wars. Occasionally, their northern territory would want to split, but thanks to the aforementioned treaty, Uncle Sam was happy to send a vessel and make sure that Columbia stayed whole.

Over in the old world, the really old world, a Frenchman, Ferdinand de Lesseps, had seen through the construction of a canal to connect the Mediterranean to the Red Sea. The Egyptian canal at Suez was a huge undertaking but in the end brought Europe and East Asia closer and saved untold time and money. If it could be done to a length of 120 miles in Egypt, then why not a short 48-mile furrow?

De Lesseps started work in 1882 and found he had enemies in the form of malaria and the land itself. His attempt to build the canal without locks didn't work and the company behind the effort declared bankruptcy in 1888.

A canal at the isthmus was devoutly to be wished. The question was would it be in Panama or Nicaragua and who would control it.

The pro-Nicaragua team was led by Alabama Senator John Morgan. He would be completely outclassed by the slick William Nelson Cromwell of the powerful Sullivan & Cromwell firm still doing business today. As important to the cause of Panama was an equally cute Frenchman, Philippe Bunau-Varilla.

Between Cromwell and Bunau-Varilla, and with men on the ground, they would foment a less-than-glorious Panamanian revolution severing the relationship with Colombia. As a mother country, Colombia was no prize, but it was still a sovereign nation that we had supported with treaty obligations.

Bunau-Varilla got himself appointed as Minister of Panama to Washington. In that capacity, he would negotiate a one-sided treaty that favored the USA.

Cromwell did very well financially with millions in fees for his efforts. Bunau-Varilla cashed out his stock from the de Lesseps successor corporation. Other than that, much of the cash trail was opaque. It is difficult to believe that J.P. Morgan, who was involved, would have been part of something without profit.

So, it all happened and was pure as the driven snow, as averred by Theodore Roosevelt: "It must be a matter of pride to every honest American, proud of the good name of his country that the acquisition of the canal... [was] as free from scandal as the public acts of George Washington and Abraham Lincoln."

There would be some disagreement on that from the press, namely Joseph Pulitzer's *New York World*. The *World* and other papers would point out holes in the story and that got under TR's skin. Roosevelt was sensitive to the accusations of his having instigated the takeover of Panama and that there had been a conspiracy. So irked was the man that he had a libel action brought against Pulitzer.

Pulitzer fought back, accusing the government of imposing lèse-majesté. The *World* had a problem: the records seemed to be non-existent. Nevertheless, he had a couple of his reporters investigate and at the last moment, they cracked the case. That was irrelevant, as the action was quashed, rightfully, on First Amendment grounds.

TR was not a man overendowed with humility, and on March 23, 1911, in California, he would give a brag of a speech wherein he near took sole credit for the canal. This contradicted his prior "America the innocent" line. Roosevelt's boasting was noticed with riots in Latin America. Columbia claimed that the former president was admitting theft and demanded compensation. Congress wanted to investigate but was diverted by Teddy's friend, Henry Cabot Lodge.

So, we had a canal for a century, but in the end returned it to Panama by treaty, and after a small contretemps with a tinhorn dictator from central casting, we've had a stable canal environment since.

Still, the whole skullduggery was probably unnecessary. Roosevelt, Secretary of State Hay, Bunau-Varilla, and Cromwell were an unworthy chapter and part of a bad neighbor policy.

14

World War I

War is not fun, but is it *stupid*? We may get people to agree that any war that could have been avoided was dumb. One may also opine that sometimes it can't be escaped, say as in resisting invasion, which means one country might have justice on its side.

Two Americans have in recent years declared at least one war stupid. The late Lt. General William Odom stated, "The Iraq War may turn out to be the greatest strategic disaster in American history." President Obama said of the same, "I don't oppose all wars. ... What I am opposed to is a dumb war."

Both men were right, but as bad as Iraq was, it bears no comparison to the folly of American involvement in World War I. Nothing good would come out of it and it would begin the nation's involvement in Europe. President Wilson's rationale seemed to stand John Quincy Adams's words on their head and change them to "America does go abroad in search of monsters to destroy."

Legend has it that when Alexander Haig asked Chinese Communist Premier Chou En Lai about the legacy of the French Revolution, Mao's right hand man answered that it was "too soon to tell." The revolution had occurred almost 200 years before the Haig-Chou discussion, but it is true we are still debating it.

If we can't agree on an event that occurred more than two centuries ago, how can we have any clear view of one that happened a mere hundred years ago? Not a bad question, but even if there can be no absolute clarity, it is not arguable that World War I is still impacting our lives.

Our current squabbles with Putin would not be happening today if the war had not occurred and Imperial Russia not been destroyed.

The events in Iraq are also the results of the so-called Great War. We are witnessing the breakdown of the Sykes-Picot Treaty. The French and British victors made up countries on the Middle East map. Had the war not happened, they would have remained parts of the Ottoman Empire. We seem hell bent on making some of 1914's all over again.

So, it is an important subject and one worth exploring as more than a century has passed. In putting the conflict under the microscope, one could do worse than consulting *The Pity of War* by Niall Ferguson.

The Pity of War is probably his most famous book and it caused quite a splash. One could argue that Britain never recovered from the First World War. Ferguson claimed the United Kingdom didn't have to be part of the conflict and that entering it was a bad idea.

Ferguson makes an excellent case. He disparages the official line of defending Belgian neutrality. The British would have themselves occupied Belgium, if convenient. They didn't want a dominant continental power. Indeed, that has always been British foreign doctrine. Belgium was good diplomatic cover.

Not so noble as another cause is the fact that the government ministers would lose their jobs if they did not opt for war. Grey, the foreign minister, and Churchill, in charge of the navy, would have resigned, and Prime Minister Asquith would have had to admit the government could not continue.

None of them wanted to have to tell their wives they were out of a job. There may be worse reasons for beginning a major conflagration that completely disrupts one's civilization, but do they readily come to mind?

Germany would probably have won without British intervention, especially in the way the French botched the first months of the war. Ferguson contends that German war aims would not have threatened UK interests. Anyway, it's hard to argue that the Britain that ended the war was much worse off than had she stood apart.

So why did the major player on the other side, Germany, feel it necessary to go to war, other than obligations to the Habsburgs? Contrary to the simplistic history taught in my high school in the 1960s, German leadership was not an evil imperial clique bent on world domination. Rather, it was a sense of weakness. The Russian and French forces were growing and improving and would eventually overtake the German military. It was a case of strike now or suffer an inevitable eclipse.

Ferguson's book is wide ranging. Some aspects of the war I had been ignorant of disturbed me. Literary figures I had admired sunk to a low level in lending their work to vilify the foe as by nature evil. Ferguson notes that religious leaders took up the enemy as the spawn of Satan trope with gusto. G.B Shaw comes off best as a consistent opponent, though with negligible effect.

Where one might disagree with Ferguson concerns American involvement. He does not see it as crucial. For this aspect one might recommend *The Myth of the Great War: A New Military History of World War I* by John Mosier. Mosier, a professor at Loyola of New Orleans, marshals evidence to demonstrate that Germany was gradually and inevitably winning until the Americans arrived.

So why did the United States go to war?

No matter how the drift to the "Great War" happened, it did and the course of the war was brutal.

The Germans, acting on their Schlieffen Plan to do an end run around the French by going through Belgium. The Germans got pretty far but seemed to run out of gas short of the Marne.

At the First Battle of the Marne, The Anglo-French attacked the Germans and sent them in retreat. After that, the front widened as entrenchment on a grand scale began. It would extend out on the Western Front from the sea to the Swiss border.

Large-scale entrenchments had happened before. Caesar at Alesia and Petersburg in our Civil War come to mind. A whole nation sliced up by a gully scraped out of its soil might have been a new departure.

This is not to say the combatants just sat in the trenches and took pot shots at each other. The desire to win generally exceeded the ability and the two sides would undertake offensives that achieved mostly slaughter of their men.

Most famous was Verdun that took place over most of 1916. Though a huge attempt by the Germans to beat the French, it became months and months of back and forth attacks and brutal artillery barrages. The main result would be over 700,000 casualties.

The Somme offensive took place in the summer and fall of 1916 and led to a million casualties and more. The allies would gain some square footage out of it. The word *victory* could only be applied said by a propagandist.

On the Eastern front, though there were trenches, it was never too widespread and the battles raged with the Germans having the better of it, despite some Russian successes such as the Brusilov offensive.

As the Schlieffen Plan was a grand outflanking maneuver, so the allies were not immune to such an idea. To that end, they came up with the Gallipoli Campaign.

The Gallipoli Peninsula is south of Constantinople in what was the old Ottoman Turkish Empire. Turkey was an ally of Germany. By landing troops on the peninsula and defeating the Turkish forces, the allies could knock them out of the war and gain control of a sea route to Russia.

It began in February of 1915 and ended in January of 1916. The French and British would try to force the straits with naval forces unsuccessfully, and would land troops for an advance up the peninsula.

The Turks, under the seconded German, Otto von Sanders, and the man who would become the Turkish national hero, Mustafa Kemal, out-generalled the allies, and in the end the game was not worth it and the occupying troops could better serve elsewhere and were withdrawn.

After a few years of continuous slaughter, one might think the sides would have come to the conclusion that their respective crusades were not worth the death of their young but rapidly aging men.

It was time to convene a new Congress of Vienna. It would not be easy, items like Alsace and Lorraine would still be sticking points, but it would have been better than any other possible future. Unfortunately, no one could see that.

The Allies had a better idea. There was a huge country to the west across an ocean with a burgeoning population and a vast economy. If they could bring in that country as their ringers, it would be quite the coup. If the war could not be automatically won, it would at least be hard to lose it.

Germany also thought she had a better idea. After Russia left the war and the treaty of Brest-Litovsk, she had her eastern front army available for a big offensive. Just march them west and charge.

The other German plan was to starve Britain with a submarine blockade. After all, starvation was a potent weapon, as starvation was happening in Germany.

So, who had the better big idea? In the long run, no one. The economist John Maynard Keynes famously stated, "In the long run we are all dead." True enough, but in the life of a nation, it's not enough. The leadership has to think about the next battle. But it should also be thinking of what will come after the battles are over. The allies, though successful in ensnaring the Yanks, would suffer much a generation later.

The President of the United States from before the outbreak of the war until after the armistice was Woodrow Wilson. At the outset, he declared the country neutral and would campaign for re-election with the slogan, "He kept us out of war." It is almost fortunate that he was unable to stand for a third term, as "He got us into war" was not going to resonate the same.

Wilson's reputation has suffered recently because it is one thing to be doing things progressives love like instituting central banking and an income tax and invading nearby countries but quite another to be more than a little biased against one's fellow countrymen of a different race.

He is, however, never found wanting for getting us into a conflict that caused over a couple of hundred thousand casualties.

On November 7, 1916, President Wilson was re-elected and was inaugurated on March 4, 1917.

On February 17, he gave a speech to Congress laying down the law on unrestricted submarine warfare. As Germany believed it was in the right to do what it needed to do in order to win, it was obvious where this would end up.

On April 6, 1917, a bit less than four months after Wilson's electoral triumph with his then battle cry, "He kept us out of war," the United States declared war on Germany.

SHE SEARCHES FOR MONSTERS TO DESTROY

Was it a necessary war? Germany had declared a zone of exclusion and was enforcing it. A blockade was in force and American ships were targeted. This was no less a blockade than what Britain placed against America in the war of 1812 or the Union against the Confederacy.

Britain itself was enforcing an effective blockade against Germany, bringing about almost famine conditions.

The morality of blockades and machinations, as evidenced by the Zimmerman telegram, are not to be belabored here. As to whether or not it was a necessary war for freedom of the seas, probably not.

It wasn't like the Barbary pirates had been an ongoing threat over generations. When the war in Europe ended, the blockade would as well.

Was there another reason? Some suggest that American banks pushed for it, as a defeated Britain and France were not going to pay back war loans all that quickly.

This is only brought up because the argument is out there. Wilson was a moralist and was as easily swayed by his crusading tendencies as by anything else. As it was, the allies were not Johnny on the spot to settle up after the war. It was for others to make the arguments for and against.

How did the country feel about the war? After the United States entered the conflict, the crusade didn't have a *Deus Vult* moment. Wilson wanted a million-man army of volunteers, but after six weeks only 73,000 had signed up. Being part of a movement to make the world safe for democracy was not selling.

The war was sold to the American populace by an official team of war promoters. One of them was the Irish-American entertainer, George M. Cohan. His stirring anthem, "Over There" is still played today. It is a great tune, but even so, a draft was necessary. Hey, somebody was going to have to pull the Anglo-French chestnuts out of the fire.

Bringing a fresh army and a fair-sized navy tipped the balance in favor of the allies. There is no need to discuss engagements and tactics. Barring a battle that would entrap and destroy a complete allied army, Deutschland was done. Whatever tactical advantages the Imperial German army might have enjoyed, a Cannae-like battle was not going to happen.

Inevitably, the Germans would need to bring an end to the war. The government sent Wilson a telegram requesting an armistice based on President Wilson's 14 points. The Kaiser had to go, and on November 11, 1918, the war ended.

1919 saw the representatives of the victorious nations assemble in Paris for a peace conference. It was not at all to be another Congress of Vienna. Germany and the other Central Powers were not allowed to attend and would have to accept the treaty as it was decided.

The peace was humiliating for Germany. She was stripped of her colonies and had her borders redrawn. Huge reparations that could not be repaid were laid on her. Ridiculously, she and her allies had to accept all the guilt for the war.

The world got Wilson's League of Nations and not much else of his high-minded program and he came home with little else to show for his efforts. The American electorate was little impressed with the result and Warren Harding won election calling for a return to "normalcy."

The world is full of Wilsonians who would try to justify the war. In answer, one might cite the words of Winston Churchill:

> *America should have minded her own business and stayed out of the World War. If you hadn't entered the war the Allies would have made peace with Germany in the Spring of 1917. Had we made peace then there would have been no collapse in Russia followed by Communism, no breakdown in Italy followed by Fascism, and Germany*

would not have signed the Versailles Treaty, which has enthroned Nazism in Germany. If America had stayed out of the war, all these "isms" wouldn't today be sweeping the continent of Europe and breaking down parliamentary government—and if England had made peace early in 1917, it would have saved over one million British, French, American, and other lives.

In his book about the *Lusitania*, Erik Larson at least hints that Churchill's machinations might have had a hand in the sinking of that ship as part of getting the Yanks into the war. We might guess that the quote was some rare sober reflection on the man's part.

One cannot truly posit an alternative history if an event had not happened. It is, however, not unreasonable to speculate about what might have happened. If Wilson had not called for a declaration of war against Germany, Adolph Hitler would have not risen to power.

Someone said that had America not entered the war, Hitler would have gone to his death raving in a Bavarian old soldier's home. That may be so, but he certainly wouldn't have died as the Führer of the German people.

Without Woody, we would not have had Dolph.

15

The Interwar Years

America became less enamored with Europe after its involvement in the war and the "peace." The nation came home and though there was a fair isolationist spirit, it still had to engage with the world in some areas.

World War I Debts

It is said of post–World War I America that it wanted to forget Europe. That was probably true, but not completely possible.

The Allied nations owed American banks money and Germany had been saddled with reparations. No one, however, was flush with cash.

The German debt was set high. The allies, claiming to have been righteous victors over the guilty Hun, felt justified in the assessment.

In 1923, Germany would default and French and Belgian troops would occupy the Ruhr to force repayment. It didn't work and the famous German inflation ensued.

Meanwhile, the war debts owed to the United States were not looking all that healthy. The debtors wished to have the loans canceled as part of the common wartime cause. The Americans weren't buying that.

What to do?

In 1923, Charles G. Dawes, a Chicago banker, headed a commission to review the situation. It presented a proposal known as the Dawes Plan. Payments would be reduced until the German economy was strong enough to afford more. The Allies would use what they got to service their debts to the Yanks. Dawes got part of a Nobel and the plan worked until it didn't.

In 1929, it was time for another committee, this one chaired by Owen D. Young, head of General Electric and a member of Dawes's group. It was also a reduction plan with the same goals.

The Young Plan also worked until it couldn't. It was doomed by the depression. Everybody but Finland defaulted.

The debt problems could be called the last battle of World War I and it was not an American victory.

The Naval Conferences

Whatever sentiment for avoiding foreign entanglements existed, it is impossible to completely ignore the greater world. The United States, bordering on two oceans and with large seacoasts, had to be at least aware of other seafaring nations.

Beginning in 1921, a series of naval conferences were held among the major naval powers of the world to regulate the amount of tonnage or ships each could build.

The first, The Washington Naval Conference of 1921–1922, was convened to prevent another war. Preventing an arms race would be in order. It would not be a bad idea to engage our two biggest rivals in naval size in such talks.

Other naval powers were invited, but the importance of limiting the increases in the fleets of the United States, the United Kingdom, and Imperial Japan was paramount.

The Five Power Treaty was agreed upon. The important aspect was, of course between the three aforementioned powers. The United States, Britain, and Japan could have tonnage in the ratio of 5:5:3.

Restrictions on overseas bases and non-restrictions on other types of ships meant that another conference would be inevitable.

In 1927, the Geneva Naval Conference was convened in the landlocked nation of Switzerland. The meeting was called to discuss extending the previous agreements to other classes of vessels not covered in the Washington conference. It was attended by the United States, Britain, and Japan.

The conference floundered on the question of tonnage and number of cruisers. Mainly, the United States and Britain were at loggerheads with the Japanese most flexible. No agreement on that issue could be reached and the conference ended.

Much in our day is mentioned about the "special relationship" between the two Anglophone nations. The disagreement was evidence that they had not ruled out that they might not be on the same side of a future conflict.

Nevertheless, both compromised on a cruiser pact in 1929, but could not solve all their disagreements regarding the heavier ships of that class.

As bureaucracies are addicted to conferences, whether or not they solve anything, another meeting was inevitable. The next one would be the London Naval Conference of 1930.

That conference ended with an agreement. The result is as described in The Office of the Historian's website:

> Although it was described as an "arms limitation conference," in actuality, the London Naval Treaty set limits above the current capacity of some of the powers involved. The U.S. Senate approved the treaty in July of 1930 over the objections of key naval officers concerned that the naval limitations would inhibit the American ability to defend its control of the Philippine islands. Then the United States actually embarked on a

shipbuilding program to make up the difference between its existing cruiser tonnage and what it was allotted under the treaty. That building ultimately helped to alleviate some unemployment caused by the Great Depression.

In 1935, the powers would meet again in London. The Japanese would walk out, but the United States, Britain, and France would agree on a six-year holiday on building larger light cruisers, and that was that for the cruiser.

A postscript to the interwar naval questions would be the Mukden incident that led to the Japanese takeover of Manchuria. That with the Japanese attack on Shanghai was seen as imperiling the Open Door Policy. This policy, promoted by America, was that China could be exploited by foreign trading nations in a way that was not unfair to those nations.

As a result of the Mukden incident, the United States came up with the Stimson Doctrine. Named after the secretary of state, it refused recognition to any treaties or agreements between the Japanese and Chinese that violated U.S. rights or agreements that we were a party to. The policy had little effect.

Due to Japanese ongoing aggression in China and violations of the final agreement of the Washington Naval Conference, the United States announced it no longer considered itself subject to the naval limitations as agreed by that treaty. This meant that a new naval arms race was in the cards as Japanese advances in China continued.

A decade and a half of trying to limit naval growth to avoid war had little to show. The three powers all had overseas territories that would necessitate sizeable fleets to protect them.

If you're going to have colonies, you're going to have to defend them.

In the end, there is little to say for all the waltzing at conferences and diplomacy. It was all for naught. Almost all the colonies are gone and what is left is hardly worth defending.

One might posit a rule for conferences: Unless all participants have a common goal, not much of value will be accomplished.

The Kellogg-Briand Pact

A treaty of nations agreeing to end war is a wonderful idea. In 1928, many nations came together to do just that, even though a "war to end war" had been fought. The Kellogg-Briand Pact eventually was signed by lots of counties.

As they say, "If wishes were horses, beggars would ride." If you know a little of twentieth-century history and are wondering how effective the pact was, you need not read further.

The Great Depression, the Neutrality Acts, and Lend-Lease

The Great Depression is generally thought to have begun with the stock market crash of 1929. Its causes are still debated among economists. To many libertarians, misapplied monetary policy is considered a major cause. To a supply sider, such as the late Jude Wanniski, protectionism as expressed in the Smoot-Hawley Tariff so stunted trade such that the world economy came to a drastic halt.

Whatever the cause, the effect was indeed drastic. A reactionary college professor of mine said to his American history survey class that both Franklin Roosevelt and Adolph Hitler came to power for the same reason at about the same time.

Such an attitude would offend progressives. No matter what, in an environment of sudden change, an electorate is looking for different answers. The right answer is not necessarily what they get.

One aspect of the Depression was an inward turning of the American nation. This would be expressed in neutrality acts. As the international situation was heating up in Europe and Asia, Americans and their representatives wished to prevent the nation from becoming involved.

The first Neutrality Act was passed in 1935. It prohibited the export of "arms, ammunition, and implements of war" to foreign nations at war, and required arms manufacturers in the United States to apply for an export license. Citizens who traveled to war zones were also advised that they did so at their own risk.

President Roosevelt, always an internationalist, did not favor the bill, but it was popular enough, he had little choice but to go along with it. The act would be renewed in 1936 until 1937 with Americans prohibited from extending loans to belligerents.

As Europe, with the Spanish Civil War, was becoming more interesting, support for neutrality was strong. The Neutrality Act of 1937 expanded the law.

Under that act, Americans were forbidden from traveling on belligerent ships, and our ships were prevented from transporting arms to warring countries even if produced outside of the U.S. The president had authority to bar belligerent ships from American waters. Civil wars would also fall under the terms of the act.

Roosevelt did get something he wanted in the renewed law. Under the cash-and-carry provision, at the president's discretion belligerents were allowed to purchase anything but arms from the U.S. They had to pay right away and had to carry them on non-American ships. Oil and some other raw materials, not being arms, were still valuable to nations in conflict. Roosevelt wanted this to deliberately aid Britain and

France if they became involved in war with Axis nations. This provision of the act was the only one not permanent with a two-year expiration.

As war started to move across Europe, the final Neutrality Act was passed in 1939 after heated congressional debate. Roosevelt got it expanded to allowing arms to be in included in cash-and-carry. Loans to belligerents were still forbidden and the goods still had to be carried in other than U.S. shipping.

Clearly, the nation was becoming a little less neutral. The Lend-Lease policy ("An Act to Promote the Defense of the United States") would move the U.S. even further away from neutrality.

War had begun in Europe in 1939. President Roosevelt wished to assist the nations fighting the Axis powers. The American people, while probably favoring the allies, were still not keen to enter another war.

The president's first bit of aid was a destroyers-for-bases deal in September 1940. This gave Britain 50 obsolete destroyers in exchange for leases on bases in British territory and was justified in terms of hemispheric defense.

Next was Lend-Lease, proposed in December 1940. This allowed the United States to lend supplies to the UK for a "consideration." It meant the administration was in the war without the fighting.

One of the better policies between the wars was Franklin Roosevelt's good neighbor policy. The U.S. had been intervening south of the border and in the Caribbean for decades. Such adventures were not popular in the non-Anglo world.

It was a better policy than what went before. One might ask, Would his cousin's canal have been built had honest dealing been the method of negotiation? Who knows? It might have happened without Cromwell and Bunau-Varilla and their skullduggery.

16

World War II

I

For the parents of the early baby boom generation, time was divided in three epochs: before the war, during the war, and after the war. World War II was so large an event that it involved almost every American, whether they were part of the armed forces or not. Time could almost not be referenced any other way.

Most households had members that were either serving in uniform or working in something defense related. Many a family, if not most, had a relative who was a casualty.

The generation affected by the conflict has mostly passed away, but the echoes in the culture are still there. Our decade-long war in Vietnam lasted longer and involved half a million troops and saw cultural upheavals at home, and yet it doesn't compare. The number of movies and books about World War II dwarf anything that has come before or after. Only the American Civil War compares in the amount of literature produced.

The generation that came immediately after the war was greatly affected by their parents' experience. Television was new and needed content. It seemed every Sunday a local Boston station would show a World War II movie. Whether it was William Bendix fighting at Guadalcanal or Van Johnson dropping bombs over Tokyo, the theme was always the same: American soldiers, sailors, or airmen fought heroically against great odds and against less brave and noble enemies.

Despite the passage of time, we are still given films and books on the subject whether it's Jack O'Connell in *Unbroken* or Brad Pitt in *Inglourious Basterds*; they were the bad guys and we were the honorable.

Just a few years after the end of World War II, we were involved in a brutal war in the Korean Peninsula. As bad as that was, there is not much public discussion about it.

Vietnam was next and there isn't a large cultural footprint other than a counter-cultural one. To cite a more recent example, our coalition to free Kuwait is little discussed.

The destruction of the World Trade Center on September 11, 2001, does compare at least because of its uniqueness and the struggle that it began is ongoing. Whether it would fade from memory if an unlikely peace ensued is up for discussion.

Is there a special reason for the persistence of World War II in the American memory and culture?

Yes.

The American victory in World War II is seen as a positive outcome and even those who might have some disagreements with that thesis have to admit, it is better that we won. Our enemy was an evil force.

National Socialist Germany was the outgrowth of resentment and racial animosity. Certainly, a better peace at Versailles would have probably meant nothing to Hitler, but the man and his regime have no excuse for what they inflicted on those nations they abused.

Our East Asian enemy was an imperialist and expansionist state involved in a campaign of conquest in China. Though the Japanese regime doesn't compare to the National Socialist state, it was not doing anything good in the world.

Maybe it was not a perfect crusade, but the better team—the United States and Great Britain—emerged in the win column.

The problems that may exist in our own glorification are not fatal. True, the Soviet Union may have contributed even more to the end result due to its blood sacrifice as it moved westward. We had other allies, but they had only a supporting role in our view.

This doesn't mean there has been no investigation of another country's contribution to the war effort, but we never see it affecting the big picture.

Though the surrender on the USS *Missouri* in 1945 did not end history, it did end operations. Nothing we have experienced since has had that sense of finality.

II

There are three questions that need to be addressed here.

First, could the United States have avoided involvement in World War II?

Second, if America had been able to stay out of the war, could that have been done without harm to the freedom and strategic position of the nation? A corollary to that question is, Did involvement in the conflict harm the freedom and safety of the American people?

Third, should we have been involved, that is, was there a moral imperative to war?

III
Background

As most people who might read this have some idea of the events leading up to the World War II, this will not be exhaustive.

Had World War I not occurred, or had ended differently, the post war history would have been different. It happened as it did and Europe was faced with an unsettled world.

The defeated Germany was now a poor but still strong country. As France was revanchist after 1870, Germany would see itself wronged by a punishing treaty.

To blame Germany completely for the war may have been fair or not. To exact retribution the way allies did would not lead to a peaceful Europe.

"This is not a peace. It is an armistice for Twenty Years."

The words of Marshall Ferdinand Foch were prophetic. The allied military leader was not denigrating the treaty because it was too harsh, but because it was too lenient.

He would have liked to see France gain the west bank of the Rhine and Germany divided up as before 1870. Indeed, such a peace might have worked as it did with a divided Germany in the Cold War.

A completely supine Germany meant a strong, maybe too strong France. That France on the Rhine business was not going to fly. So, there it is, a mean-spirited peace, harsh enough to spark thoughts of revenge and not harsh enough to make them impossible.

Out of this mess would arise Adolph Hitler. He was not inevitable and with circumstances other than actually occurred, he may have never been anything other than a small-time rabble-rouser, but they didn't.

Foch would be proven correct, and Hitler's arrival would seem inevitable.

IV

Events happen in history as they happen and it is impossible to "change history." Nevertheless, we can say with confidence that a peace without a German defeat, even if not an outright victory, would have never seen the rise of Adolph Hitler.

That, of course, is now irrelevant. Hitler did arrive and was the chief actor in the march to World War II.

He was not, however, the only man on stage. The British and French and Polish and Czech and Soviet as well as Italian governments were all there and were all players as the world moved to war.

A.J.P. Taylor's *The Origins of the Second World War* does not rehabilitate Hitler, but does put him in perspective. He makes the case that man was not always the master of events he seemed but had a knack for patience and often was willing to just wait for events to go his way.

The English military writer, B.H. Liddell Hart, seems more respectful of Hitler's genius in his rise to power and the undoing of Versailles. The man with the plan, perfect or not, did accomplish the mission.

The Czech president, Edvard Beneš, was, as noted by Taylor, a supremely skilled diplomat. Though he had some good innings, He lost against Hitler. Realist though he was, Beneš underestimated Hitler in that for the German leader, there was no way the drama would end without the Sudetenland becoming German.

Maybe it was because he didn't realize he was fighting Chamberlain and Daladier who saw injustice in Versailles and justice in Hitler's desire to reunite the Sudetenland with Germany.

Had Beneš* saw that there was no way out if he was going to preserve his country and that all his diplomatic skill would avail nothing, he might have fought. After all, his country had a modern, well-trained army and air force.

But, he didn't. Hitler seems to have been best at knowing where he wanted to go and what he was willing to do to get there.

Even going to war for Danzig was not fatal to Hitler or Germany. France and Germany could render no aid to Poland

and were not willing to make the effort to advance against Germany from the west.

The brilliant execution of the campaign against France in 1940 strengthened his position. All things being equal, he should have been able to stand on the defensive and waited out the English. But he didn't.

England, after Dunkirk, could also wait, but there was not much else she could do.

So, who would win? In the end, neither. Even though she would survive the war and be part of the taking of the surrender, Britain would be much diminished.

Germany would be bombed out and occupied, and the author of its war would be dead by his own hand.

Hitler decided to attack the Soviet Union. He had allied with Stalin to destroy Poland, but suspected his fellow totalitarian. Would he have been better to just stand on the defensive and be ready if Stalin had decided to move west? We shall not know. One can look elsewhere for a discussion as to whether or not Hitler had to do anything.

On June 22, 1941, Operation Barbarossa was launched. The Germans had initial successes, but became bogged down before Moscow and would never be able to deliver the knockout punch.

Hitler's next move would prove to be his worst. Germany had an alliance with Japan, and upon the Japanese attack at Pearl Harbor, the Third Reich declared war on the United States on December 11, 1941.

The United States had been neutral before its entry into the war. Its neutrality, however, had been in favor of Britain. The Roosevelt administration wanted to get into the war against the Axis, but short of an attack by the Germans, would not have been able to find support to enter the conflict.

The Japanese solved that conundrum.

*Beneš would be able to take some satisfaction in that Berlin was rubble and lovely Prague was intact at the end of the war.

V
Japan and America: Getting to War

In a sense, the war between the United States and Japan began on July 8, 1853. On that date, Commodore Matthew Perry led his squadron into Tokyo Bay to begin the process of opening the hitherto isolated Japan to western trade whether they wanted it or not. This set Japan on a course to become the other big Pacific power.

The Japanese did not want the opening, but they apprehended reality and took to modernization, and unlike the Chinese, were able to avoid the exploitation suffered by the Middle Kingdom.

By the twentieth century, Japan had become an industrial and military power. Upon victory over the Russians in the first decade, she had become the major power in East Asia.

Now, was it inevitable that we would come into conflict with the Empire of the Rising Sun? Japan was an imperialist power. They had taken over Korea and were part of the scramble for influence in China. In 1895, they began to rule in Formosa. One might say, also, that America after the war with Spain was also a colonialist state. We were also an Asian power with our Philippine conquest.

The Japanese archipelago lacked most of the natural resources needed for her growing industries. Japan also felt a need for lebensraum. This didn't necessarily mean conflict had to develop.

Whatever Japan intended in Asia, it is hard to believe that it was her desire to fight the United States. According to writer and academic, Robert Higgs, things started to heat up with the election of Franklin D. Roosevelt. Higgs claimed that FDR disliked the Japanese.

Roosevelt didn't pay much attention to foreign affairs for the early part of his presidency. Higgs claims that it was after the New Deal's decline that FDR looked outward.

According to Higgs,

> In June 1940, Henry L. Stimson, who had been secretary of war under Taft and secretary of state under Hoover, became secretary of war again. Stimson was a lion of the Anglophile, northeastern upper crust and no friend of the Japanese. In support of the so-called Open Door Policy for China, Stimson favored the use of economic sanctions to obstruct Japan's advance in Asia. Treasury Secretary Henry Morgenthau and Interior Secretary Harold Ickes vigorously endorsed this policy. Roosevelt hoped that such sanctions would goad the Japanese into making a rash mistake by launching a war against the United States, which would bring in Germany because Japan and Germany were allied.

The administration, if it wanted war, needed this. The American people were not interested in going to war. The America First organization was popular and though supported by some dicey groups (whose support they did not seek), had the same sentiment of the people of being against getting into war.

Indeed, Roosevelt felt it important to dissemble and state at an address in Boston on October 30, 1940: "And while I am talking to you mothers and fathers, I give you one more assurance. I have said this before, but I shall say it again and again and again: Your boys are not going to be sent into any foreign wars."

It would take some maneuvering to get the public to accept war. Nothing short of an attack on the United States would probably work. The administration set to work.

So believes Robert Stinnett in his book, *Day of Deceit: The Truth About FDR and Pearl Harbor*. The author had done many years of research that advances the idea that the Roosevelt administration had the McCollum Plan to push Japan into attacking.

According to Stinnett, Lt. Cmdr. Arthur H. McCollum came up with the plan to provoke the Japanese into attacking.

The eight steps of the McCollum plan were:
A. Make an arrangement with Britain for the use of British bases in the Pacific, particularly Singapore
B. Make an arrangement with the Netherlands for the use of base facilities and acquisition of supplies in the Dutch East Indies
C. Give all possible aid to the Chinese government of Chiang-Kai-Shek
D. Send a division of long-range heavy cruisers to the Orient, Philippines, or Singapore
E. Send two divisions of submarines to the Orient
F. Keep the main strength of the U.S. fleet now in the Pacific in the vicinity of the Hawaiian Islands
G. Insist that the Dutch refuse to grant Japanese demands for undue economic concessions, particularly oil
H. Completely embargo all U.S. trade with Japan, in collaboration with a similar embargo imposed by the British Empire

Stinnett's book is controversial and has been attacked by reviewers and Historians. This is understandable. If he is right, the American government conspired to start a war against the wishes of its people. Who wants to believe that?

Without researching through government documents, Liddell Hart made his reasonable case long before Stinnett wrote his book:

> Since 1931 the Japanese had been expanding their footholds on the Asiatic mainland at the expense of the Chinese, who were weakened by internal conflict, and to the detriment of American and British interests in that sphere. In that year, they had invaded Manchuria and converted it into a Japanese satellite. In 1932 they invaded China itself, but in the effort to establish their control of that vast area they became enmeshed in the toils of guerrilla warfare, and sought a solution of the problem in further expansionist moves, southward, aimed to shut off the Chinese from outside supplies. Following Hitler's defeat of France, the Japanese took advantage of her helplessness by getting her to agree, under threat, to their "protective" occupation of French Indo-China.
>
> In reply President Roosevelt demanded, on the 24th July 1941, the withdrawal of Japanese troops from Indochina—and to enforce his demand he issued orders on the 26th for freezing all Japanese assets in the U.S.A. and placing an embargo on oil supply. Mr. Churchill took simultaneous action, and two days later the refugee Dutch government in London was induced to follow suit—which meant, as Mr. Churchill has remarked, that "Japan was deprived at a stroke of her vital oil supplies."
>
> In early discussions, it had always been recognized that such a paralyzing stroke would force Japan to fight, as the only alternative to collapse or the abandonment of her policy. It is remarkable that she deferred striking for more than four months, while trying to negotiate a lifting of the oil embargo. The United States government refused

> to lift it, unless Japan withdrew not only from Indo-China but also from China. No government, least of all the Japanese, could be expected to swallow such humiliating conditions, and utter loss of face. So there was every reason to expect war in the pacific at any moment, from the last week of July onwards. In these circumstances the Americans and British were lucky to be allowed four months grace before the Japanese struck. But little advantage was taken of this interval for defensive preparation.

From Liddell Hart, it appears that we did want war and didn't prepare for the opening blow that was necessary to seek the support of the people for the conflict.

No matter, the war came and we were in it. As grand strategy, we could have done worse. Getting in late made sure that others, allies and enemies, were not fresh, while we were at full bloom with an untapped manpower.

As the world's largest industrial economy, we could provide for our own material needs as well as our allies. We were also our own Saudi Arabia. No having to scramble for petroleum or converting coal into aviation fuel as the enemy had to.

True, the Russians put more men into the battle than we did and slugged it out on a larger scale than the Germans. There are two aspects of that.

First of all, we didn't have to be involved at all. If we hadn't bugged the Japanese and let them go on their not-so-merry way in China, they probably would have left us alone.

Second, if we were not there, Russia would have probably been defeated. Her early losses in men and material would have in all probability been too dire to recover from. Our provision of supplies may not have been as much as they manufactured on their own, but it was important.

That we didn't put as many men in battle may not mean Volgograd would have become Hitlergrad, but without us, the name of Stalingrad would have been much more short-lived.

As Charles De Gaulle supposedly wrote in his diary on the night the U.S. got into the conflict, "The war is over." It was, but it would be years a dying.

There's no point in a detailed military history of the war. The basic outline is known to all. Suffice it to say, after the declaration of war against the US, Germany and Italy faced an enemy that had only one big task: keep the alliance together and the major states from collapsing. As the big players, the US, the USSR, and the United Kingdom were not going to sink. All that was necessary to destroy the National Socialist regime was that no one was tempted to make a separate peace.

This accomplished, the economic might of our great republic and the manpower advantage would lead inexorably to first the surrender of the Italian fascist state in September of 1943 and eventually, Hitler's suicide and the German surrender on May 7, 1945.

The war was not done. The Japanese had been losing at least since the Battle of Midway. Their initial run of victory meant they had a lot of territory to lose. As in the Western theater, the Anglo-American edge in men and material would be the deciding factor.

A devastating submarine campaign and the allied island-hopping strategy bled the Japanese while bringing us closer to the home islands.

Rather than invade those islands, the United States dropped two of the newly developed atomic bombs on Hiroshima and Nagasaki.

As agreed, and at this point, with little cost, the Russians declared war on Japan and invaded and conquered Manchuria in short order.

Bowing to the inevitable, Imperial Japan surrendered on the decks of the battleship USS *Missouri* September 2, 1945.

The enemies of the allies were brought low and vanquished. Germany would be occupied from one end to the other in zones by the United States, UK, France, and the USSR. Japan would suffer a similar fate, being shorn of all her possessions and with American occupation under General Douglas MacArthur as Supreme Commander for the Allied Powers.

It was total victory.

Or was it?

True, our country came out of the war with all its cities intact and suffered no territorial bombing save Pearl Harbor. Other than a landing on a couple of Aleutian Islands, no ground had been occupied.

American factories made a rapid transition to peacetime production and the feared return of depression did not occur.

So, all was well?

One would think that the successful completion of a war meant that one could bring all the troops home and forget about the enemy. True, we would have to clean out the apparatus of the old regime as the fight against National Socialist and the militarist regime of Japan had the aura as a crusade against evil.

There was a problem, as there usually is.

The Soviet Union had been our ally in the war in Europe. Its ruler had well before the war directed a state that had led to deaths on a scale greater than in Hitler's Germany. Should we have had qualms about being their ally?

The British prime minister, Winston Churchill, put the case for allying with a government that was by his lights criminal:

> No one has been a more consistent opponent of Communism for the last twenty-five years. I will unsay no word I have spoken about it. But all this fades away before the spectacle which is now unfolding. The past,

with its crimes, its follies, its tragedies, flashes away....
The Russian danger is therefore our danger, and the danger of the United States, just as the cause of any Russian fighting for hearth and house is the cause of free men and free peoples in every quarter of the globe.

Never at the loss for a bon mot, Winnie would also quip in the matter. "If Hitler invaded hell, I would make at least a favorable reference to the devil in the House of Commons."

The acceptance of Stalin and the Soviets as full partners would mean that for the United States, victory could not be complete. If Churchill's refusal to unsay his words meant anything, they meant that after the war, all his pre-war opposition would have to rise again to the surface, and statesmen of his ilk would find themselves facing a large and powerful enemy.

If the United States stood for much the same and also opposed the Soviet Union, our indefinite occupation of Western Germany, with Britain and France, gave us a border with the Soviets.

In Asia, we occupied all of Japan, but across a body of water was our first post–World War II conflict in Korea to remind us the victory was incomplete.

One might come to the opinion that the two biggest post-war winners were Japan and West Germany. They were freed from all of what was required of states pretending to the status of "Great Powers." They no longer had to maintain large military establishments. In effect, the U.S. Air Force served as the Luftwaffe and our fleet functioned as the stand-in for the Imperial Japanese Navy.

Without having to spend much money on defense, both countries managed to have "economic miracles."

We should have had such a victory.

The other non-communist European nations, as part of the North Atlantic Treaty Organization or NATO, were also able to do well out of the peace. They could be part of an alliance that saw them paying relatively little on defense while relying on the United States to do the major spending.

NATO was formed in response to the Soviet's blockade of the Western occupied Berlin in 1948. To have to have an outpost surrounded and adrift in the Soviet zone was not exactly a wise agreement to make in setting up the post-war administration, but that's what happened.

The Soviets blocked surface travel, and so the West, mostly Americans, supplied Berlin by air.

The Cold War was off and running. We would be facing the Soviet bloc as a bloc until that union dissolved.

The question is finally, might a better foreign policy have allowed us to avoid involvement in World War II? One could think so. It is true that the U.S. was within its rights to not sell petroleum supplies and other material to the Japanese in the years leading up to the war. However, any freezing of assets owned by Japan, if financial in nature, might have been questionable.

Getting back to Liddell Hart's remark, was there anything that we could wisely do to avoid war with Japan and thus Germany as well? At the very least, we could have avoided the appearance of belligerency while insisting on our rights to not trade.

Assuming we could have avoided war with the Axis, what would the post-war world have looked like? We should posit a worst case.

Without the events of December 7, we can assume the Japanese would have adjusted and continued their war in China and eventually brought it to a conclusion that would have been in their favor.

Germany would have continued the war that began with Operation Barbarossa. Britain would continue resistance. With the help of the Empire, they could have held out unless

German submarine warfare improved to the point of completely isolating and starving Britain.

Without America in the war, Britain and Germany might have sparred around the edges, such as North Africa, but with little decisive result. Germany would probably have beaten the Soviet Union, but even there, she might have come to a draw.

Worst case, the USSR collapses, and to avoid starvation due to a successful submarine campaign, Britain negotiates and keeps her now restive empire.

So, Japan reigns supreme in Asia and Germany from France to Siberia. Would they now turn their sights across to oceans to engage us?

Post bellum, Germany would have needed to spend time making sure Eastern Europe stayed suppressed. If they were unable to conciliate the West of the continent, they would have to do the same there. A withdrawal from France would have been possible and probable. Reality could not have escaped even as romantic a nation as the Gauls, and they would have acquiesced, even if they didn't happily accept the situation. Even so, Deutschland would have had their hands full for no little time.

Japan, during her war in China, despite losing ground to the allies in the Pacific, was able to prosecute a successful offensive during and until the end of 1944. The empire's ability to digest China was surely possible. If the Manchus could lord it over the Middle Kingdom, surely, His Imperial Majesty could have ruled as a Chinese emperor if his government pursued a politic strategy.

So, the world would have continued, always being a place of some danger for any country, but no worse than usual in the American nation. The necessity of being prepared for all eventualities always presents itself for all countries.

The last question presents itself. Did we have a moral obligation to enter the Second World War? No matter how all wars start, they eventually become crusades. It did not take the Allies in World War I to demonize their fellow dynasts as "the Hun." Well, Hitler was the Hun and a racial fanatic. Was it our duty to bring him to his end?

That we ended up allying with an entity run by someone with a higher body count should at least give us pause, especially as we would be the enemy of said entity for most of the rest of the twentieth century.

The United States suffered over 400,000 military deaths in the conflict. Did it really solve anything more than our being in World War I did?

It certainly did not bring permanent peace, as many young Americans would find out a few years later.

17

The Cold War Arrives

Teachers who break up recess fights on the schoolyard with the words "violence solves nothing" are wrong. Violence solves a lot. In the last century, the surrender in Europe meant an end to the German dream of dominating Europe. The ceremony on the *Missouri* also signaled that Japan would not be allowed to rule the waves in the Pacific.

Violence also creates problems at its end, such as how would the victors sort themselves subsequently.

In 1945, we faced the Soviet Union in Berlin and on a line in Germany. The question was how would we confront or conciliate them. Contain was what our side decided as the course.

There was debate as to who started it. The Gouzenko Affair revealed a large Soviet espionage apparatus in the West. The affair had an effect on opinion, but what country does not spy on others?

Much was made of ideology of the USSR. True, it had a worldview that posited that the class struggle would end in the dictatorship of the proletariat and the withering away of the state. It was the duty of the country of the revolution to help it along, but did that mean in a power struggle with the West?

In the end, the who-started-it question is not as important as the situation the two entities found themselves in 1945. Just the fact that they were so big and powerful and faced each other meant confrontation. The question of could it have been avoided by the United States as we might have avoided World War II is more complex. Because we did not avoid it, we found ourselves in a several decades struggle.

The Cold War warmed up in 1948. The Allies introduced the Deutsche Mark to replace the decrepit Reichsmark. The Soviets opposed this measure and blockaded the allied sectors of Berlin.

The Allies supplied Berlin with an airlift. It was a logistically huge effort and was successful. Neither side wanted war so there was some restraint. In the end, the Soviets allowed land traffic and that round was over.

The 1948 coup that ended democratic government in Czechoslovakia did nothing to allay allied suspicions.

The game was on and it would be move and counter-move until the Soviet Union collapsed.

18

Korea

Our next conflict would be the undeclared Korean War. At the end of World War II, the Soviets occupied the northern part of the Korean Peninsula and we the south. Consequently, a Marxist government was set up in the north under Kim Il-sung.

We had a government under Syngman Rhee in the south who had been elected by a mere 92.3% of the voters.

The North Korean regime ran so well that Soviet forces were able to leave in 1946. The Rhee government was not as well organized.

Kim had built up a strong and competent military. Rhee's army, like the rest of his government, was corrupt and inefficient.

Whatever the ideological differences of the two men, they both had at least one goal in common. Each wanted to reunite the country, just not together.

According to an essay by Professor William R. Polk, "The event that appears to have precipitated the full-scale war was the declaration by Syngman Rhee's government of the independence of the South. If allowed to stand, that action as Kim Il-sung clearly understood, would have prevented unification."

The long and short of it was that the North Koreans were ready for war and the South was not. In June of 1950 war began.

The South Korean forces crumbled and the Americans were driven into the southern province of Pusan, holding on to a tiny area.

Resistance at Pusan stiffened, halting the heretofore-victorious northerners. The Americans and their United Nations allies, under American commander General Douglas MacArthur, made an amphibious landing on the western coast of the Korean peninsula, outflanking the enemy.

It was a great victory, but it took some time to take Seoul. No matter, much of the North Korean army was stranded in the South and the war was turned around, for the time being anyway.

Now, MacArthur moved north to bring about the reunification of Korea. The beaten North Korean army was not able to stop them and quickly they approached the Yalu River on the Chinese border.

Both China and the Soviet Union were alarmed. Stalin would not commit troops; he had never been enthusiastic about the adventure anyway.

The Chinese sent 300,000 south to stop the American juggernaut. On October 25, 1950, they were sent as "volunteers" rather than as official army to a formal direct clash with the United States. Lightly armed as they were, they squashed what was left of the South Korean army and drove U.S. forces out of the north.

That the American slam-dunk was blocked unexpectedly was a shock. Truman declared a state of emergency and MacArthur called for using atomic bombs. This is interesting, as MacArthur didn't support the use of nuclear weapons on the Japanese.

Nukes didn't happen, and MacArthur was replaced by General Matthew Ridgeway under whose leadership the situation was stabilized.

The U.S. Air Force began a bombing campaign of vast devastation. The bombs for the next couple of years were more than had been inflicted on Japan in the recently concluded war.

Korean cities saw greater damage than German and Japanese cities that had been firebombed. As to the deaths suffered, quoting the Polk essay:

> Canadian economist Michel Chossudovsky has written that LeMay's estimate of 20% should be revised to nearly 33% or roughly one Korean in every three killed. He goes on to point to a remarkable comparison: in the Second World War, the British had lost less than 1% of their population, France lost 1.35%, China lost 1.89% and the U.S. only a third of one percent. Put another way, Korea suffered roughly thirty times as many people killed in 37 months of American carpet-bombing as these other countries lost in all the years of the Second World War.

Eventually, negotiations began to reach a ceasefire. Negotiations were protracted, but the armistice was signed on July 27, 1953.

According to Mr. Polk,

> The North set about recovering from devastation. It had to dig out from under the rubble and it chose to continue to be a garrison state. It was certainly a dictatorship, like the Soviet Union, China, North Vietnam and Indonesia, but close observers thought that the regime was supported by the people. Most observers found that the memory of the war, and particularly of the constant bombing, created a sense of embattlement that unified the country against the Americans and the regime of the

South. Kim Il-sung was able to stifle such dissent as arose. He did so brutally. No one can judge for certain, but there is reason to believe that a sense of embattled patriotism remains alive today.

Rhee continued to rule the South until the army had had enough. The army would rule until the Korean people agitated for reforms and elections. Korea is now an economically and industrially advanced nation. Hyundai and Samsung are international powerhouses.

And yet there is no peace on the Korean Peninsula. The demilitarized zone at the 38th parallel is where the North and South meet to resolve any problems, but it is just an armistice.

However, the arrival of Donald Trump shook things up on the peninsula. You may recall that Trump began his administration threatening "fire and fury" while the North Koreans threatened missiles. In the end, it was just some bombastic saber rattling from Trump, so things eventually calmed down. Kim Jong-un, the DPRK Supreme Leader met the South Korean President Moon Jae-in for an inter-Korean summit.

In June of 2018 Kim and Trump met in Singapore. Not until a few years ago did anyone think that could happen. Kim was amenable to dismantling of the North's nukes if the United States took some reciprocal steps.

Kim and Moon have had more meetings and things seem better between the two countries. Trump is gone. How events will play out, time will tell.

19

The 1950s

The 1950s

The 1950s in America were to many a golden age. Life was not unpleasant for many Americans, and what for most of history had been considered the working class could think of themselves as middle class and contemplate suburban home ownership. Since then, there has been some revisionism, but the legend endures for many.

Some have characterized the decade as culturally dull, while others may celebrate that as a pleasant tranquility. The same people who call the era boring will extol the beats as pioneers.

No matter how domestic life played out, we still had to have a foreign policy and the 1950s did not lack for one.

The Cold War that began after the end of World War II continued through and after Korea. An arms race ensued with the Communist bloc as the Soviet Union obtained nuclear weapons. The decade would end with presidential candidate John F. Kennedy calling the Eisenhower administration out for a "missile gap," that turned out to be overblown.

The Mosaddegh Coup

The United States did have its adventures overseas. In 1953, a coup was engineered to overthrow the democratically elected government of Prime Minister Mohammad Mosaddegh in Iran.

What could be the reason to overthrow a government that was elected by principles our nation supposedly holds sacred? Oil.

Mosaddegh was a reformer who had put some land reforms into place. Doing so did not endear him to the upper classes. That, however, would not be a fatal move. Taking on the Anglo-Iranian Oil Company, or AIOC, was another matter.

As prime minister, Mosaddegh proposed nationalizing the AIOC. The AIOC would, of course, respect Persian national sovereignty and negotiate just compensation and leave the enterprise under Persian control.

Not likely.

There was too much involved. Britain was no longer the British Empire it was in the eighteenth and nineteenth centuries. They had been well bloodied in two epic struggles of the twentieth century wherein they had to bring in their ringers, i.e., the United States to pull their chestnuts out of the fire. They were going to have to do that again.

At first the Brits stamped their feet, threatened, and did blockade and boycott the Iranians. They withdrew technicians, which reduced production. This was effective, but Iran did not back down.

The British were not to be thwarted, but with reduced resources, MI6, the Secret Intelligence Service, outsourced the coup to the Central Intelligence Agency run by Allan Dulles, brother of Secretary of State John Foster Dulles.

The rationale for U.S. involvement was the specter of a communist takeover by the Tudeh Party. To say the least, this was a smokescreen, as admitted by Dean Acheson. Maybe it wasn't follow the money but follow the oil, but in the end, there's little difference.

The CIA put into action Operation Ajax. Point man for the op was Kermit Roosevelt, grandson of Teddy, who was no stranger to such adventures. The CIA engineered protests and bribed army officers and eventually Mosaddegh was removed, the Shah ensconced, and the oil flowed. To keep the lid on, a secret police, SAVAK, was put in place.

It looked to be the perfect operation. Our man was firmly in power. Surely whatever promotions resulted were deserved.

The lid on Iran may have looked securely in place, but the truth was otherwise. Persia would come back into focus in 1979 with a vengeance.

The Suez Crisis

The building of the modern Suez Canal in the nineteenth century was an engineering marvel and a boon to world trade. The reduction in shipping time made the passage from Europe to the Indian Ocean faster and easier. Who controlled the canal would be of no little geopolitical importance.

In 1951 Egypt unilaterally abrogated the Anglo-Egyptian Treaty of 1936. In 1954, Britain agreed with Gamel Abdel Nasser's Egyptian government to withdraw her troops. This was completed in 1956.

When the United States and Britain withdrew an offer to fund the Aswan Dam project, Egypt under Nasser nationalized the canal.

The British were not happy with that and sought French support. The French suspected Nasser was aiding Algerian rebels and were thus onboard.

On October 26, 1956, the Israelis struck against the Egyptians in the Sinai. Their foreign minister, Abba Eban justified it thus:

> *During the six years during which this belligerency has operated in violation of the Armistice Agreement there have occurred 1,843 cases of armed robbery and theft, 1,339 cases of armed clashes with Egyptian armed forces, 435 cases of incursion from Egyptian controlled territory, 172 cases of sabotage perpetrated by Egyptian military units and fedayeen in Israel. As a result of these actions of Egyptian hostility within Israel, 364 Israelis were wounded and 101 killed. In 1956 alone, as a result of this aspect of Egyptian aggression, 28 Israelis were killed and 127 wounded.*

We do not have the Egyptian counter-arguments and make no judgment as to whether they exist or not.

Two days later the French and British invaded and took control of the area around the canal.

It was not a stunning victory. Egypt was a minor country with a not very advanced military establishment fighting three enemies at once. In the end, it would be a defeat for the invaders.

The Soviets, looking to expand influence in the Arab world, would butt in. They had been supplying Egypt weapons via Czech proxies and would help build the Aswan dam. Nikita Khrushchev, then head of the Soviet Union, condemned the invasion and threatened to send nuclear missiles upon the Western Europeans if the invaders did not withdraw.

So, what was the involvement of the United States?

President Eisenhower was for a negotiated settlement and against military intervention. After the Anglo-French-Israeli intervention he responded in a measured manner. He warned the Soviets to back off. The president also rebuked the invaders and insisted they withdraw. All three had no choice but to comply, especially the British, as they were in need of financial assistance.

Eisenhower's reputation soared. Britain and France were reminded of how badly they had lost World War II, as they had no choice but to follow America's lead while the official losers, Germany and Japan, were having their "economic miracles."

U.S. policy would change in the coming years and we would not be as loved in the Arab world.

Around the time of the Suez Crisis, The Hungarians rose against their government. Other than some small response in the United Nations by Secretary of State Dulles, and coverage by Radio Free Europe, there was little that the U.S. could do. The CIA was caught flat-footed.

Latin America
The Overthrow of the Guatemalan Government 1954

Guatemala was a corrupt state under U.S.-backed dictator, Jorge Ubico. In 1944, Ubico was removed after a popular uprising led by two army officers, Jacobo Arbenz and Francisco Arana.

Land and labor reforms were instituted. Real problems would ensue when the reformers came up against the power of the United Fruit Company.

United Fruit had been adversely affected by the regime's liberal labor policies. That a banana republic was not acting like a banana republic would not do.

United Fruit lobbied the U.S. government for help. The Dulles brothers—John Foster was Secretary of State and Allan headed the CIA—had ties to United Fruit and were onboard. That there were communists in Guatemala was also a consideration, or excuse.

President Eisenhower authorized Operation PBSUCCESS to engineer a coup. It was a full on heavy-handed effort to overthrow an elected government, and it succeeded.

It was a betrayal of everything we believed about our own battle to liberate the non-free-world countries. It would breed resentment in Latin America, unsurprisingly.

Our action was a vindication of Smedly Butler's "war is a racket speech" and book. The anti-communist crusade melded with crony capitalism.

The Cuban Revolution

I vaguely remember as a child a *Time* magazine cover with a picture of Fidel Castro in a heroic pose. In the immediate aftermath of his successful revolution, he seemed to have taken power as the successor to a corrupt dictator.

Eventually, two views of the man coalesced in American minds. Either a bogeyman to those on the right or a saint to people more to the left. Whether or not Castro was a net benefit to the Cuban nation will be argued by historians forever and probably from ideological viewpoints. What is not in dispute is the ancien régime headed by Fulgencio Batista deserved to lose.

In *The Godfather Part* II there's a famous scene at Hyman Roth's birthday party where Michael Corleone talks about Cuban rebels. Michael notes, "I saw an interesting thing happen today. A rebel was being arrested by the military police, and rather than be taken alive, he exploded a grenade he had hidden in his jacket. He killed himself, and took a captain of the command with him." Michael further notes, "The soldiers are paid to fight. The rebels aren't. ... They can win." Hyman Roth dismisses the insurgents: "This country's had rebels for the last fifty years. It's in their blood, believe me, I know. I've been coming here since the '20s."

We all know how that worked out, except that *Godfather Part* II is fiction. The real story is much more interesting. It is the tale of hard, calculating men who thought they had made a country their wholly owned subsidiary and find out otherwise. Oh, the part about the rebels being willing to die and thus potential winners? That was true.

The Batista government, a firm ally of the gangsters, was becoming more repressive and hated every day. Its enemies, however, seemed pitifully inept. The big star of the revolution, Fidel Castro, had been captured after an attack on a barracks in 1953.

Despite the tyranny, the regime looked secure. Real-life mobsters—Meyer Lansky, Charles "Lucky" Luciano, et al.—invested heavily in Cuba. They made Havana their corrupt playground with its casinos and other dens of iniquity.

Out of jail in an amnesty, Castro started organizing. The new efforts did not seem impressive. His little army set sail from Mexico in an unseaworthy ship. Landing with 82 seasick men, he headed for the hills. Betrayed by a guide, Batista's forces ambushed his little band. With 16 left it didn't look good. The casino owners must have been thinking like Hyman Roth as he spoke to Michael Corleone.

Fidel and his sidekick, Ernesto "Che" Guevara, had made their last mistake. Batista had started making his. The revolutionaries would cultivate the population while the government would become more repressive. The rebels would grow in numbers while defections would plague state forces.

Until near the end, Batista would vow to keep up the fight. Then, on New Year's morning, 1959, the dictator took off without telling his mob allies. Talk about holding the bag!

Time has shown Castro to have done many of the things he complained about in the Cuban ancien régime. He has political prisoners, news is censored, and he was until recently a dictator. Yet, he meant what he said about the casinos and closed them down when he could. The mob was booted out, never to return. The losses sustained by the criminal element were staggering. So bad were they that Meyer Lansky who had invested vast wealth in Cuba would leave an estate of $57,000 according to *Havana Nocturne* author, T. J. English.

We were not done with Cuba, nor is Cuba done with us.

The new regime, never warm and fuzzy, started televised executions of its enemies. It was not as easy to have sympathetic magazine covers.

It wasn't just casinos. Cuba began nationalizing U.S.-owned properties in Cuba. The Eisenhower administration began trade restrictions. Cuba looked to the Soviet Union for assistance against the *yanquis*.

On January 3, 1961, the Eisenhower administration closed the embassy and ended diplomatic relations.

In the 1960s we would have a lot of Cuba to think about.

20

Cuba Heats Up

The Bay of Pigs

On January 20, 1961, John F. Kennedy was inaugurated president. He would not be in office long until a crisis would occur. Anti-Castro Cubans would land at a place called the Bay of Pigs.

It would be a debacle, for not only was it a failure as the insurgents were captured, but it involved of an arm of the American government that would have to shoulder the blame.

Planning began during the previous administration of Dwight Eisenhower. When Castro took power, Cuba was an economic colony of the United States. It was not just the mob owned hotels, casinos, brothels and other establishments. American interests owned many of sugar plantations and the majority of the cattle ranches, mines, and utilities.

The idea of local control could only be popular at the outset. It did not, however, set well with the American government. Worse, Castro suggested other Latin countries be more assertive. Ike responded by authorizing the CIA to recruit and train Cubans living in Miami exile to train to overthrow Fidel.

Castro established diplomatic relations with the Soviet Union and the United States prohibited the importation of sugar from Cuba. As most of the sugar went north, it would be necessary to find a new buyer or the island's economy would sink.

To prevent that, the USSR would buy the Cuban sugar. Washington responded by breaking diplomatic relations and stepped up preparations for the invasion.

Allen Dulles would have Richard Bissell, Deputy Director for Plans, take charge of the anti-Castro program. The CIA would foment a plan to kill Castro using the Mafia. As the man died of natural causes many decades later, one can deduce that effort was a failure.

Planning went forward for an invasion and would go operational on April 15, 1961. An attempt would be made to destroy the Cuban air force on the ground using surplus American B-26 bombers. The Cubans knew about the plans and the planes were moved. The bombers would be useless.

On April 17, the invasion force would land at the remote Bay of Pigs. It was botched from the beginning and soon Castro's men had the invaders pinned on the beach. Unexpected coral reefs sank some boats. Paratroopers landed in the wrong place. Final score: 114 killed, over 1,100 taken prisoner in less than a day of battle.

The CIA and Bissell probably thought Kennedy would not leave the invasion in the lurch and would order the military to come to the rescue. That was never going to happen. Dulles had to go and both did.

Kennedy still wanted to see Castro gone and would approve the espionage and sabotage project known as Operation Mongoose. Outright war was not part of the plan.

It would be useful to note that when Kennedy met Eisenhower at the White House on the incumbent's last day, the president-elect asked Ike, "Should we support guerilla operations in Cuba?" Eisenhower replied, "To the utmost. We cannot have the present government there go on."

Despite Ike's words, that government has survived to this day, but so have we despite the failure to remove Castro.

The Cuban Missile Crisis

On October 14, 1962, an American U-2 high altitude spy plane flying over Cuba photographed a Soviet SS-4 medium range ballistic missile under assembly.

On October 16, the president was informed and the administration would deal with the Cuban Missile Crisis for the next couple of weeks.

U.S. nuclear missile power was superior at that time. Having nukes in Cuba would significantly alter the balance of power because the Soviet weapons could hit the eastern United States.

Khrushchev sent the missiles to Cuba to level the playing field. Nations bordering the Soviet Union and its Warsaw Pact Allies had missiles based in them that could quickly attack the Eastern Bloc countries.

The missiles in Cuba also could be seen as an insurance policy against another attempt at overthrowing the Castro government.

For the Kennedy administration, nuclear missiles in Cuba were not to be tolerated. They question was how to get them out without starting a bigger war that could go nuclear.

After deliberating, the president and advisors came up with a number of possible courses of action, among them, invasion and bombing of the missile sites.

Kennedy decided on a naval blockade to prevent delivery of more missiles. Along with that was an ultimatum that the existing missiles would have to be removed.

On October 22, 1962, the president spoke to the nation. In a television broadcast the president notified the American people about the decision to blockade Cuba as well as the willingness to use force to end the threat to national security.

For those alive at the time who heard the president's address, it would be a tense period as they waited in hope and trepidation for the crisis to be resolved. There would be a showdown at sea and an American U-2 spy plane would be shot down. It appeared nuclear war was imminent.

In the end a compromise would be arranged: Khrushchev offered to remove the missiles if we would remove ours from Turkey.

Kennedy would agree, but never made it public that he had agreed to remove the missiles from Turkey.

At the time, the country believed it was on the brink of war. Both the Soviet and American governments were aware of the danger and held back from going too close to the cliff edge.

Both sides seemed to realize the seriousness of the emergency. The next year, a "hot line" was set up to bring about direct communication between the two governments to defuse confrontations that might arise.

Cuba, a little bit of the iron curtain 90 miles off our shore, would continue to bother us, but we were not going to invade. We were each other's bête noire. Cuba would support "liberation movements" and we would oppose them. Otherwise, it was not pleasant but relatively stable.

21

The Berlin Crisis of 1961

After World War II, defeated Germany was occupied by France, the Soviet Union, the United Kingdom, and the United States. The arrangement worked well enough except that the Soviet Zone, the local worker's paradise, began hemorrhaging workers. As the border between the zones was not as strict as the national borders of other East Bloc countries, nationals of those nations were able to flee west through Germany.

The loss of the professional classes was noticed and something needed to be done and the East German government did it. The border was tightened in the early 1950s culminating with the erection of a fence across Germany between the Russian Zone and the rest of the occupied country built ostensibly with the purpose to keep out spies and smugglers and other nefarious characters. One supposes that those who desired to migrate and be part of a workers' state would be able to apply at official checkpoints. Figures on such requests are not known.

This left the still relatively open border of occupied Berlin. That would have to be tightened up, as the brain drain of professionals was getting worse.

In 1958, the Soviets issued an ultimatum demanding the other powers withdraw from Berlin so that it could become a free and demilitarized city. Thus, the Western nations would have access only with the permission of the East German government.

The United States, the UK, and France were not leaving, and in 1959, Khrushchev withdrew the ultimatum. There were meetings and negotiations and Khrushchev would come to the United States for a visit.

Things looked okay. Khrushchev and Eisenhower appeared to get along in their meetings. The two men agreed to discuss the matter again at the scheduled Paris summit in May of 1960.

When an American pilot, Francis Gary Powers, flying a U-2 spy plane was shot down over the Soviet Union, the summit was cancelled.

In June of 1961, the new president, John F. Kennedy, met with Khrushchev at the Vienna Summit. It did not go well. The Soviet premier again issued his ultimatum to make a separate peace treaty with East Germany and thus ending access to Berlin to the three other parties except by East German permission. Khrushchev set a year-end deadline.

The other powers responded by saying that an East German–Soviet treaty would not affect the Western status on Berlin.

After the debacle at Vienna, President Kennedy delivered a televised speech on the 25th of July. The president noted that U.S. intentions were peaceful and we recognized Soviet security interests and that we were willing to come back to the table.

Kennedy also noted that he was asking Congress for more money and troops.

Needless to say, the Soviet leader was not amused. At the Black Sea resort of Sochi, Khrushchev told Kennedy's disarmament advisor, John J. McCloy, that the military buildup threatened war.

Meanwhile, the East German regime was dealing with too many people heading for the exit. In a stealth manner, they stockpiled material to build a wall. Construction began in August of 1961. In response, the president called up reservists.

The four-power agreement on Berlin allowed that allied personnel could move freely in the sectors of Berlin. In October of 1961, the U.S. Chief of Mission was stopped at Checkpoint Charlie.

The president's special advisor, General Lucius Clay, decided to show American resolve by sending a diplomat to be escorted in East Berlin by military police.

We were upset that the Soviets were not doing their part to avoid confrontation and the Soviet commandant was not happy that our tanks were at the border and we were trying to send armed military personnel across the checkpoint.

The Soviet commandant Solovyev warned: "I am authorized to state that is necessary to avoid actions of this kind. Such actions can provoke corresponding actions from our side. We have tanks too. We hate the idea of carrying out such actions, and are sure that you will re-examine your course."

A standoff would ensue. From October 27 to October 28 Soviets and Americans faced each other with live rounds and orders to fire if fired upon.

Clay wanted to bulldoze parts of the wall, as he was sure it would show the Soviets. Cooler heads prevailed, and Kennedy and Khrushchev were kept informed of events on the ground. The two leaders came to an agreement, and so troops and tanks were moved back.

The wall stopped the movement of people east and west (really, almost all west) and could be a death trap. Even so, the East/West confrontation over the city stabilized until the wall was removed in 1989 in the wake of the Soviet Unions' impending demise.

22

The Vietnam War

When did the Vietnam War start? For American adults or those who grew up during the conflict, there can be different answers. Was it after the French left and we took up sponsorship of the southern regime? Was it when we started sending advisors? Was it when the Tonkin Gulf incident occurred? Or when the first American combat troops arrived?

Can there really be a set date? Probably not for Americans. In retrospect, it appears to have been a drift into the conflict.

For the Vietnamese, it may be in 1858 when the French arrived and set up the country as a colony.

As to when it ended, there is little doubt. When the Tank 390 crashed the gates of the presidential palace on April 30, 1975, it was all over.

It would dominate the news for much of the 1960s, and when it was done, there would have been much change, not least in how the United States makes war.

The End of the Democratic U.S. Army

What does one mean by a "Democratic Army?"

A democratic army is one with broad participation of the citizenry. Sparta may have been a nation that was an army, but Athens enrolled young citizens to be called up in military service. Rome, for most of the Republic, counted on its citizens for defense.

The eighteenth century saw armies that were more professional, but with the French Revolution, and its levée en masse, large national armies composed of citizens and the national identity that went with it became more the rule.

In a rare moment of near lucidity while pretending to be a college student, I remember the professor quoting the Prussian field marshal and statesman, Helmuth von Moltke the Elder, to the effect that future wars would require the state to propagandize the citizenry to engage them in whatever crusade the nation was involved in. I have tried without success since to find the exact quote. A paraphrase of what I recall is this: "The age of cabinet war is behind us. All we have now is a people's war."

No matter, the two world wars of the last century more than proved the point that if you are going to have mass democracy, the voting plebs had to be engaged.

For America, the Civil War, World Wars I and II, and Korea were all democratic wars. To fight them, they had to be crusades. In such wars the people need to be propagandized unceasingly. Dissent must be opposed, if not suppressed.

The conflict to save the union would become a war against slavery. Both ideas lend themselves to making a war a cause better than the war itself. The tariff as a tax on the South was not mentioned.

For the South, the war to keep men enslaved could only be sold to a non-slave owning majority as a war for freedom from (federal) tyranny.

A democratic army does not mean that the people rally to the cause en masse. It is true that there were large enlistments at the beginning of the Civil War on both sides, but as the war progressed, it is necessary to take people into service by compulsion. It is not as brutal as press gangs, as in Britain's slave navy, but being done by a state bureaucracy, it is far more difficult to avoid.

Our next major war, Word War I, a war of choice, followed the pattern more so. There was no Fort Sumter to wave the bloody shirt for. The Germans were portrayed as the vilest people to have ever populated Europe. The Hun was the name they were saddled with.

True, strategically, it is always good to enter a war after your enemy has had a few years of seeing their men slaughtered and people starving, not that anyone was shrewd enough to think in those terms.

Woodrow Wilson would get the declaration of war, but the people were not so moved to fly to the colors, ergo the draft would have to be utilized. Still, it would not be resisted in any effective manner and dissent would be suppressed. The war would be prosecuted until the successful end.

World War II would follow the pattern of the previous war, but on a grander scale. It was made easier due to the fact that the primary villain almost appeared to have been sent by central casting. Whether or not his speeches made sense in German is beyond the knowledge of anyone who does not speak that language. To a non-speaker watching his ranting, it would have been easy to see him as a wild-eyed fanatic.

Even so, the Roosevelt administration had no success in ginning up war fever and the president had to assure moms and dads that he had no intention of sending their boys over to fight.

Japan, whether goaded into it or not, solved FDR's dilemma by attacking Pearl Harbor, no less in the act as the way it was carried out. The "sneak attack" was a propagandist's dream. Many enlisted and among those who were drafted, there was negligible resistance, if any.

Propaganda was pervasive and the news outlets were cooperative.

SHE SEARCHES FOR MONSTERS TO DESTROY

Like World War I, America was strategically aided by coming into the war after everyone else was bloodied. It meant the enemy would be at least somewhat weaker and allies friendlier (with the possible exception of the Soviet Union) but under no illusion would they be considered anything but junior partners. That war would see a united country dominant in the world outside of the Soviet Bloc.

The next war with engagement of our army was Korea. We were in it from the beginning instead of waiting for an opportune moment to join. However, the army we sent was made up of conscripts and volunteers. We would not win that one and the Republican candidate won handedly as a victorious general and with the promise of ending the Korean conflict.

Though the bombing of Korea surpassed the scale of bombing in the Pacific campaign of World War II, we put near a million men in the field. The best we could do was a stalemate.

The Korean conflict saw no mass protests other than the defeat of Truman. We were probably not as united as at the end of the previous war. Would a state policy of total propaganda have led to a victory in Korea? It didn't happen and was not going to happen.

Vietnam would see the end of a citizen army fighting our wars. It would begin with the draft system securely in place and would end with registration but with conscription ended. Clearly, those in charge of operating the narrative, if there was anyone in charge, were not doing the job.

The Vietnam War was mostly of the era known as "The Sixties." It began with Kennedy's election and ended more or less in the early 70s. It was a time of mass college attendance and with that, a student population that was not interested in being part of the developing war. There was much experimentation with different lifestyles and psychoactive substances.

If a World War II veteran had slept from 1945 until 1968 and woke up in a college town, he would not have thought himself to be in the same country he had served.

Of course, if he had woken up in a small mid-American town differences would have existed, but they would not have been as stark. The attitude against the war and what was called the "counterculture" was in college towns more than anyplace else.

The students were abetted in their sentiment by many professors. Crane Brinton, in his book, *The Anatomy of Revolution*, discussed the alienation of the intellectuals. Though not all of the professoriate abetted the antiwar students, there were many who did with names famous even today.

There was consternation concerning the unfairness in the system of conscription, and so a lottery system was begun. Then on January 27, 1973, the Selective Service, the government agency overseeing the draft, announced that there would be no more draft calls.

One still had to register with Selective Service, but there would be no more draft. Anti-Vietnam War sentiment waned as we were on the way out anyway.

What has that meant for the structure of the military?

We now fight our wars with an all-volunteer army. Also, we've had lots of wars. The wars are open ended and with no chance of "victory." One might posit that we did have a triumph of sorts in the downfall of Saddam Hussein and our role in the fall of Qaddafi, but that was just pushing Humpty Dumpty. None of our horses and men has been able to put anything back together again.

We persisted with a democratic army in Vietnam for over ten years. We have kept saving the world since September 11 and for much longer than that with our professional force. Indeed, it looks like we shall be doing this forever if we can.

The current system was inevitable if the Cold War were to continue with our opposition to the Soviet Bloc. The communist Chinese had moved away from the Soviets and though not our ally, were a counterweight.

The antiwar sentiment that ended the draft meant that we would have to rely on volunteers. We have done that and continue to do so with the end of the Soviet Union.

There's a problem with our military situation. We're at war but not at war. It isn't necessary to have total mobilization of the kind that we had for the two world wars or even for what we had for the Civil War, but support is still necessary.

The drumbeat must be kept up, but not too, too much. One has Ben Affleck making PSAs for the wounded and all that, but the presidents don't meet the coffins from the planes. One is reminded of Margaret Thatcher meeting a plane bearing the coffins of British soldiers from Ireland. Support plummeted and the prime minister did not do it again. We are not going to make that mistake either. Our adventures need only the right amount of support. How long we can keep this up remains to be seen.

The War

There is no need to have an exhaustive rehash of the war's history. We all know the outcome. In 1954, the French left and per the treaty signed at Geneva, the country was divided at the 17th parallel. Ho Chi Minh and the communists set up a government in the north. The Emperor would reign over the south.

There was to be a nationwide vote for reunification in 1956.

Bao Dai was removed as emperor in 1955 by the anti-Communist premier, Ngo Dinh Diem, and the South became, officially, the Republic of Vietnam. The election never happened.

As part of the Cold War, we would support the regime in the south. Trained and equipped by the United States, South Vietnamese government forces cracked down on opponents. Around 100,000 were arrested. Many were mistreated and/or killed.

Armed resistance against Diem was carried out starting in the later 1950s by the Viet Cong. Opposition to the government was under the umbrella of the National Liberation Front (NLF). The NLF claimed to be on its own and mostly non-communist. The United States assumed it was controlled by Hanoi.

As a child in the late '50s, I saw on American television a news segment that highlighted the southern government's success against anti-regime guerrillas. The theme, that the opposition was on the run, would have given one the feeling that the government was in control. Maybe they were at the time.

South Vietnam was seen by the United States as a "domino." According to the domino theory, if South Vietnam fell, Laos would go next—then Cambodia, then Thailand, and then Burma, all tumbling like a row of dominos.

Under that assumption, the Kennedy administration increased military and technical aid to South Vietnam. Troops, other than advisors, were not sent.

The Diem government faced protests by members of the Buddhist majority. Diem, a Roman Catholic favored his co-religionists and this led to unrest. The mass protests included dramatic acts of self-immolation by saffron clad monks.

Dissatisfied with Diem's handling of the war and the Buddhist resistance, a group of army officers planned and carried out a coup against Diem whom they executed on November 2, 1963.

American government had knowledge of the coup and may have provided encouragement. Not soon after, President Kennedy was assassinated. Madame Nhu, sister-in-law of Diem, who lost her husband in the coup, sent a condolence letter to Kennedy's widow that was not without some bitter commentary.

Needless to say, the coup stabilized nothing. As the situation continued unsettled, the Johnson administration increased military and economic assistance.

In August of 1964, an event that led to a large escalation of American involvement occurred. At the time, news outlets reported that North Vietnamese torpedo boats had attacked American destroyers in the Gulf of Tonkin. The president ordered bombing raids against North Vietnamese military installations.

More importantly, Congress would pass the Tonkin Gulf Resolution giving the president broad war powers.

When everything came to light years later, the incident was hardly a *casus belli*. Indeed, the first shots fired were from the destroyer USS *Maddox*. No matter, the administration would run with it.

In the next year, the United States would begin the bombing campaign code named Operation Rolling Thunder. The campaign would see vast amounts of explosives dropped on the north. The bombing destroyed much of North Vietnam, but did not bring the enemy to its knees. It would also see them accrue bargaining chips in the form of captured aircrews.

Even though Johnson defeated Goldwater by portraying his opponent as a war-monger in the 1964 presidential campaign, he would nevertheless decide to send combat troops to Vietnam in late July of 1965. At the time, there was no large-scale opposition to the move.

The American troops that were sent to South Vietnam went on search and destroy missions and racked up great body counts. Large scale bombing of "free fire zones" took place. Yet despite all that the enemy was still in the field, fighting on with no sign of being beaten.

The North Vietnamese and allies in the south were able to resupply via the famous Ho Chi Minh Trail. It was never stopped by any method of interdiction.

Tet

The administration and General William Westmoreland, who commanded U.S. forces in Vietnam, held that the American strategy of attrition was working. So, when seemingly out of nowhere, the North Vietnamese and their southern allies began an offensive, it was a shock to the American public.

Intelligence did have knowledge something was up but not the scale and plans. Beginning on January 30, 1968, attacks began across much of the south. The attackers were not able to take any amount of territory and were driven off sooner or later. The South Vietnamese military responded to the challenge unevenly, but no unit would break or defect.

Fighting in Hue would take place over a few weeks and would be one of the bloodiest battles of the war.

Though the North Vietnamese and their allies had not been able to hold any territory, Tet was a propaganda victory for them. It would change the perception of the war among the American people. There would be an increased attitude of skepticism toward official comments.

Khe Sanh

The siege of Khe Sanh began about the time of Tet but is separate, as it lasted a lot longer. It was seen in the American media as an attempt at a replay of the defeat of the French at

Dien Bien Phu. Khe Sanh would not fall. Casualty figures for the PAVN (People's Army of Vietnam, the North Vietnamese army) and the Marines are still disputed.

The siege would be broken and the base closed. Khe Sanh was an outpost not really worth it to either side. It did have some value as a diversion away from cities in Tet.

Protesting

While the fighting was going on in Southeast Asia, a protest movement against the war had arisen in the United States. It began among leftist students on various campuses. The burgeoning counterculture added fuel to the fire. Even students and others who may not have been naturally enthusiastic protestors came on board, as they were not interested in being drafted.

In October of 1967, 100,000 protesters crowded the Lincoln Memorial and many of them would march on the Pentagon. Some were arrested after a confrontation. Martin Luther King, Jr. came out against the war in the same year.

A February 1968 Gallup poll showed more people against the war than for it.

By the end of 1967, Lyndon Johnson was expected to be his party's nominee for another term. However, the war was catching up with him. At first, it looked like there would be no opposition to his nomination.

Minnesota Senator Eugene McCarthy took up the challenge and announced his candidacy. The odds were long, as he had little support from party leaders. It was do or die, and he put all his resources into the first-in-the-nation New Hampshire primary.

On January 26, 1968, the senator began his run with an address at the Saint Anselm College Stoutenburgh Gym.* An antiwar following coalesced behind him. In the cold north, the dedicated arrived and worked with dissident democrats to build support for the candidacy.

On March 12, McCarthy both lost and won the New Hampshire primary. True, the president received 49% to the insurgent's 42%. Everybody, noticed, however, that the senator, with no party support had done well. Among those who noticed was Johnson.

> *The author was in the audience and at the time and thought McCarthy's quest quixotic at best.*

Realizing the battle to be re-nominated and elected for another term would be difficult and not certain of success, on March 31, 1968, in an address to the nation, Johnson withdrew from the race.

Senator Robert F. Kennedy, brother of the assassinated president, announced his candidacy in a move that was looked upon as opportunism by supporters of Senator McCarthy. Kennedy, after a grueling campaign, won the California primary. On the night of that win, he was assassinated.

The party regulars would rally around Vice President Hubert Humphrey. He would get the nomination instead of Senator McCarthy even though he did not contest the primaries.

In the general election, the Republican nominee, Richard Nixon would win.

While not the "peace candidate" that Nixon said he was, it has been said that he had claimed a secret plan. That is in dispute, but he could hardly say that he had no idea what he was doing.

No matter what he said or planned, once in office, Nixon owned the war. Those who had protested yelling, "Hey, hey, LBJ, how many kids did you kill today" now had someone else to oppose and they did it with greater fervor.

Paris Peace Negotiations

In his speech on March 31, President Johnson announced a halt to bombing in much of the north and called for peace talks. Talks would start in May in Paris. They would continue until a ceasefire was enacted. Mostly, however, they were at an impasse. The North Vietnamese saw them as part of a policy of "fighting while negotiating." It wasn't a bad strategy.

Vietnamization

The Nixon administration continued with the peace talks, but pursued a policy of "Vietnamization." This would be training and supplying the South Vietnamese so that they could take over more and more of the war.

The war would continue on with many twists and turns. There was the massacre of civilians at My Lai and the deaths of protesters shot by guardsmen at Kent State. Negotiations continued, much of it secretly, between Henry Kissinger and the North's Le Duc Tho.

The huge 1972 North Vietnamese offensive in the South failed and an agreement was drafted by fall. The Saigon government rejected it. Bombing raids against Hanoi and the harbor at Haiphong were undertaken.

In January of 1973, the final peace agreement was concluded. We got our prisoners back and they got a ceasefire in place. Our troops came home.

The North would complete their long game by biding their time until 1975. No matter what reassurances we might have given, we were not going back. When they began the final offensive, nothing could stop them until the tanks crashed into the presidential palace.

Aftermath

Nobody doubts that we lost in Vietnam. All the equipment and treasure spent to halt Communism was gone. The north took possession of all the ordnance left behind. The money squandered among defense contractors and numerous other wasted accounts had evaporated like melted snow.

Gone, all gone, but it could have been worse. We could have scored the same tie that we achieved in Korea. That would have been a debacle. Had the north agreed to a permanent ceasefire on the border, we would still have troops and planes and PXs and condom-dispensing machines all over South Vietnam. There would be brass on the border taking meetings ad infinitum with the North's officers. We would be forever rebuilding the south. Swiss banks would be awash in skimmed cash from all the associated boondoggles.

Ah, but that was not the case. When the last of our boys left, we were gone. We had bled buckets and lost billions, but when we finally said au revoir, it was over. We even had a measure of revenge, as Hanoi had its own Vietnam in Cambodia. All the dominos did not exactly domino.

In the end, it was one of the few places we got to leave. It was almost as if we left no forwarding address and they changed their phone number.

We could forget about the place, which is more than one can say about most of the other spots we're stuck in.

23

Post-Vietnam

After the end of the Vietnam War, an incident occurred that spoke volumes about the hapless Ford administration. The cargo ship *Mayaguez* was seized by Khmer Rouge forces, and as it was being held, the Marines retook it.

It was a confused affair, but after the ship was retaken and the crew released, there was a smug picture of President Ford and Henry Kissinger with aides seeming to exult over the incident. All we had done in Vietnam had been undone and these men were gloating over what had been hardly more than a booby prize.

Ford would get a bump in polls, but nothing could save his unelected presidency. The next president, Jimmy Carter, tried to project a different image. His regime continued to be shy about foreign commitments. He didn't save the Shah of Iran, but that didn't matter too much, as his regime probably could not have been salvaged.

Our history with the Persians, based significantly on our destruction of the Mosaddegh government, could only be seen as an error. True, the Shah had a few decades as our man, but it was all swept away with the coming of Khomeini.

When the dying Shah was admitted to the United States for medical treatment, the American Embassy was occupied and its Marine guard held hostage. The Carter administration was unable to resolve the crisis diplomatically and an attempt at rescue militarily failed.

Afghanistan

In April of 1978, local Afghan communists led by Nur Muhammad Taraki overthrew the government that had previously overthrown the king. The Taraki regime attempted reforms in education and land distribution accompanied by executions. A revolt ensued against the government and Taraki was deposed by the brutal Hafizullah Amin.

By December of 1979, the Amin government had lost so much control of the country that the Soviets invaded, executed Amin, and installed Barbrak Karmal as president.

Even before the Soviet invasion, the U.S. government had considered activity to help the insurgents in concert with Pakistan. Whether this was part of a plan to draw the Soviets to intervene or not is an interesting question. Zbigniew Brzezinski, who was Carter's National Security Advisor, would claim that "We didn't push the Russians to intervene, but we knowingly increased the probability that they would."

Brzezinski was a hardliner and certainly pro-Polish in outlook. This is hard not to sympathize with. The Poles were tortured by the National Socialist occupation regime and then were betrayed by the Western Allies. They would be unhappily part of the Warsaw Pact until the end of the Soviet Union.

A campaign that was the Soviet Union's Vietnam could only be supported by an American who was also a Pole. Without our support, the mujahideen might have collapsed quickly and the Soviets may have been able to then deal with the Poland's Solidarity trade union. Whatever the cause, the USSR became fully involved in a war against mujahidin in a land known as the "graveyard of empires."

It is certain that if we had not assisted the Pakistanis and their clients, the events of September 11 would never have happened. The Soviet system was in decline. It was being threatened in Poland by the strike of Solidarity. Without American help, would the efforts of the Pakistanis and the money of the Saudis been enough to tip over the Soviets, or would they have prevailed in Afghanistan?

All of this is impossible to say. What Carter's successor called the "evil empire" would implode, but Francis Fukuyama author of the End of History, was wrong and history did not end and not on a completely fortuitous course.

During the Carter administration, two major diplomatic events occurred: the Camp David Agreement between Egypt and Israel that has led to a long cold peace between the two countries (but did not begin to solve the issues of the Middle East), and the establishment of relations between the People's Republic of China and the United States.

The 1956 Suez Crisis had seen the United States gain some credit in the Arab world, as the Eisenhower administration made the invaders give back. We would not always seem as evenhanded.

In 1967, the Israelis and a coalition of Arab states fought the Six Day War. The Israelis were victorious on all fronts and ended up occupying the West Bank of the Jordan River, the Gaza Strip, and all of Jerusalem as well as most of the Golan Heights.

The Arabs never admitted defeat and the Israelites began settlements on the occupied lands. Since the 1967 war, the United States has been seen by the Arab world as a sponsor of, if not an ally, of Israel. The Soviet Union became more involved with the war's losing side.

1967 made clear the weakness of Arabian military power. It seemed that Israel was so dominant that, other than propaganda pronouncements, Arab states would have little course of action other than to understand and accept the reality on the ground.

Thus, it was no little shock when the Arabs attacked on October 6, 1973, which was also the holiest day of the Jewish year. The conflict, which became known as the Yom Kippur War saw initial Arab success.

Most surprisingly was the Egyptian crossing of the Suez Canal. The feat was pulled off secretly and efficiently. At the same time, the Syrians retook the Golan Heights.

Though the Israelis were thrown back on the defensive, they recovered and retook the Golan. On the Egyptian front, they pulled off the impressive coup of crossing the Suez Canal and striking into Egypt proper.

An October 25th ceasefire ended the war.

In the war, the Arabs proved they could fight well against the Israelis, if not decisively so. The United States showed its hand as being firmly the sponsor of Israel as the Nixon administration unstintingly resupplied the Israeli military during the war.

From the beginning of Carter's presidency in 1977, his administration sought to bring peace to the Middle East. Though he and his Secretary of State Cyrus Vance worked hard to engage the regional powers, in the end he had only Egypt and Israel to work with.

Egyptian President Anwar Sadat really started things moving with his visit to Israel and speech before the Knesset, the Israeli legislature. Israeli Prime Minister Menachem Begin returned the visit, but the process stalled.

President Carter invited the two men to come and negotiate at Camp David, the presidential retreat. The two men agreed and the summit began on September 5, 1978.

The negotiations at the retreat went on for 13 days. In the end, there would be what is known as the Camp David Accords leading to an Egyptian-Israeli peace treaty.

The rest of the Arab world did not sign treaties and Egypt would be expelled from the Arab League. Anwar Sadat would be assassinated. Still, the pact is in force, though it has been referred to as mentioned a cold peace. All things considered, it was a great accomplishment for Carter. Begin and Sadat would get the Nobel though. The former president, after some campaigning, would receive one in 2002.

One might note, as important as it was, that the Middle East remains even more of a problem today for the United States, and as long as we stay, will always be so.

Our recognition of the PRC (People's Republic of China) was to see them as a counterweight to the Soviets. How really useful that was in the long run will be debated by historians. It has certainly not been of much value to the American factory worker.

24

The Reagan Revolution

The election of Ronald Reagan saw a higher polarization among the electorate than even the beginning of the Nixon presidency. If you were a liberal, you feared a man who was about to start a nuclear war with the Russians. Conservatives saw him restoring a hollowed out military and bringing prosperity.

True, the Carter presidency saw a devastating inflation and this moderated under Reagan. As to who goes the credit is open to debate, as Fed Chairman Paul Volcker was a Carter nominee. Volker is given much of the praise for the moderation.

The new administration got off to a great start even before Reagan took office. The Iranian hostages were released in what seemed like a response to a new reality. This is still debated, but it appeared so at the time.

The early perception of the Reagan administration as hardline bears some truth, yet as time went on, progress in relations would occur with the Soviet Union, though in 1983 he would call it an evil empire.

The administration made much of increasing defense spending on different programs, most notably the Strategic Defense Initiative. Skeptics dubbed SDI as "Star Wars" and characterized it as expensive and unworkable. Nevertheless, it concerned the Soviets, which may have been its most important aspect.

Central America
Nicaragua

In Central America, toward the end of the Carter administration, the dictator of Nicaragua, Anastasio Somoza, was overthrown by the Sandinista National Liberation Front, or FSLN. Whether or not the Sandinistas deserved to win is a question much debated in right and left circles.

What is in little doubt is that Somoza deserved to be deposed. His family had ruled Nicaragua undemocratically for decades. The Somoza-run country was more or less a U.S. client until it was no longer tenable to support him.

The new government itself was not into the electoral thing and would soon be accused of human rights abuses and would be opposed by a militia known as the Contras that was funded and trained by the CIA. The U.S. government also did not approve of the Sandinista support of other revolutionary movements such as the one in El Salvador. The close relationship with the Cuban government was not about to win the Sandinistas any favor in Washington other than with some in Congress such as House Speaker Jim Wright who wished to be his own foreign secretary. The ethically challenged speaker would resign under a cloud in 1989.

How one felt about the Contras mostly depended on ideology. People on the left saw them as tools of American imperialism while on the right they were viewed as opponents of a murderous regime. Congress, with a Democratic majority, was not in favor of supporting the insurgents. Under the Boland Amendment, funding for arming the Contras was stopped.

The administration got creative in providing arms for the Contras, and when it was exposed and became known as the Iran-Contra affair, it became a scandal.

Basically, the project was to sell arms to the Iranians, whom the administration had not been shy about characterizing as terrorist supporters, then use that money to support the Contras. The administration justified this by claiming the executive branch could run foreign policy as it wished. How confident they were that this was all kosher was questionable as it was all done in secret.

When it all came out, it damaged the administration. National Security Advisor, Admiral Poindexter, would be convicted of lying to Congress, though the convictions would be reversed on appeal. National Security Council staffer Oliver North, a Marine lieutenant colonel, was convicted of various felonies that would also be overturned.

Official investigations found no evidence that President Reagan had any knowledge of events. If so, he might be criticized for not being aware of what were significant programs on his watch, even if that gave him plausible deniability.

The Boland Amendment would be repealed, but the Contras would not win. A ceasefire was agreed to in 1988 and elections were held in 1990 that saw the electoral defeat of the Sandinistas and the presidency of Violeta Chamorro.

The violence was over and politics resumed. As of 2021, Daniel Ortega serves as president of Nicaragua and has done well for himself in politics, moderating much of his revolutionary fervor (there have been protests against his regime in the last few years).

The question becomes whether or not all our anti-Sandinista activities were a waste of time. The ruling Somoza family deserved ouster, but they had been sponsored, if not created, by the United States. FDR is supposed to have said in

1939 of the father of the last ruling dictator, "Somoza may be a son of a bitch, but he's our son of a bitch." We had a long run of controlling events in that land. Now that we don't, are we any worse off?

True, a nation that accounted itself the enemy of our system supported the Sandinistas and their desire to spread revolution. Maybe they would have succeeded and a socialist collective from Tierra del Fuego up to the Rio Grande would have been organized.

Or maybe it was mostly a waste of time and money.

El Salvador

The other regional civil war in which the United States was involved in was El Salvador's. This was a brutal conflict that ran from late 1979 until the beginning of 1992. We supported the government and Cuba and Nicaragua backed the Farabundo Marti National Liberation Front or FMLN. The war concerned the usual stew of upper and middle classes against peasants, students, and workers.

For much of the war, the country's president was Jose Napoleon Duarte. He was the moderating face of the government, while death squads continued to operate. In the end, after negotiations, peace broke out. The FMLN disbanded and security forces were much reduced. Today, the president is a member of the FMLN party.

The results in a polarized nation such as El Salvador are not a little surprising. Again, the question is, was our involvement necessary? Did it really benefit us?

Grenada

The small island nation of Grenada had a leftist government that had overthrown a previous one. In 1983, the lefties were overthrown by a further lefty group with mayhem and murder ensuing.

The United States, with regional urging, invaded Grenada to close down the playground. They battled some Cuban troops and that was that. Not a major geopolitical happening.

The Falklands/Malvinas War

The Falklands/Malvinas War was not a big event and afterward was quickly forgotten, certainly by the American public. It did pose a policy question that the United States spent little time thinking about. When a conflict involves a hemispheric neighbor and a European power, do we support the neighbor, the European power, or stay out of it altogether?

"The first panacea for a mismanaged nation is inflation of the currency; the second is war. Both bring a temporary prosperity; both bring a permanent ruin. But both are the refuge of political and economic opportunists."

So said Ernest Hemingway.

Hemingway was not thinking about the Argentines when he made the above observation. Argentina seemed to always be having a battle with inflation, so one might wonder why it took them so long to find a war.

The military government of Argentina had suppressed opposition, but had not been running a particularly stellar economy. The nation had always claimed the British-occupied islands to the east and as they were far enough away from Great Britain, maybe an invasion would work? After all, the Brits were constantly downsizing their military. The Argentines decided to go for it, and on April 2, 1982, invaded and took the islands. The British would dispatch a task force and take them back.

Could they have done it without our support and should we have given it?

Initially, the United States appeared to play honest broker, hoping to mediate the dispute. Our NATO treaty obligations to Britain did not require that we support them in the South Atlantic. The Rio Treaty did not require that we support Argentina, as they were the attacker, not the attacked

What that kind of meant was that the United States would try diplomacy until it was obvious that the Argentines were not leaving—and then we would support the British.

A *Guardian* article of September 5, 2002, averred that the UK could not have won without U.S. help, "Margaret Thatcher would have lost the Falklands war in 1982 if America had failed to provide crucial missiles to bolster British air defenses, according to an adviser to the former prime minister."

Lord Renwick of the British embassy at the time said in a BBC documentary that he was tasked with going to the Pentagon and asking for the latest 105 Sidewinder missiles. The Brits wanted them within 48 hours. To get them would mean taking them from frontline U.S. units.

Lord Powell of Bayswater, Lady Thatcher's key foreign affairs adviser, said that Britain would have lost the war without such assistance.

Richard Perle, then an assistant U.S. defense secretary at the time, confirmed Powell's assertion, "Britain would probably have lost the war without American assistance. That's how significant it was."

What can we conclude? If it is necessary for the United States to be in NATO, and if that trumps hemispheric concerns, certainly it is necessary to keep an important ally happy.

There are some questions to be answered. Our "special relationship" with the United Kingdom in the twentieth century can be defined as Britain gets into a war they cannot win and then inveigles the United States to pull their chestnuts out of the fire.

Indeed, the special relationship is more important to the British than to us. The same *Guardian* piece had it that Margaret Thatcher, the "Iron Lady," was miffed that we had even pretended even-handedness between Britain and Argentina. Your average Yank could be forgiven for thinking that took a bit of nerve from a supplicant.

One hopes that the United States got something out of the support given the UK that has not been mentioned. Otherwise, it was not a good deal. Sure, they would send a well-trained unit to help us out in one of our adventures, but what little we get from them hardly compares to a century plus of favors we have done.

Special relationships never work to the benefit of the United States.

To answer the question of what would have been the best course of action, staying out entirely would have. I doubt Argentina holds a grudge. I suspect its citizens realize the war itself was a mistake. Its only plus was that it hastened the departure of the junta. The economy is still a mess and probably always will be.

The Brits would have been miffed, but so what? Being the Brits, they are unable to know when to stop. They should have negotiated a peace in World War I instead of calling in the ringers. They probably would have carried on until they had taken back the sheep farm and ruined their economy and the Thatcher economic miracle in the process. Good lesson.

No, we had to support our NATO associate. If you're going to be an empire, you have to keep the satraps happy.

And, we can just put aside that little Doctrine of Monroe.

Afghanistan and the Middle East

After World War II the United States was never not involved in the Middle East, but over time, we have become much more so.

We have had a long relationship with the Kingdom of Saudi Arabia (KSA), as there are shared interests. We both want to be able to keep the huge petroleum resources flowing: KSA to sell and the rest of the world to buy.

Saudi Arabia, as a monarchy with a conservative religious outlook, could only be suspicious of the Soviet Union and its official ideology.

Our relations with Iran have been discussed elsewhere and have continued to be a problem.

In the Middle East, the administration became involved in the Lebanese hall of mirrors. In August of 1982, U.S. Marines were dispatched to Beirut as part of a multi-national force or MNF to oversee the Palestinian Liberation Organization's evacuation of Beirut.

In September, the PLO left under the protection of the MNF and afterward the Marines left Beirut. The situation deteriorated in Lebanon, and Marines were ordered back.

The United States was not seen as even-handed and there was no little animosity toward them. Whatever the perception, the Corps had guidelines to make the situation even more dangerous. Marines were required not to keep rounds in the chamber and other rules. It was a dangerous situation.

On October 3, 1983, a truck laden with explosives and driven by Iranian national Ismail Ascari crashed into the building used as a Marine barracks and detonated the explosive charge.

In the bombing, 241 American servicemen were killed. A short time later, the French barracks suffered a similar attack.

It was horrific, and both the French and the United States pledged to stay the course and retaliate against the perpetrators. In the end, the malefactors could not be identified with certainty.

U.S. forces remained and the battleship the USS *New Jersey* provided support offshore. On February 7, 1984, President

Reagan would order the withdrawal of the Marines. It was the end of a rather misguided episode. The impossibility of unraveling the Gordian knot of the Middle East should by now be evident. Leaving was the best idea. We should have not forgotten that lesson.

Afghanistan

The Reagan administration would continue to pursue a policy of supporting resistance to the Soviet-backed Afghan government. It was a rather roundabout process. Steve Coll, author of *Ghost Wars: The Secret History of the CIA, Afghanistan, and Bin Laden from the Soviet Invasion to September 10, 2001*, in an interview on *Democracy Now* describes it thus:

> Well, it of course begins in 1979 when the Soviets invaded during the Carter administration, and it really swelled between 1981 and 1985. Essentially, under Bill Casey, the CIA created a three-part intelligence alliance to fund and arm the mujahideen, initially to harass Soviet occupation forces and eventually they embraced the goal of driving them out. The three-way alliance in each of the parties had a distinct role to play. The Saudi, their intelligence service primarily provided cash. Each year the congress would secretly allocate a certain amount of money to support the CIA's program. After that allocation was complete, the U.S. Intelligence liaison would fly to Riyadh and the Saudis would write a matching check. The U.S. role was to provide logistics and technological support as well as money. The Saudis collaborated with Pakistan's intelligence service, ISI, to really run the war on the front lines.

Whatever could go wrong? Again, per Mr. Coll:

Certainly, there were people in the early 1980s involved in the program who were aware that many of America's favorite clients were fundamentally anti-American in their outlook. But it was only in the late 1980's as the amounts of money and guns and really the success of the jihad began to swell that clients such as Gulbuddin Hekmatyar and Abdul Sayyaf, who were two of the most vehemently anti-American leaders of the jihad began to explicitly turn their propaganda pamphlets, at least their rhetorical efforts, against the United States as well as against the Soviet Union. As that began to happen ... there were individuals inside the U.S. bureaucracy, at the state department, elsewhere, who began to warn that the United States needed to change its political approach to this covert action program, that they needed now to start getting involved in the messy business of Afghan politics and to start to promote more centrist factions and to negotiate compromise with the Soviet-backed communist government in Kabul to prevent Islamist extremists from coming to power as the Soviets withdrew. These warnings, when you look at them with the benefit of hindsight, are quite prescient and certainly were strongly given, but they languished in the middle of the bureaucracy and were largely ignored by both second term Reagan administration and the first Bush administration, Bush 41.

So, the ball was dropped. Could there have been an intelligent policy that allowed the war to wind down and for all factions to have found a spot to rest on within a government that included everyone and excluded no one? I doubt Mr. Coll means that. Maybe what the United States needed was a point at which it could successfully just bug out. It is worth noting, the only successful exit strategy we executed in the twentieth century was from Vietnam.

The End of The Cold War

There is an area of foreign policy where Ronald Reagan performed brilliantly and it was so unexpected. As mentioned above, the 40th president began his first term perceived as John Wayne riding in as the sheriff to clean up the town after the last office holder had let the place go to ruin. Of course, if you were not his partisan, his arrival was seen as the entry of a bull in a China shop.

Both sides never really gave up their prejudices and still believe him as either the man who put American power back on track or the unreconstructed cold warrior.

Neither wants the truth: that Reagan worked with Soviet General Secretary Mikhail Gorbachev to bring about the end of the Cold War. Reagan did what he could to bring about conciliation and was met more than half way by Gorbachev.

Authors Jack Matlock and Suzanne Massie both give Reagan credit though Massie seems to award more to Reagan than does Matlock (who cites Reagan giving the greater share to his counterpart). Does it matter who gets a little more?

Suzanne Massie had been the wife of Robert K. Massie who had written about Nicholas and Alexandra, the last Russian tsar and his wife. He had credited her with much of the research. Her book, *Trust but Verify: Reagan, Russia and Me*, gives an account of her travels in the later stages of the Soviet Union. Matlock's account is that of a Reagan administration insider and eventually ambassador to Moscow. Her affection for Russia, if not for the USSR, shines through no more than when she notes that Gorbachev was the first ethnically Russian head of the country. Praise for Reagan however is unstinting.

Gorbachev had reasons for seeking a rapprochement with the West. The Soviets had a war that was draining them in Afghanistan. In Poland, they faced a union movement in

Solidarity that they had not been able to quell. Their economy and agriculture were in decline, as usual. The big money earner, oil, was in a price slump. It dawned on many in the Nomenklatura that things had to change.

Gorbachev was the man to do it, if he could. He would pursue the policies of Glasnost and Perestroika.

Glasnost was a slogan calling for increased openness and transparency in the Soviet Union. Perestroika means restructuring. Two such slogans do inherently contain danger as they admit the system of "scientific socialism" is not working at least up to the fever pitch of efficiency as envisioned by its theoreticians. A call for transparency implies that the political climate is or has been opaque.

It is easy to chortle about the pervasive regime secrecy; our nation has not always been forthcoming with information. Decades after the event, we only recently saw the release of the JFK file with some objection. Even now, some pages are still held back. It was not without a lot of heel dragging that the redacted pages of the September 11 report were given up. Speaker Ryan made sure that certain interested parties, such as the American people, were not privy to the occult secrets of the Trans-Pacific Partnership.

The last head of the Soviet Union had good reason to look for an opening. It is to his credit that the "Gipper" pursued peace with his counterpart despite opposition in the administration.

The two met in a summit in Geneva in November of 1985. The meeting produced no big surprises, but both men worked to produce a relationship that would be built on.

Their second meeting in the Icelandic capital, Reykjavik, is portrayed by some as a disaster or an event that saw Reagan hang tough on SDI. True, the talks collapsed but there had been enough progress made that work could continue. It may not have seemed as conciliatory when he spoke loudly in Berlin, "Mr. Gorbachev, tear down this wall," but it was coming.

The final summit would take place in Washington in December of 1987. The General Secretary came to the American capital to sign the Intermediate-Range Nuclear Forces (or INF) Treaty. Gorbachev also hoped to persuade President Reagan to work on further arms limiting in a Strategic Arms Reduction Treaty (START). Those negotiations would happen, but in the next administration.

Reagan would pass into history. His grassroots base would always believe he stood tall against the foreign menace.

25

The Elder Bush Presidency

In foreign policy, the George H. W. Bush administration was active. The diplomatic initiatives with the Soviet Union would continue. There would be two wars. The Communist Party would lose power and the Soviet Union itself would dissolve.

The other large Marxist state, The People's Republic of China, would suppress a large protest and demonstration in Tiananmen Square. The seemingly popular uprising ended and the Communist Party remains in power to this day in what is a mixed economy. The Chinese were able to accomplish the reforms that the Soviets could not. President Bush would condemn the PRC's action, but that changed nothing.

Poland would stop being a communist country, and in November of 1989, the Berlin Wall came down. To anyone alive when it went up, it seemed a symbol of the permanence of the East Bloc.

That bloc appeared a military behemoth that, short of instigating a civilization-destroying war, would last forever. More disintegration was up ahead.

The next month, President Bush would meet with President Gorbachev off the coast of the Island of Malta. They discussed issues, but no big agreements were reached. Both men declared the Cold War over.

In June of 1990, the two men would meet in Washington to sign a broad arms reduction agreement that would scrap significant portions of their nuclear arsenals.

Meanwhile, the foundations of the USSR were crumbling. The periphery was trying to leave and the center, as embodied by the Gorbachev regime, was limited in the amount of repression it could contemplate. The rebellious Boris Yeltsin, who had left the Communist Party, was elected in June of 1991 as head of Russia in the Soviet Union.

It was an unstable situation and the boil was about to be lanced. A group of hard-liners mounted a coup in August of 1991, kidnapping Gorbachev and announcing the new regime on television. The necessary ingredient in the attempt would be the willingness of the military to enforce the coup. When that did not happen, it was over.

By December, Gorbachev resigned, and in January the Soviet Union was replaced by the loose "Confederation of Independent States."

It was a promising time for the world. Unfortunately, despite some good efforts on the part of many statesmen, it hasn't worked out all that well.

Part of the reason that post-Soviet relations have not gone as smoothly as the world would have desired is the aggressive policy of enlisting old Warsaw Pact states in NATO. There is much dispute about this, but declassified documents from the National Security Archive at George Washington University give evidence that Gorbachev had received assurances that NATO would not move "one inch closer" to Russia. According to the archive:

> U.S. Secretary of State James Baker's famous "not one inch eastward" assurance about NATO expansion in his meeting with Soviet leader Mikhail Gorbachev on February 9, 1990, was part of a cascade of assurances about Soviet security given by Western leaders to

Gorbachev and other Soviet officials throughout the process of German unification in 1990 and on into 1991, according to declassified U.S., Soviet, German, British and French documents posted today by the National Security Archive at George Washington University (http://nsarchive.gwu.edu).

The documents show that multiple national leaders were considering and rejecting Central and Eastern European membership in NATO as of early 1990 and through 1991, that discussions of NATO in the context of German unification negotiations in 1990 were not at all narrowly limited to the status of East German territory, and that subsequent Soviet and Russian complaints about being misled about NATO expansion were founded in written contemporaneous memcons and telcons at the highest levels.

https://nsarchive.gwu.edu/briefing-book/russia-programs/2017-12-12/nato-expansion-what-gorbachev-heard-western-leaders-early

One would hope that the Bush administration bargained in good faith. A buffer of states between Russia and NATO may not have worked out well. After all, buffer nations between the USSR and Germany didn't work out as well either, but what we have now is an ongoing low-key war.

Panama

The Bush administration would go to war against the country that the United States had a hand in creating. Panama, formerly part of Columbia, had become independent not without machinations by U.S. American business. Also, the government wanted to see a canal built at a thin point of the isthmus connecting the two American continents.

The treaty leasing the Canal Zone to the United States, never too popular in Panama, was interpreted as being for 99 years.

In 1964, Panamanian students entered the zone to fly their national flag per agreement. They were jeered by American students and their parents and school officials. Rioting broke out and 20 Panamanians were killed. Clearly, the citizens had no little resentment for the force that they saw as an occupying power.

As time got closer to the final year, the Panamanians wanted to end the lease and gain sovereignty over the Canal. Negotiations began in 1977 and were completed in August. Panama ratified the treaty by referendum in October of 1977 and the United States Senate did the same in March of the following year.

Under the Torrijos–Carter Treaties, the canal and properties were to change hands by the year 2000.

Omar Torrijos was the strongman and dictator of Panama. His reign and life ended when his plane went down on July 31, 1981.

After Torrijos's death, there was a period of jockeying for power. By 1983, Manuel Noriega emerged as the new leader. Noriega was your basic *caudillo*, and did all the strongman stuff, such as press suppression and electoral manipulation.

Noriega's relationship to Los Norteamericanos was complicated, to say the least. The Panamanian officer had ties with American intelligence going back to the '50s and became a "full-fledged source" for army intelligence in the '60s according to a *New York Times* article dated January 6, 1990.

According to Reuters after his death:

> With the knowledge of U.S. officials, Noriega formed "the hemisphere's first narcokleptocracy," a U.S. Senate subcommittee report said, calling him the best example in recent U.S. foreign policy of how a foreign leader is

able to manipulate the United States to the detriment of our own interests.

Which would have been a reason to oust him.

The administration gave four reasons for the invasion:
- Safeguarding the lives of U.S. citizens in Panama. In his statement, Bush stated that Noriega had declared that a state of war existed between the United States and Panama and that he threatened the lives of the approximately 35,000 U.S. citizens living there. There had been numerous clashes between United States and Panamanian forces; one U.S. Marine had been killed a few days earlier.
- Defending democracy and human rights in Panama.
- Combating drug trafficking. Panama had become a center for drug money laundering and a transit point for drug trafficking to the United States and Europe.
- Protecting the integrity of the Torrijos–Carter Treaties. Members of Congress and others in the U.S. political establishment claimed that Noriega threatened the neutrality of the Panama Canal and that the U.S. had the right under the treaties to intervene militarily to protect the canal.

The reasons seem just, but in a sense a bit late. Noriega's drug trafficking and electoral and human rights shenanigans had been going on for almost as long as he had been in power.

The war itself was not much. The Panama Defense Force was not long in the field and collapsed quickly. Bipartisan support was supplied by Congress and that was that.

Noriega, after taking refuge in the Vatican mission, eventually surrendered. He was tried in the U.S. and duly convicted and served his time. After that he would be jailed in France and Panama and die incarcerated. If there is a handbook for how to behave and attain longevity as a dictator, the chapter on Noriega would be a how not to.

Post Noriega some things have not changed. It is a still a place to launder money from the drug trade. Bank secrecy, not beloved at all by the U.S., continues. A facade of normalcy at least exists as there is no dictatorship and elections take place regularly. No comic opera *El Jefe* reigns.

The First Iraq War

The libertarian writer, Jacob G. Hornberger, wrote in a 1990 essay that there were four reasons given for the justification of the war against Saddam Hussein. The first is that it was necessary to restore the Emir of Kuwait and family to power. Second, we had to stop "a budding new Hitler." Third, that "Iraq would capture a large portion of the world's oil market and, therefore, control the price of oil. Finally, "to make the world safe."

It will soon be three decades since the beginning of the First Gulf War. What is hard to believe is that a sufficient amount of the American public, let alone Congress, bought the given reasons.

The first reason turned Wilson's "Make the world safe for democracy" on its head. With all our free world propaganda and paeans to representative government, the senior Bush and his minions did not dare claim to be making the world safe for despotism, but that was what was happening for Kuwait, and by extension, the Saudis and Gulf statelets.

The second, the new Hitler, is tiresome. Hornberger points out that Ho Chi Minh once held that office. Indeed, one can take one's pick: Pinochet, Gaddafi, Assad. That none of them have the capacity to take over the world (nor did Dolph, if one wants to be honest) does not register. They are all so terrible, that if not opposed, will do something bad. That they have no capacity to invade or even do serious harm to the American republic hardly registers.

The third reason, that Hussein, who already sat on an ocean of petrol, would get more and control the price of oil, might have some truth. However, granting the possibility that he could, we must also allow he was not completely irrational. The purpose of having the oil is to sell it and one can only do that if one will come to terms with a willing buyer.

In truth, the man did not control the price of oil. There were many other OPEC producers and they would have been capable of countering Saddam's efforts if inclined. Of course, he might have decided to make further conquests of oil states, but in the end, he would still have to sell it.

The last reason, to make us safe, is almost not worth bothering with. To think we were safer after the war than before is dubious. The first and second attempts at destroying the World Trade Center are evidence of that.

All in all, the few men we lost in the Gulf the first time around were like the bones of Bismarck's Pomeranian grenadier.

The United States and Iraq had a complicated history. After the Camp David Accords, Iraq took the lead in having Egypt expelled from the Arab League. The United States also was not happy with Iraq's support of terrorist groups, such as Palestinian organizations.

Much of that would change during the Iran/Iraq war. We would not have a formal agreement, but it is hard to argue that we weren't de facto allies. Diplomatic relations were restored and Saddam's regime received military support.

The Iran/Iraq war began with an Iraq invasion of its enemy in 1980. Iraq started hostilities without a declaration of war and quickly gained territory. The Persians repelled their enemy, regained the territory and went over to the offensive. It is possible, if not probable, that Iran would have won without the material support for Iraq that the United States and the West supplied along with Arab countries.

The support would prove crucial in bringing about an end to the war. The success in the final Iraqi offensive led the Khomeini regime to agree to give it up. It ended in August of 1988.

Henry Kissinger had famously said, "It's a pity both sides can't lose." The result of the conflict was that he got his wish. In real terms, the people of both countries lost, and badly.

How bad it was did not deter Saddam Hussein from another war. Iraq accused Kuwait of stealing Iraqi oil via slant drilling.

The Hussein regime also owed $14 billion to Kuwait that had helped finance the war. It is understandable that Saddam might have resented this. Iraq had fought the war and suffered the losses, but had Iran won, the Sunni Arab countries would have been in a weaker position versus their Shia neighbor.

On August 2, 1990, the invasion began. In a couple of days most of Kuwait had been overrun by the Iraqi Republican Guard. Kuwaiti forces fell back to neighboring countries and Saddam announced that Kuwait had become the 19th province of Iraq.

Why did Saddam Hussein think he could get away with the invasion without opposition, especially from the United States? He had been our ally of sorts during the previous war and would have had to at least take into consideration the U.S. attitude in the matter.

Iraq maintained that Kuwait had been lopped off from it by the Anglo-Ottoman Convention of 1913. It is true that the Brits got a protectorate over some Ottoman land and, though there was no Iraq at the time, it would be understandable that an Iraqi patriot would resent a loss of part of the homeland. That Iraq itself is an artificial state carved out of the Middle East by foreign powers after World War I begs the question as to what is an Iraqi patriot?

As to American opinion on the matter, it is possible Saddam thought the United States would not oppose his actions on attaining his new province.

According to a *New York Times* article, Confrontation In The Gulf; U.S. Gave Iraq Little Reason Not to Mount Kuwait Assault," Saddam might have thought he had a green light:

> *In the two weeks before Iraq's seizure of Kuwait, the Bush Administration on the advice of Arab leaders gave President Saddam Hussein little reason to fear a forceful American response if his troops invaded the country.*
>
> *The Administration's message to Baghdad, articulated in public statements in Washington by senior policy makers and delivered directly to Mr. Hussein by the United States Ambassador, April C. Glaspie, was this: The United States was concerned about Iraq's military buildup on its border with Kuwait, but did not intend to take sides in what it perceived as a no-win border dispute between Arab neighbors.*
>
> *"In a meeting with Mr. Hussein in Baghdad on July 25, eight days before the invasion, Ms. Glaspie urged the Iraqi leader to settle his differences with Kuwait peacefully but added, "We have no opinion on the Arab-Arab conflicts, like your border disagreement with Kuwait," according to an Iraqi document described as a transcript of their conversation.*
>
> *Portions of the document, prepared in Arabic by the Iraqi Government, were translated and broadcast by ABC News on Sept. 11 and were the basis of accounts by The Washington Post and The Guardian of London. The State Department "declined to confirm the accuracy of the document, but officials did not dispute Ms. Glaspie's essential message."*

> As those and other details of the Administration's diplomacy have unfolded in recent weeks, its handling of Iraq before the invasion has begun to draw strong criticism in Congress, even among those who generally support the Administration's military action in the Persian Gulf. Some lawmakers have asserted that the Administration conveyed a sense of indifference to Baghdad's threats.

Events around the Glaspie meeting are still discussed today. No matter what happened, the United States was not indifferent to the invasion after it happened.

The United States issued an ultimatum that Iraq would have to evacuate its military from Kuwait by January 15, 1991. Iraq faced condemnation from major world powers. The UN Security Council passed a resolution condemning the invasion.

Negotiations would fail and the Bush administration would begin Operation Desert Shield on August 2, 1990. Troops and equipment were sent to Saudi Arabia in a huge buildup.

The administration's actions seemed to have popular support. There was the last squeak of the anti-war left with the slogan "No blood for oil," but it didn't amount to much. Congress took its time in debating the issue. This lead John Chancellor, the longtime NBC news anchor to take the body to task in a broadcast of January 2, 1991:

> Everybody hopes the crisis in the Gulf doesn't inflict serious damage to American forces there but there has already been one important casualty—the U.S. Constitution. For almost half a year, as this country prepared for war, the Constitution has been ignored. There hasn't even been a debate in the Congress on the situation in the Gulf much less a declaration of war, and we'll soon have 430,000 troops out there.

We've heard a lot of talk about constitutional theory, that the president has authority to commit forces without Congressional approval etcetera, etcetera. But that's beside the point. The real reason for no debate is that they're all scared. The Republicans are scared that a close vote on a declaration of war would encourage Saddam Hussein. The Democrats are scared that voting against the war might make them look like defeatist wimps if war starts and George Bush wins. So, it's let the other guy, or the other party take responsibility. The democrats who control the Congress won't call a special session to debate war or peace. The Republican president won't use his powers to call one.

The Gulf Crisis is the perfect occasion for a debate about going to war. This is no unexpected emergency like the start of the Korean War. It's been five months since Kuwait was invaded, plenty of time for reasoned discourse. There is still time, in fact. Let them obey the constitution. We're risking American lives in the Gulf to uphold the rule of law, why should we ignore it here at home?

Chancellor always seemed to be self-righteous, but his commentary was dead on. The Constitution most often seems to be honored in the breach by those who have sworn an oath to uphold and defend it. Congress would pass the resolutions, and the president would sign them on January 14.

On January 17, 1991, a five-weeks aerial and naval bombardment began with ground operations commencing on the 24th of February. With superiority in men, materiel, and logistics, there was little question of the outcome. Most Iraqi forces were destroyed or captured. The borders were restored.

A cease-fire was called by the United States on February 28, after 100 hours of operations. It has been said that President Bush was surprised by how rapid the offensive was and ended it without Saddam even asking, Why didn't they go all the way to Baghdad and destroy the Ba'ath regime?

There would be many good reasons for that, but nothing seems to have been well thought out. The Bush administration encouraged the Iraqi people, or at least the Shia and Kurds, to rebel via radio broadcasts by the president on clandestine stations. It would have not have taken much to get the people to rise up.

In one of the most disgraceful acts of our history, the Bush administration would then pull the rug out from underneath the rebels. Saddam was allowed to slaughter them unmercifully. His generals were shocked when General Schwarzkopf told them they could use their helicopters with their rockets.

There was fear that the Iraqi state would disintegrate if the rebellions succeeded. The U.S. would not be so wary of that in its next Mesopotamian war.

There was little that Saddam had to end up agreeing to. He had to agree to the Security Council's resolution to give up weapons of mass destruction as well as pay damages for the occupation of Kuwait.

How much was really settled is opened to question. The Iraqis did their best to resist inspections. The coalition had to institute no fly zones for some protection of Kurds to the north and Shia to the south.

So, American policy would limp along until a few years into the new millennium. George Bush probably thought it a roaring success.

He certainly loved being "leader of the free world." If you saw one of his pressers during the Malta Summit, he was happy being a guy bantering with the reporters—though he certainly was not in control of them.

Ah, but he was not the in-control guy he thought he was. Having promised the voters "Read my lips, no new taxes" with passionate emphasis, he abandoned his pledge. George never got it. The little people didn't like being tossed aside like Iraqi peasants and they would toss him aside no matter how wonderful his 100 hours war appeared to be.

In the years that followed, U.S. and British aircraft continued to patrol skies and mandate a no-fly zone over Iraq, while Iraqi authorities made every effort to frustrate the carrying out of the peace terms, especially United Nations weapons inspections.

26

The Clinton Administration

The former Massachusetts senate president, Billy Bulger, said of Bill Clinton's speech at the 1988 Democratic Party convention, "I was a young man when Bill Clinton started speaking." The infamous Whitey Bulger's brother was no youth at the time.

Clinton was an interesting character and that he became president with baggage that might not (or might) be excused today, is in its own way fascinating. That he made it through two terms, let alone one is not without interest. The controversies that dogged him, including impeachment, were not sufficient to sink him.

Then again, it should not come off as a surprise. The focus on the "it's the economy, stupid" aspect of his campaign got him elected, and an improving situation in that area got him re-elected. Whatever he did or did not do worked.

Clinton was not known as someone with a deep knowledge or interest in foreign policy. Unlike his predecessor, who had served as Director of Central Intelligence and Chief of the U.S. Liaison Office to the People's Republic of China (before we did ambassadors with the Middle Kingdom), he had no experience of the subject and would have to learn from others. There was a lot to learn.

Somalia

One of the last acts of the George Bush administration was to send troops to Somalia. The mission was to combat famine and protect food supplies. American soldiers would become embroiled in the factional warfare of the country. Bodies of American soldiers were dragged through the streets. Support for the mission tanked.

The Secretary of Defense, Les Aspin, would resign over controversy that the troops had not received adequate equipment. That may have helped keep soldiers alive, but would not have effected too much in the long run. Somalia would not now be a completely functioning state and our troops would just be wasting time.

Then the inexperienced Bill Clinton did something smart, something brighter than any foreign policy maneuver executed by either Bush. He got the troops out of Somalia in 1994. It was the first exit strategy since Vietnam and it was a good one.

There was nothing to be gained by staying. Clinton, being an adept political guy, knew a loser policy when he saw one. There was no upside and he got it.

The First World Trade Center Bombing

On February 26, 1993, a bomb exploded in a parking garage below the World Trade Center in Manhattan. There were six deaths and over a thousand injured, but the building stood and would reopen.

The perpetrators, Ramzi Yousef and his accomplice Eyad Ismoil, were captured and extradited after fleeing overseas. Yousef was able to continue his terror career for a few years before being caught in Pakistan.

The two will never get out of jail, but the question is how they got into the country and were allowed to stay. Ismoil overstayed a visa and it doesn't appear an effort was made to apprehend him.

The bombing should have been a wakeup call that there was an organization that believed itself at war with the United States. It doesn't appear that the effort was made to make sure people who should not have been here were not admitted. The proof of that would be apparent a few years later.

Haiti

There must be something in the air in Haiti or Washington that causes the United States to feel the need to intervene in Haiti. Sometimes it might be a mercenary. Smedley Butler, the Marine general who fought there said of his time, "I helped make Haiti and Cuba a decent place for the National City Bank boys to collect revenues in."

The Clinton administration's efforts can be characterized as humanitarian, but like all other American efforts, changed little for the long run.

There was another aspect of the Haitian situation that could not be ignored, the refugees. In 1991 a Haitian general, Raoul Cedras, had overthrown the government of the elected president Jean-Bertrand Aristide. As a result, Haitians in the thousands sought to leave Haiti. Few were allowed to land in the United States.

In September 1994, we invaded. The president, in an address, explained to the American people the reasons:

> Now the United States must protect our interests, to stop the brutal atrocities that threaten tens of thousands of Haitians, to secure our borders, and to preserve stability and promote democracy in our hemisphere and to uphold the reliability of the commitments we make and the commitments others make to us.

High minded and meaningless, but ya gotta say something.

As the troops were en route, a delegation led by President Carter was trying to persuade Cedras to go. Cedras agreed and left Haiti with his associates and Aristide returned to office.

Not much was really accomplished and U.S. troops would be gone by 2000.

Rwanda

In 1994, the hatred of the Hutus for the Tutsi people in Rwanda broke out into genocidal murder. Neither the world nor the United States moved quickly to stem the killing.

Clinton received criticism for American inaction. In 1998 while in Africa he apologized for what had not been done.

Should the United States have loaded the troops onto transports and made Rwanda our project? In light of the fact that our overseas endeavors usually come a cropper, the temporary success would have meant us being there forever and sooner or later, not loved for it.

The genocide would end with the successful campaign of the mainly Tutsi Rwandan Patriotic Front. The RPF regime may not be an optimum solution, but it also not the worst that could have happened.

Africa is better off without a permanent Rwandan occupation.

Clinton and the Balkans

When the Soviet Union went away, we should've too, at least from Europe. We should have considered the USSR's collapse as victory and thus the chance to leave. Our NATO buddies should have been told, Okay, guys and gals, we're taking off. You have a few years to work out your modus vivendi for the next millennium, but, you're on your own.

How naive that such a sentiment would have been. All those bureaucrats out of work, Pentagon planners with nothing to plan, a president who couldn't refer to himself as "Leader of the Free World" (granted it does not have the ring of a Dux et Imperator, but we still pretend to be a republic; it will take a while until even Princeps appears). So, we still had our Cold War commitment, without a cold war. No problem, we would eventually give ourselves one.

Otto von Bismarck said of involvement in the Balkans that it was "not worth the bones of a single Pomeranian grenadier." Bill Clinton didn't have Pomeranians to deploy, but he did feel the necessity to intervene. How much American involvement actually improved the situation among the peoples of the broken Yugoslavia is hard to say, but the peace has held since. That the people of the United States got nothing out of it has never seemed to matter.

In the wake of the end of the Cold War and the demise of the Soviet Union, the functional Yugoslavia started breaking up. The country may have worked, but it was a patchwork of nations that did not love the big state.

Slovenia quickly got out. Croatia fought its way out and Bosnia declared independence on March 1, 1992.

Bosnia had the same problem as Yugoslavia did. There were three main ethnic groups: Serbs, Croats and Bosniaks. The Bosniaks were Slavic Muslims. The Serbs wanted out and set up their own parliament and republic before the Bosnian independence vote. The only group with a marked allegiance to Bosnia were Bosniaks.

The situation became a war of the three parties. The Serbs, best armed at the beginning, occupied a lot of the country and would ethnically "cleanse" areas that came under their control. They perpetrated a massacre at Srebrenica and put the capital, Sarajevo, under siege.

Europe was not excited to intervene. The UN forces on the ground that had not protected Bosniaks at Srebrenica were at risk and some bombing might do more harm than good.

President Clinton pushed NATO to intervene more vigorously and brought about a sustained bombing campaign. Assistant Secretary of State, Richard Holbrooke, would push the warring parties to a peace conference resulting in the Dayton Peace Accords.

The fighting ended and a large peacekeeping force was deployed. Elections were held and the region stabilized without the loss of one American soldier, let alone a Pomeranian grenadier.

Kosovo

While Bosnia had been part of federal Yugoslavia, Kosovo had been part of Serbia. Intervention would be against a nation that didn't threaten us or anyone else in NATO. It was a Wilsonian, "make the world a better place" endeavor. Maybe it did. Maybe it didn't.

Just after World War I Yugoslavia was the Kingdom of the South Slavs. The South Slavs known as Serbs looked on Kosovo as a homeland and it was lost in the battle of Kosovo in 1389 to the Turks, but never forgotten.

There was another ethnic group in Kosovo. The Albanians began migrating to the region after Turkish rule started. They didn't have much in common with their Serb neighbors and were not Slavs.

The Serb/Albanian divide was also a religious one. The Serbs were overwhelmingly Orthodox Christian and the Albanians were Muslim.

Albanians wanted autonomy and, even when not stated, complete separation. This was something that for the most part, the Serbs resisted.

In 1960, the government in Belgrade began to allow more autonomy for Kosovo, and in 1974 the Yugoslav constitution accorded the region the status of "federal autonomous region." Happiness, however, was not to reign. In 1981 troops were sent in to deal with Albanian student riots over living conditions. There were deaths and some non-Albanians fled.

In 1987, the hardline nationalist, Slobodan Milosevic, was elected Serbian president. Two years later he would lead a rally among Kosovo Serbs promising to never give up control of the region.

The leaders of the Albanians in Kosovo declared independence from Serbia and the Serb government dissolved the regional government in 1990. In September 100,000 Albanians were sacked and a general strike resulted.

In 1992, the Albanians would proclaim a republic and journalist and scholar, Ibrahim Rugova, was elected president. As one might suspect, the following years would see tension continue to rise.

By 1995 a paramilitary organization, the Kosovo Liberation Army (KLA), announced its fight for independence. In 1998, open warfare between the KLA and the Serbian police would lead to a brutal crackdown by the Serbian government against an organization they characterized, not without some justice, as terrorist.

NATO was noticing the severity of Serb measures to suppress the KLA. Milosevic was told to stop the crackdown or else.

In 1999, the air campaign against Yugoslavia began. It would last 78 days and lead to Milosevic agreeing to withdraw Serb forces from Kosovo. They would be replaced by the Kosovo Force known as Kfor, which consisted of NATO and non-NATO countries contributing troops. Russia was one of the non-NATO participants, and an incident at the outset on June 11, 1999, almost led to a crisis, but a cooler head prevailed.

The Russians had expected to have a sector independent of NATO and were upset when that did not happen. On June 11, a column of around 30 Russian armored vehicles with 250 soldiers came down through Serbia. They headed for the airport at Pristina to get there ahead of NATO.

American General Wesley Clark, NATO Supreme Allied Commander Europe, was not happy with the Russians being there and wanted the airport runway blocked. He met with the British commander of Kfor, Lieutenant General Mike Jackson. Jackson refused and reportedly told Clark, "I'm not going to start the Third World War for you." Humanity can probably agree, even if General Clark did not, that that was probably a good thing. Pristina, not to mention Kosovo itself, was hardly a worthy place to start a nuclear war over. (Jackson hadn't been so reticent about violence when troops under him murdered innocent Irish people at a demonstration in Derry on January 30, 1972, that became known as Bloody Sunday.)

UN Resolution 1244 reaffirmed the commitment of UN member states to the sovereignty and territorial integrity of Federal Republic of Yugoslavia and the other states of the region. Without such language, Serbia might have continued to resist and there would not have been Russian support. There was also language about a "Kosovo status process." No matter what was said, there were few who were naive enough to believe that when the time came, the Kosovars would not be allowed to scoot. Sure enough, in 2008 the Kosovars declared independence and that was that.

Kfor still exists. The American footprint on the ground, Camp Bondsteel, is the big presence in Kosovo. In a post at G2mil, blogger Carlton Meyer asks ,"Why Does Camp Bondsteel Still Exist?" He then describes the facilities:

> *Camp Bondsteel was constructed to house American peacekeeping forces soon after Kosovo achieved independence from Serbia in 1999. It can hold up to 7000 soldiers, which makes it the largest U.S. base in the Balkans, and employs hundreds of locals. The post exchange is the largest military shopping complex in*

southeastern Europe with everything found at Wal-Mart, and the U.S. military spends millions of dollars each year to ship all items from the USA. The base also has the best hospital in Kosovo, a movie theater, three gyms, two recreation buildings that have phones, computers with internet, pool tables, and video games. It has a chapel with various religious services, a huge dining facility, a library, a fire station, a military police station, an education center where college classes are offered, two cappuccino bars, a Burger King, a Taco Bell, an Anthony's Pizzeria, a barbershop, a laundry facility, a sewing shop, and a Thai massage parlor.

Just the Thai massage parlor would get some troops to extend their deployment if asked. Meyer suggests the place isn't needed, as we have another base not too far away.

More important to ask is why did it ever exist to begin with? There was never a reason to choose between the Serbs and Albanians.

Nobody ever asks whatever happened to the anticipated peace dividend? You can see where part of it went at the camp.

Today, the Kosovo state is not a shining example of nation building. In a February 1, 2016, article at Antiwar.com, Justin Raimondo, wrote about the nature of governance in the statelet. Raimondo, Antiwar.com's editorial director at the time, avers that Kosovo is a mafia state as noted by the Council of Europe. Hashim Thaçi might as well be called godfather. Justin quotes *The Guardian*:

> Kosovo's prime minister is the head of a "mafia-like" Albanian group responsible for smuggling weapons, drugs and human organs through eastern Europe, according to a Council of Europe inquiry report on organized crime.

> *Hashim Thaçi is identified as the boss of a network that began operating criminal rackets in the run-up to the 1998-99 Kosovo war, and has held powerful sway over the country's government since.*
>
> *The report of the two-year inquiry, which cites FBI and other intelligence sources, has been obtained by The Guardian. It names Thaçi as having over the last decade exerted "violent control" over the heroin trade. Figures from Thaçi's inner circle are also accused of taking captives across the border into Albania after the war, where a number of Serbs are said to have been murdered for their kidneys, which were sold on the black market.*

Toward the end of his presidency, Bill Clinton was reported to be wondering about his "legacy." He might want to sneak into Pristina and load up and haul away the statue of himself that stands over the main square. Tearing down the Bill Clinton Street Sign might also be a good idea.

Whether or not the U.S. government learned anything from the Albanian adventure is hard to say, but someone did. An October 16, 2017, *Diplomat* article, "What North Korea Learned From the Kosovo War," by Samuel Ramani gave the lesson the DPRK gained:

> *From Pyongyang's vantage point, NATO's restrained military intervention in Yugoslavia demonstrated that the United States was only willing to carry out military interventions if they resulted in few casualties.*
>
> *The low cost of an air war in Kosovo encouraged a NATO military intervention. However, U.S. policymakers viewed the prospect of sending ground troops to Yugoslavia as unacceptable, as a full-scale war against Belgrade could have triggered a retaliatory escalation from Russia and drawn Washington into a Vietnam-*

style quagmire in the Western Balkans. Therefore, by developing sophisticated missile systems and nuclear weapons to up the ante of any conflict on the peninsula, North Korean officials concluded that they would be able to safeguard themselves from both a Kosovo-style limited military intervention and regime change mission.

For the North Koreans, so far so good. As to the United States, at least the first half of Talleyrand's observation, "Ils n'ont rien appris, ni rien oublié," is probably correct.

That is not to say Clinton didn't have some success. The Good Friday Agreement has generally held though the age of Brexit may test it. Still, the legacy is light, which in the history of our foreign policy is not the worst reputation, as we would learn from his successor.

27

George W. Bush and The Beginning of The Eternal War

It seems like another life when one tries to think of the campaign for presidency of George W. Bush. After two wartime administrations, it's hard to remember that he ran on a platform suggesting a humble foreign policy. Yet that is what he told the American people. What happened was not what was promised. It is best described by Stephen M. Walt in a September 18, 2016, *Foreign Policy* article:

> Next, consider the 2000 election. Running against Vice President Al Gore and lacking foreign-policy experience, George W. Bush sounded a modest and realistic note throughout the campaign and relied on the so-called Vulcans, several of whom had decidedly realist pedigrees. He promised Americans a foreign policy that would be strong but "humble," and both he and his advisors chided Clinton and Gore for their misguided efforts at "nation-building." In short, Americans were told that Bush would focus on great power politics, avoid messy quagmires in countries of marginal strategic importance, and keep our powder dry.

Bush's good intentions were blown off course completely by two distinct factors. First, instead of relying on realists from the Brent Scowcroft/Colin Powell wing of the Republican Party, he allowed Dick Cheney to populate his administration with neoconservatives who had greater ambitions and even worse judgment than the Clintonites. Second, the 9/11 attacks allowed the neocons to convert Bush to their misguided worldview and pave the way to the disastrous quagmires in Iraq and Afghanistan. Instead of giving Americans the foreign policy they had voted for, Bush, Cheney, and the neocons gave them the absurd goal of trying to transform the Middle East and then spread liberty throughout the world. We all know how well that worked.

On September 11, 2001, an event occurred that is called by its date shorthand: 9/11. We all know of the two planes that slammed into the two World Trade Center towers as well as the plane that hit the Pentagon and one that came down in a Pennsylvania field.

There will always be inside job controversy and whether or not Building 7 was set up. Though anything is possible, one can find more than enough reading material from other sources to entertain them forever. If you are looking for that here, you will be disappointed.

Suffice it to say, 9/11 proved the late Harry Browne correct when he said, "...we have a very strong national offense, but a very weak national defense." All the missiles and planes and ships and overseas bases did nothing to stop a tiny band of operatives from coming to the United States and killing thousands while destroying the two tallest structures in New York City. Whatever the causes were, 9/11 happened. It should be plain to everyone that our response has not led to anything but more strife.

Before 9/11 Al Qaeda should have caught our attention. To a certain extent, it did. After the 1998 embassy bombings in Africa, President Clinton struck at a camp in Afghanistan and pharmaceutical plant in Sudan without great effect.

There never seemed to be much going on concerning the terror threat, at least in the national news. The men who would perpetrate the most devastating attack on American soil by foreign actors since the War of 1812 would prove Harry Browne, if not a prophet, correct.

Could Al Qaeda have been stopped? Maybe, but the administration did not have its eye on the ball, and maybe they were not even aware there was a ball to have their eye on.

To outline the events before 9/11 we look to Major Danny Sjursen:

> *Much of the necessary information—certainly the warning signs of what was going to happen that September 11th—were already there. If, that is, one cared to look. History is contingent, human beings have agency, and events result from innumerable individual decisions. The CIA, the FBI, and even the Bush administration knew (or should have known, anyway) that an attack of some sort was coming.*
>
> *As the 9/11 commission report painfully detailed, none of those agencies collaborated in a meaningful way when it came to preventing that day's attacks. Still, there were warnings ignored and voices in the dark. When Richard Clarke, counterterror czar and a Clinton administration holdover, requested through official channels to deliver an emergency briefing for Bush's key foreign policy officials, it took four months just to arrange an audience with their deputies. Four more months elapsed before President Bush received a briefing titled, "Bin Laden determined to strike the U.S." Unimpressed, Bush quickly*

responded to the briefer: "All right... you've covered your ass now." Barely more than a month later, the World Trade Center and the Pentagon were burning.

One might dispute Major Sjursen's writing on some details. What is damning are the words "All right... you've covered your ass now."

So, the deed was done and the United States would have to respond. The Bush administration demanded that the Afghan Taliban government hand over Osama Bin Laden who they named as perpetrator and expel Al Qaeda.

The Taliban government refused extradition without evidence of bin Laden's role and did not expel Al Qaeda. The U.S. government saw this as a delaying tactic.

It may have been true, but had another country demanded the U.S. give up a suspected criminal the legal niceties would be observed and a high-profile person of interest would not be sent packing before generating large fees for his or her attorneys.

The extradition of Turkish cleric Fethullah Gulen has been demanded by the Erdogan government. Whatever the merits of the case, The U.S. has not budged. Turkey is not happy, but has not bombed or invaded us.

The U.S. began operations soon enough and allying with an already existing insurgency ended the Taliban state. Then we stayed and stayed. The events can be summed up in a blog post the author wrote in 2006.

> *Los Angeles Times reports that we are losing in Afghanistan. Of course, they are highlighting the obvious, but I guess that has to be done over and over again as few of us get it the first time. I would not wish to repeat what the Times is saying. Let's focus on another aspect of the Afghan war. It was a fool's errand from the beginning.*

Remember the heady days after 9/11. Well, I do, but how clearly? Good question. I'm having more and more senior moments all the time. I remember the general tone being, "We gotta get those bastards." We started bombing Afghanistan and cooperating with the Northern Alliance, a group of freedom loving patriots who quoted from the collected works of Bill Bennett. With our air support, they turned the flank. We sent troops in and chased the remnants of the Taliban out and installed a government and freed women and all that noble stuff.

It was all a waste. All of it. We did not get the self-confessed mastermind of every bad thing that has happened to us. That evil Taliban is back. What people forget is that the Taliban was not defeated. They retired in some order. Certainly, good enough order that they were able to regroup and return to battle. Not only that it looks like Round 15 of a 15 rounder and what looked in the early rounds like a mismatch with that big lanky guy from the West landing a few roundhouse rights has changed. That cagey boy from the East got on his bicycle and just circled around, landing a jab here and there, staying out of reach, while wearing the big guy down. In the final round, the betting has shifted, big time. This is how the Afghan Kid has won all his fights, seemingly a pushover in the early going then coming back later on. And, he has won all his fights (maybe the contretemps with Big Alex can be called a draw, but that's about it).

But of course, this time it was going to be different. Right. Anyone who thought the GIs giving out nylon stockings and chocolates thing was going to work this time was nuts. Actually, all that ranting about "United we stand" was little more than the raging of a drunk in a bar. Trust me, it's been a long time, but it's a subject I know something about.

So, I can hear no one say, though they might, what would have been your great plan, smart guy. Well that's the thing. I have no illusions about my genius, but all too many of my country's leaders do. If, by some bizarre circumstance, I had been invited I would have laid out the options thus, "Scenario one, we can invade that country and try to capture bin Laden. To do it right so that he can never come back if he escapes, it will take hundreds of thousands of troops and several decades to change the culture and more likely our culture will change. Oh, we will probably leave without actually effecting the desired change. Scenario two, I would withdraw all our troops from overseas and secure our borders.

By now, if you are awake, you are saying, does this guy want to just give the terrorists a pass? No, I want to win. This hardly seems what our foreign policy wonks want, as even still they appear to be hell bent in desiring to take us into one labyrinth after another.

The most intelligent strategy I have ever heard was best explained in a letter to the Antiwar.com letters page years ago. It was posted by George D. of the UK, 'the terrorists could have been hunted one-by-one by having a special task force that deals with it, like Israel did in hunting the Nazi war criminals, without going to war with the country that provided shelter for them.' Such a policy would need focus over a long term and could not be a TV war and no party out of power would have been able to resist accusing the administration of doing nothing.

> *No, the Afghan thing will continue on until the inevitable and like the Brits and Russians, we shall leave, maybe with some face saving fig leaf, but we shall leave.*

This post is perhaps a bit flip or glib, but it remains valid.

We would eventually get Osama. What role he had left is hard to say, but if he had discernible effect on operations, his loss probably changed little. Al Qaeda was small before 9/11. Now there is Al Qaeda in many places. Clearly, the results of invading Afghanistan have not solved anything.

Yet we remain with no idea what victory is or could be.

This is illustrated in an article retired U.S. Army officer and foreign policy expert Daniel L. Davis in *The National Interest* on April 28, 2018:

> *The results of the past seven years have proven my assessment to have been correct, yet every effort to end the failing mission and return the troops to their home stations continues to be intensely resisted. Major suicide attacks—like the one on Sunday that killed fifty-seven people—continue to plague Kabul, and as the most recent report from the Special Inspector General for Afghan Reconstruction (SIGAR) confirms, measures of American involvement have been overwhelmingly negative.*
>
> *SIGAR's report revealed it hasn't mattered whether it was in the security realm, the economic sphere, or domestic government corruption, the evidence overwhelmingly confirms mission failure. Yet America's military involvement there has no set of metrics it seeks to accomplish and thus no criteria the accomplishment of which could ever signal an end to the mission.*

Nevertheless, we persist.

28

The Second Iraq War

"The invasion of Iraq may well turn out to be the greatest strategic disaster in American history."

The statement of the late Lieutenant General William E. Odom as to whether or not it was the worst error can be debated. What is not really up for discussion is the fact that the invasion was a disaster.

In the sense of support, the invasion had many fathers and some mothers. One positive aspect of the Internet is that it lasts forever (so far) such that it is difficult to run away from one's record and the catastrophe that Iraq was and is.

Donald Trump claims to have not been for it. Some aver proof he was. Whatever the truth is, his predecessor, Barack Obama was clearly and forthrightly against it in 2002.

> I don't oppose all wars. And I know that in this crowd today, there is no shortage of patriots, or of patriotism. What I am opposed to is a dumb war. What I am opposed to is a rash war. What I am opposed to is the cynical attempt by Richard Perle and Paul Wolfowitz and other arm-chair, weekend warriors in this Administration to shove their own ideological agendas down our throats, irrespective of the costs in lives lost and in hardships borne.

What I am opposed to is the attempt by political hacks like Karl Rove to distract us from a rise in the uninsured, a rise in the poverty rate, a drop in the median income—to distract us from corporate scandals and a stock market that has just gone through the worst month since the Great Depression.

That's what I'm opposed to. A dumb war. A rash war. A war based not on reason but on passion, not on principle but on politics.

Now let me be clear. I suffer no illusions about Saddam Hussein. He is a brutal man. A ruthless man. A man who butchers his own people to secure his own power. He has repeatedly defied UN resolutions, thwarted UN inspection teams, developed chemical and biological weapons, and coveted nuclear capacity.

He's a bad guy. The world, and the Iraqi people, would be better off without him.

But I also know that Saddam poses no imminent and direct threat to the United States, or to his neighbors, that the Iraqi economy is in shambles, that the Iraqi military a fraction of its former strength, and that in concert with the international community he can be contained until, in the way of all petty dictators, he falls away into the dustbin of history.

I know that even a successful war against Iraq will require a U.S. occupation of undetermined length, at undetermined cost, with undetermined consequences. I know that an invasion of Iraq without a clear rationale and without strong international support will only fan the flames of the Middle East, and encourage the worst, rather than best, impulses of the Arab world, and strengthen the recruitment arm of al-Qaeda.

I am not opposed to all wars. I'm opposed to dumb wars.

The man who would become the forty-fourth president of the United States spoke clearly and intelligently. For some of us, they were the finest words he spoke and most memorable. His voice, however, was lonely while the chorus was loud for intervention.

The list of people who were gung ho reads as a who's who of those who were considered heavy hitters among intellectuals of various heft. Andrew Bacevich gives a good list in the May/June, 2018 issue of The American Conservative:

> A *remarkably broad swath of establishment worthies signed onto this project with evident enthusiasm. Call it the Lewis-Ledeen coalition, extending all the way from the eminently respectable Bernard Lewis to the eminently disreputable Michael Ledeen. Or, better still, call it the Pax Americana cartel.*
>
> *From his perch at Princeton University, Professor Lewis took to the pages of The Wall Street Journal to argue that it was "Time for Toppling." According to Lewis, a renowned authority on the Islamic world, not only Iraqis but all Arabs and also Iranians would welcome liberation at the hands of U.S. forces. He dismissed out of hand the notion that "regime change in Iraq would have a dangerous destabilizing effect on the rest of the region, and could lead to general conflict and chaos."*
>
> *A regular contributor to National Review, Ledeen viewed the possibility of war with all the delight of an eight-year-old playing with his first set of toy soldiers. Ledeen differed with Bernard Lewis on one point only: If invading Iraq destabilized the region, then all the better. "One can only hope that we turn the region into a cauldron, and faster, please." If ever there were a region*

that richly deserved being "cauldronized," wrote Ledeen, it was the Middle East. He emphasized that deposing Saddam was just a first step. After it finished with Iraq, the United States should go on to "bring down the terror regimes" in Iran, Syria, and Saudi Arabia. This, he concluded, represented America's true "mission in the war against terror."

The roster of writers, editors, and talking heads subscribing to the Lewis-Ledeen school of American statecraft is long and impressive. A partial list of prominent members runs the gamut from A to Z, beginning with Ken 'Cakewalk' Adelman, and including Peter Beinart, William Bennett, Paul Berman, Max Boot, David Brooks, Tucker Carlson, Thomas Friedman, at least two Goldbergs, Sean Hannity, Victor Davis Hanson, Christopher Hitchens, several Kagans and Kaplans, William Kristol, Charles Krauthammer, Rich Lowry, the Rev. Richard John Neuhaus, Bill O'Reilly, George Packer, Richard Perle, Anne-Marie Slaughter, Andrew Sullivan, Leon Wieseltier, and George Will, with Fareed Zakaria bringing up the tail end.

The nominally conservative National Review endorsed the idea of invading Iraq as did the nominally liberal New Republic. The editorial pages of The New York Times, Wall Street Journal, and Washington Post were positively gung-ho to go after Saddam. As for The Weekly Standard, it's a wonder that younger staffers eager to join in the fun didn't rush off to their local Armed Forces Career Center to enlist.

In terms of intellectual firepower, the Pax Americana cartel both outnumbered and outgunned the antiwar camp. True, Michael Moore, Brent Scowcroft, Edward Kennedy, and the Dixie Chicks expressed opposition to *the war. So too did Pope John Paul II, who to the dismay of Catholic neoconservatives denounced the coming invasion of Iraq as "a defeat for humanity.*

In this instance, if in few others, the left-leaning *Nation* magazine agreed with the right-leaning pope. And standing shoulder-to-shoulder with *The Nation* was its ideological opposite: the brand new *American Conservative*.

The bunch of choristers is still with us for the most part and their failure has not hurt employability.

The administration itself was doing its best to sell the American people that the Hussein regime was building, if not possessed of, weapons of mass destruction. They were also throwing other bits of propaganda against the wall to see what might stick. Does anyone remember anthrax?

That was pushed for a short while. the late Boston talk show host, Jay Severin, pushed that line. One afternoon he breathlessly intoned that it was reported that the anthrax involved in letters sent had the "footprint" of an Iraqi lab and that if it did have that footprint, then, "We are at war with Iraq." Cut to a break.

To his credit, the next day he did admit the scare was not all it was cracked up to be. Anthrax as a cause of war faded as there was no there there. No matter, the WMD trope was working well enough.

The intellectuals and commentariat signed on to the war for various reasons, but most seemed to at least have bought the fig leaf of WMD, which was necessary as a cause because, as Paul Wolfowitz put in an interview, it was "the one issue that everyone could agree on."

Such a statement implies that there were others, but go with the one that works, and they did.

The critics of the war, sparse and unloved as they were, did suggest there were other reasons (e.g. oil) but they never got much traction. Still, among the left there was enough residual "all we are saying is give peace a chance" sentiment that it had to be addressed or at least gestured to.

Ted Kennedy and Russ Feingold and several others would vote against the invasion, but it was forlorn. We were about to invade another country and the anti-war demos were sparse compared to Vietnam.

Not that they lacked for enthusiasm that was at times almost delusional. I remember some granola acquaintances enthusiastic about a demonstration they were going to in New York. The members of the little band were insulted when I told them they had no chance of halting the juggernaut and that the people who wanted the war were going to have it, and that was that. Of course, that was discounted, but such is life. If common sense had ever prevailed in this country the slogan would have been, "Forget the Maine." Contriving a war has a history here.

If there had been a contest for most ludicrous comment in support of the adventure, it would have been a crowded field, but the gold would have to go to Condoleezza Rice's "we don't want the smoking gun to be a mushroom cloud."

So, war had been decided. How was it to be fought?

On the world stage, Hussein would have to be painted as the worst evil since, well, the worst evil since. Surely, Godwin's Law must have been invoked more than once.

At Defense, Donald Rumsfeld and General Tommy Franks were doing the hard work of planning a war. Rumsfeld bugged Franks to pare down the number of troops to be included in the projected invasion.

The slender strength of the force would not mean that it was in danger in any sense. Our superiority in men and materiel meant there was no chance of our losing. That was not possible and the American government would have never contemplated such an adventure unless a "cakewalk" was projected.

The plan finalized, and the forces were arrayed. Saddam was given an ultimatum by Bush to depart. He did not. But the question was, Where was he going to go? No matter, the president gave the order for the operation to go forward. On March 19, it began.

Other than a few glitches and minor setbacks, it all went as well as can be expected. The men did their part and the equipment worked and on April 4 the Airport outside Baghdad was occupied. Tanks were in the city the next day. By the ninth organized resistance was done.

It was not exactly the toppling of a Stalin statue, but the Iraqi leaders image was taken down. The event was a bit stage managed supposedly to give the photos the appearance of a larger crowd.

As a victory it was, if not perfect, well done and the men behind it might have been forgiven for believing the future looked bright. The war itself, however, has never completely ended.

With the governmental collapse, civil order ceased. The Iraqi people rose up not against the old regime as they had in the previous Gulf War, nor against the new force, but against stuff. The looting was immense. A *Los Angeles Times* article of April 11 stated that Baghdad had become "a lawless frontier."

On May 1, 2003, President Bush landed on the aircraft carrier USS *Abraham Lincoln* to speak and declare the end to major combat operations. It was a victory lap decried by some as too theatrical and wasteful. Had it truly been an end to war with only a little tidying up to do, any criticism would have seemed mere carping.

The banner on the carrier, "Mission Accomplished," is still controversial. Was it just the banner for the crew of the ship as it was coming home after a long deployment having performed as required? Or was it to congratulate the president for a successful war? Maybe we can recycle a former cabinet secretary and ask, "What difference at this point does it make?"

Whatever was meant, the war itself was not over.

In reforming the Iraqi nation, the method to be followed would be wholesale. A Coalition Provisional Authority was set up to administer the country. L. Paul Bremer was appointed Provisional Coalition Administrator and compared himself to Douglas MacArthur's role in post-war Japan. His comparison to Doug's shogunate did not really hold up.

On May 23, 2003, he would issue the order dissolving the Iraqi Army and other Ba'athist entities. The decree would be controversial.

That the army had been disbanded did not mean it had completely stopped fighting, or at least a significant part of it had not. As Canada's *National Post* put it in a May 23, 2015, article by Davide Mastracci quoting Iraq analyst Sajad Jiyad, a senior researcher at the al-Bayan Center for Studies & Planning in Baghdad:

> *Thousands of the old professional and well-trained soldiers, unemployed and bitter, went on to drive a violent insurgency that saw guerrilla attacks, suicide bombings and improvised explosive devices (IEDs) used to kill thousands of U.S. and Iraqi troops, as well as Iraqi officials and civilians.*
>
> *The post-invasion insurgency involved a tactical alliance between terrorist groups, such as al-Qaida in Iraq, former Ba'athists and Sunni tribes. Despite substantial ideological differences, the partnership was driven by a shared interest in reclaiming control of Iraq from U.S. forces.*

That tactical alliance would turn out to be formidable.

Immediately after the order to disband the army, more than 250,000 soldiers and officers were put out of work overnight.

Those below the rank of colonel received a one-month severance package and were able to enlist in the new army; higher-ranking officers were barred from both.

Jiyad calls the decision a "catastrophic" mistake that "gave every reason to a vanquished enemy—battled-hardened Ba'athist officers—to fight the U.S. and further destroy Iraq."

Thousands of the old professional and well-trained soldiers, unemployed and bitter, went on to drive a violent insurgency that saw guerrilla attacks, suicide bombings, and improvised explosive devices (IEDs) used to kill thousands of U.S. and Iraqi troops, as well as Iraqi officials and civilians.

The post-invasion insurgency involved a tactical alliance between terrorist groups, such as al-Qaida in Iraq, former Ba'athists, and Sunni tribes. Despite substantial ideological differences, the partnership was driven by a shared interest in reclaiming control of Iraq from U.S. forces.

As the insurgency continued, it had become obvious even to the sleeping public that we were not winning. Something had to be done. Enter "The Surge." It may be ancient history to most of us that in 2007 we sent over 20,000 additional men under the hero du jour, David Petraeus. His command of the troops would turn the tide of battle. Or so the headlines would have it.

In the words of Ira Gershwin, "It ain't necessarily so." In his *Ghost Riders of Baghdad: Soldiers, Civilians and the Myth of the Surge*, Major Daniel Sjursen laid out what happened:

> *First, by late 2007, an Iraqi sectarian civil war (although few military officers or supporters of the administration dare use the term) had raged on for almost two years. Millions of people were forced from their homes or left the country in fear. Tens of thousands were killed. One result was an ever-greater segregation of the opposing ethnic and religious communities. A once heterogeneous Baghdad became largely dominated, and other Iraqi*

cities became similarly Balkanized. Few truly mixed neighborhoods or towns remained. Before 2006, estimates had placed the city's district breakdown as 40 percent Shia, 20 percent Sunni, and 40percent mixed. By mid-2007 half the Sunnis had left and 60 percent of neighborhoods were solidly Shia. Thus, by the time of the Surge, much of the work of death and displacement was complete. Violence began to decrease as the opposing groups settled into geographically separated armed camps. We watched this firsthand. In November 2006, it was still possible to find streets in Salman Pak and southeast Baghdad with alternating Sunni and Shia households. By the time we began formal census taking in late 2007, that was a thing of the past.

Sjursen has more about how non-crucial the Surge was:

Second, in 2006, months before the Surge, one American army armored brigade astutely exploited growing tensions between Sunni tribal leaders and Al Qaeda extremists in far western Anbar province. This unit laid the necessary foundations for an eventually expanded policy of placing former Sunni insurgents on the American payroll to battle AQI fighters. Many of our new allies were themselves former insurgents and had undoubtedly killed American soldiers in the recent past. Occupation is an ugly business. In the bad old days of 2006, whether such a policy had long-term benefits or would portend future national unity was beside the point. What mattered was lowering violence. This breakthrough long preceded the Surge and was not dependent on the thirty thousand extra troops. The Tribes didn't turn because of more troops—2006 was pre-Surge—and besides most of these Sunni leaders hated and had once attacked Americans.

One almost thinks of Narses heading into the Hippodrome with a bag of gold to bribe the blue and green factions into loyalty to the Byzantine emperor.

> *Third, the most violent and effective Shia militia, Moktada Al Sadr's Mahdi Army called a unilateral ceasefire in August of 2007. Internal strife, factionalism, and loss of central control had contributed to decreased effectiveness among the Mahdi Army for several months. It is hard to overestimate the importance of this self-imposed armistice. Sadr's units were responsible for the great majority of EFP attacks on American convoys. These were deadliest and least avoidable weapons in the vast insurgent arsenal and struck absolute terror in the hearts of U.S. soldiers. The addition of Petraeus and his thirty thousand troops had only limited influence on the Mahdi Army ceasefire, which served as a reorganizational tool for Sadr rather than a sign of surrender. The pressure of additional 'boots on the ground' undoubtedly played some role in convincing Sadr to lay low, but it was neither the primary reason nor a long-term solution.*

Sjursen comes to a conclusion he admits is speculation but sounds reasonable. "I think many Iraqis-on both sides of the divide-simply got tired of the violence. Collectively, they inched up to the abyss throughout 2006, reached the edge in early 2007 and took a step back."

The major makes the point that the Surge was going to be labeled a success no matter what. Politicians do that and no one should be surprised. Short of losing every trooper sent to the theater of operations, victory was bound to be declared.

So, did anyone win? Sjursen pronounces, not without reason, Iran was the victor. The Shia dominated government is allied with the Iranians and influenced by them.

According to Sjursen, "Iran remains the strongman in the region, no longer balanced by a countervailing Iraqi Arab power."

Iran is still a horrible bogeyman to many American pundits and certainly to the Trump administration. Saddam Hussein was not a warm, cuddly guy, but if you needed someone to be your flank guard on the Persians, he filled the bill.

The late General Odom's prediction can be argued as to the use of the word "greatest." Entering World War I might be that. One cannot argue, however, the enormity of the 2003 blunder.

The war continued at a less hectic pace and in November of 2008 a status of forces agreement between the United States and Iraq was agreed upon. The agreement was to run three years and in that time, American forces would withdraw from Iraqi cities by the end of June 2009. All U.S. combat troops were to be out of the country by the end of 2011.

America was heading for the finish line. The Bush administration passed away and Obama came into office. Like Bush, who had first campaigned as a man for a modest foreign policy, he was at least the relative peace candidate. The new president would not have a "bring it on" moment, but war would not go away.

President Obama kept to the timeline negotiated by Bush and al-Maliki. There were negotiations to leave a residual force in Iraq, but they foundered when a new status of forces agreement could not be reached.

So, our troops left. The president would pay tribute to the soldiers who had served on December 14, 2011, at Fort Bragg. He would claim we had left a "sovereign, stable and self-reliant" Iraq. It was as successful as Vietnamization.

The Shia government would go back to discriminating against the Sunni and that would lead to trouble later. When it did, the chorus of Republicans and their supporters blamed Obama.

Typical was a Massachusetts talk show. The host, Howie Carr, and guest Ann Coulter were going after the then president on September 22, 2014. Ann had a lot to say about how Barack had blown it:

> *The war in Iraq. Everything that was done under Republicans was fantastic. We took Iraq. We flipped it. They voted. They showed us their purple fingers. We had established a government. And then, oh ho, a Democrat gets elected, pulls every last U.S. troop out. The war was over. It was done. We had won. All you had to do was leave troops behind, and a Democrat comes along and wrecks it.*

"All you had to do was leave troops behind." What kind of victory is it if you have got to garrison the place forever? Of course, it is never said that it is forever, but we are not too quick on the exit ramp.

Ann didn't get that if they voted and "showed us their purple fingers" and had a sovereign government, they had a right to reject a Status of Forces Agreement and we would have to leave.

We would leave an imperfect state that would see the rise of ISIS and near collapse of Iraq. The big question is, Did we have to go back in?

We did go back in. With the rise of ISIS, the American military would return to Iraq.

ISIS was dealt with, more or less. President Trump announced withdrawal from Syria in December of 2018. It wouldn't happen, but shortly after that announcement, according to Al-Masdar News, The United States built two bases in Iraq along the Syrian border, as reported by a Syrian state news agency.

According to Colonel Lang, "The generals' club is probably at work in this, seeking to limit the effect of Trump's order for

U.S. forces to withdraw from Syria." That seems reasonable. Not to say there is a deep state, or even deep generalship.

On December 26, 2018 Trump visited troops in Iraq for which the mainstream press found fault. That was not unexpected. As security was tight, the Iraqis were not informed and were miffed. Many news outlets reported that Iraqi lawmakers demanded the withdrawal of U.S. troops as a result. More eternal recurrence as in the aftermath of the Soleimani assassination the Iraqi legislature is again making the same demand.

That they mean it and we acquiesce is devoutly to be wished.

29

Libya

"It is worse than a crime—it is a blunder"

The words above are attributed wrongly to Talleyrand. The Duke d'Enghien was executed by a French drumhead court after being abducted from over the border and brought back to France by dragoons.

Whether or not it was a blunder can be debated, but the quote has lived on in history.

In recent times, the destruction of the Libyan state can arguably be described as a blunder and one of far greater proportion, if not impact, than the Duke's. Blunder it was, but the crime aspect might also be considered. Will history say, "What were they thinking?"

Libya has for the most part been ruled by other states. From the sixteenth century on the Ottoman Empire held sway. In the early twentieth century the Italians took it over with tribal opposition.

With Italy's defeat in World War II, Libya would be given independence under King Idris, who was chief of the Senussi religious order and had opposed the Italian occupation.

The king would establish relations with the United States and Britain allowing bases. With the discovery of oil, he oversaw the establishment of that industry and the enrichment of Libya.

It was not all peace and concord in his kingdom, and frustration at corruption and dependence on Western powers was rife. In 1969, while the king was in Turkey for medical treatment, he was deposed by Lieutenant Muammar Gaddafi.

Gaddafi immediately did well out of the coup, instantly promoting himself to colonel. He would never make general, but who needs that when you also become Brotherly Leader and Guide of the Revolution.

The colonel would consolidate the regime and dominate it for several decades. He would work to spread revolution by supporting movements outside Libya and attempted military adventures elsewhere.

He was known for confrontation far and wide, and not least with the United States. The back and forth continued and included an air strike on April 15, 1986. The raids and Gaddafi's defiance led to a boost in popularity for Reagan in the United States and for Brother Leader in the Arab world.

After the infamous Lockerbie bombing that killed all the passengers and crew of an airliner, Libya slowly became a less confrontational state.

Over the ensuing years, Libya sought rapprochement with the world culminating in the decommissioning of the country's chemical and nuclear weapons programs. Did this leave it toothless going forward?

Relations with the United States improved. Gaddafi came to terms with the European Union to stem immigration from below the Sahara. Agreements with Berlusconi's Italian government would help with Libyan infrastructure. The country under the strongman seemed to be a member of the concert of nations.

Then came what has become known as the Arab Spring. Any fence-mending Gaddafi had done would prove to have been for naught.

NATO would engage against him and set up a no-fly zone. What would the role of the United States be?

President Obama had been given the Nobel Peace Prize for something or nothing at the beginning of his administration. He had continued on in Afghanistan with more troops, but his administration was not doing too much earth shattering. Libya would change that.

The lead in taking America into the contest would be led by then Secretary of State Hillary Clinton. According to Ben Norton writing on March 2016 in *Salon*:

> *Sec. Clinton pressured a wary President Obama to join France and the UK in the war, the Times reported. Vice President Biden, National Security Adviser Tom Donilon and Defense Secretary Robert Gates, among others, opposed the war effort. Numerous government officials recalled that her hawkish enthusiasm was decisive in the 51–49 decision.*

Thus, we joined in another crusade under the rubric R2P, or Responsibility to Protect.

Mr. Norton was critiquing articles that appeared in the *Times* about the Secretary's role.

From what he wrote in *Salon*, it appears that the woman was enthusiastically for war. Odd that the criticism that has been leveled at Clinton is mostly from the left.

Norton cites a *Jacobin* magazine article "Worse Than Benghazi" by David Mizner to drive home the point. Mizner's title notes that the later incident that led to an ambassador's murder pales in comparison to the war that Clinton championed.

> *According to Mizner, Hillary was so in favor of war that she made sure that any attempt to halt the conflict before the destruction of the regime was accomplished would be short-circuited. Mizner wrote: "On March 17, 2011, the*

United Nations Security Council passed Resolution 1973, authorizing a no-fly zone over Libya and 'all necessary measures' to protect civilians. That same day—as revealed by Pentagon audio tapes obtained by The Washington Times—President Qaddafi's son Seif tried to call a U.S. general to try to negotiate a ceasefire."

And what happened with that? "Never mind that the UN resolution had urged diplomacy, Secretary of State Hillary Clinton instructed the Joint Chiefs of Staff not to negotiate with the Libyan government."

Further, "Qaddafi proposed a seventy-two-hour-truce, then said he would step down to allow for a transition provided that NATO agreed to maintain the Libyan army, lift sanctions against him and his family, and provide them safe passage."

A way to a solution was found?

"Was the offer genuine and workable? We'll never know, because Clinton shut down the negotiations."

Hillary Clinton was going to own it all, from the second of the *Times*' articles, there is a quote that puts her in front of it, "The timeline, her top policy aide, Jake Sullivan, wrote, demonstrated Mrs. Clinton's "leadership / ownership / stewardship of this country's Libya policy from start to finish."

The war went on, and not all that well. Despite the heavy airstrikes, Gaddafi's forces were holding out. According to a posting by Patrick Bahzad at the *Sic Semper Tyrannis* blog of Colonel Lang, Gaddafi's men "had kept their defensive posture and had been able to cut off any advance of the rebels from the East along the Mediterranean Coastal strip. With supply lines for the government forces still open through the Western border, there was no end in sight for the war. People in high places were getting nervous and impatient ..."

It was going to be a tough, dirty job so we had to go to the tough, dirty fighters to get it done. Who would that be: the

Seals, Rangers, Green Berets, SAS? No, it would be the Cheese Eating Surrender Monkeys. That is a nickname for the French originating on *The Simpsons*:

Mr. Bahzad wrote of the French:

> *Asked one day what the difference had been in fighting first the French and later the U.S., Vietnamese general Nguyên Giáp stated that in a guerrilla war—something we call today "asymmetric warfare"—fighting the Americans was "peanuts, compared to fighting the French." Not that the U.S. grunt was less of a fighting man, but the French—probably due to their having to do more with less—used every dirty trick in the book to get the job done. They still failed after the debacle of Dien Bien Phu, which was another of those examples of overconfidence that French military history is riddled with.*

Libya was not Verdun, but a puzzle to be solved and the Gauls would be the go-to team. "Regarding the war in Libya however, the traditional ability for 'out of the box thinking' that is sort of a trademark of French COS on the ground was key to unlocking a situation that looked dangerously close to heading for compromise at the negotiating table."

In hindsight, the negotiating table might have been the better result.

The French masterminded the operation utilizing several different outfits one of which was the "February 17th Martyrs Brigade," under the command of a former Al Qaeda fighter, Abdelhakim Belhadj. They were the most, if not the only, battle-hardened rebel group.

So, the regime collapsed, the leader dispatched, and the famous video of Secretary Clinton callously intoning "We came, we saw, we died" and then laughing will live forever on YouTube.

And they lived happily ever after. No, again we have Peter Patrick Bahzad on the aftermath,

> However, the nature of the campaign, the number of the groups and forces present on the ground, the diversity of their sponsors and interests would prove too much for the victorious revolution of Libya ... Soon the country would descend into chaos and anarchy and the much vaunted "February 17th Martyrs Brigade" would take part in other less heroic action, on the 11th of September 2012 ...

Not that efforts weren't made to put the country back together again, but we were going to not learn that lesson of Iraq again. It is easier to break a country than put it back together. From the *Times*:

> After decades in exile, some leaders were more familiar with American and European universities than with Libyan tribes and the militias that had sprung from them. Others, like Mr. Jibril, were suspect in some quarters because of previous roles in the Qaddafi regime. It was increasingly evident that the ragtag populist army that had actually done the fighting against Colonel Qaddafi was not taking orders from the men in suits who believed they were Libya's new leaders.

Shoulda seen it coming.

Reports were coming in that all was not well and factions were demanding this and that, but little was done. The *Times* article puts it succinctly, "Such alarming reports might have been expected to spur action in Washington. They did not."

While there was minimal violence, the radar screen was what Libya was not on.

Militias would need to be disbanded. They were not. With no lack of different groups, elections could only mean so much. Other problems in the Middle East came up on the screen to push Libya off.

Factional fighting increased. Mrs. Clinton did see the problem and, according to the *Times*, "pressed for the administration to do more, asking the Pentagon, for example, to help train security forces. But she was boxed in by the president's strictures and the Libyans' resistance."

The proliferation of weapons was an ongoing problem that was impossible to control even with a $40 million program. How bad was it? The *Times* goes on: "'There was one arsenal that we thought had 20,000 shoulder-fired, surface-to-air missiles, SA-7s, that basically just disappeared into the maw of the Middle East and North Africa,' recalled Robert M. Gates, the American defense secretary at the time."

Weapons from Libya have been found in Syria and other parts of the region as well as Africa.

Was it predestined to go south? "In a sense, it was lost from the beginning," said Gérard Araud, France's ambassador to the United States and an early advocate of the intervention. "It was the same mistake you made in Iraq. You organize elections in a country with no experience of compromise or political parties. So, you have an election, and you think that everything is solved. But eventually tribal realities come back to haunt the country."

The deterioration meant that there would be the possibility, if not probability, of an event.

An attack occurred, supposedly instigated by the militant, Ahmed Abu Khattala. Ansar al-Sharia, a Salafist militia, would lead the charge. As a result of the attack, the ambassador, J. Christopher Stevens, Foreign Service Officer Sean Smith, as well as CIA contractors Tyrone S. Woods and Glen Doherty were killed.

In the aftermath, there would be investigations to affix and assess blame. Hillary Clinton took complete responsibility, but charges were leveled about trying to blame a video that attacked Islam rather than the militants involved.

Outlets more favorable to the administration have been kind to Mrs. Clinton while those not so inclined disagreed. What happened is debatable, and the words Mrs. Clinton uttered before a Congressional committee are apropos: "What difference, at this point, what difference does it make?"

What is true is that someone took their eye off the ball. That is understandable if there are so many balls in the air at one time. The United States is involved in a few exotic locales and even a truly stalwart Secretary of State can expect one of the orbs to crash no matter how good a juggler he or she is.

Libya is not as bad as it was, but it is hardly a center of order. As of December 2017, the Libyan National Army had defeated the last pockets of Islamists in the Battle of Benghazi that had been going on since 2014. That it took that long may not seem that impressive, but with all the factions in the country to contend with, organizing a national force is an accomplishment. Still, there are problems with human trafficking as a transit point from Sub-Saharan Africa to Europe. Also, many native Libyans have few qualms about enslaving the Africans of a different race.

Libya has been a broken country since 2011. The old adage, "The road to hell is paved with good intentions" applies here. Certainly, one must hope the intentions were noble as the results were ruin for the people of that benighted nation that went from being the most prosperous African country to a disaster.

With a sea of oil beneath the sand, it should have been easy to attain a relatively high standard of living even though some countries that are as blessed with the stuff cannot. Nigeria has not eradicated poverty and Venezuela is having problems.

Petroleum exports are back to respectable levels, but it is doubtful the wealth is being spread around. There was never any real reason for United States involvement. A shoddy exercise

30

Syria

When did the Syrian Civil War begin?

Some might say in March of 2011 when protests began. Others might say 2006 was the start, at least in an embryonic sense. In that year, according to a CBC (Canadian Broadcasting Corporation) article at their website:

> The U.S. State Department acknowledged Monday it has been funding opponents of Syrian President Bashar Assad, following the release of secret diplomatic cables obtained by WikiLeaks that document the funding.
>
> The files show that up to $6.3 million US was funneled to the Movement for Justice and Development, a London-based dissident organization that operates the Barada TV satellite channel, which broadcasts anti-government news into Syria. Another $6 million went to support a variety of initiatives, including training for journalists and activists, between 2006 and 2010.
>
> Asked point-blank by reporters whether the United States is funding Syrian opposition groups, State Department spokesman Mark Toner told a news conference Monday, "We are—we're working with a variety of civil society actors in Syria with the goal here of strengthening freedom of expression."

Time magazine had reported in a December 19, 2006, piece by Adam Zagorin of the beginnings and how the Bush administration had funded the National Salvation Front run by Amar Abdulhamid. The group included the Muslim Brotherhood. That the United States would be part of a group that the Brotherhood was a member of speaks volumes. MB is not a pacifist front.

With that in mind, it is difficult to think that at least some in the U.S. government did not have an inkling of where it was all headed.

According to a March 5, 2007, *New Yorker* article by Seymour Hersh, the U.S. government was stirring the Sunni-Shia pot with the purpose of opposing Iran. Iran and Hezbollah in Lebanon were Shia. The Syrian state was led by the Alawite minority, which had an interesting theology, but were recognized as Shia and were not beloved at all by the Sunni oil states. They were at least de facto allies of Iran.

According to Hersh, "The U.S. has also taken part in clandestine operations aimed at Iran and its ally Syria. A by-product of these activities has been the bolstering of Sunni extremist groups that espouse a militant vision of Islam and are hostile to America and sympathetic to Al Qaeda."

Al Qaeda, the organization that had killed thousands of Americans on American soil was now getting a pass, at least sort of. It may not have been Oceania that has always been at war with Eurasia, but it didn't smell too good.

Conveniently, a drought occurred. The Turkish dams upstream didn't help. The rural poor lost much of their livelihood and fled to the cities. By 2011 things seemed to be falling into place for those who wanted to see the end of the Syrian regime.

Depending on who you believe, peaceful demonstrations broke out against real injustices and the Syrian authorities used harsh tactics to suppress them, or amongst the demonstrators, some of whom were armed and fired at the police. Naturally the police and troops responded with more firepower.

Rightly or wrongly, media coverage did not favor the government. Still, the Syrian regime appeared more resilient than expected. Assad was not as hated as he was made out to be. Reforms were undertaken and opposition rebels were not the Boy Scouts despite the good press.

To beat Assad, more would be needed. The Saudis and Qataris worked to recruit jihadis, and the CIA channeled Saudi money to bring in arms and ammo. Exiles would be built up as the external future government.

This would take its toll. The government would need to retreat to conserve its forces. Thus, rural areas would fall to the rebels. The population there fled to cities or other countries. Insurgents in cities were difficult to dislodge without property damage.

With help from Iranians and Hezbullah, the army was reformulated for fighting the insurgents. Local paramilitaries took over the areas where insurgents were flushed out by the army. The Russians provided supplies.

Team Insurgency was not a smooth-running machine. The word "team" is not warranted. There were many groups, but most of them had a knack for upsetting the locals who were not up to their standards of religious purity.

Pictures of a jihadi eating an executed man's liver and other images of atrocities were not exactly from the Dale Carnegie playbook, as the president of Syria never felt the need to partake of the inner organs of his enemies.

The proposed government in exile did not operate like clockwork other than possibly twice per day.

Efforts to build a Free Syrian Army to be able to install a non-extreme, post-Assad government were well funded but success was severely limited.

The Thin Red Line

At a press conference on August 20, 2012, President Obama announced:

> I have, at this point, not ordered military engagement in the situation. But the point that you made about chemical and biological weapons is critical. That's an issue that doesn't just concern Syria; it concerns our close allies in the region, including Israel. It concerns us. We cannot have a situation where chemical or biological weapons are falling into the hands of the wrong people.
>
> We have been very clear to the Assad regime, but also to other players on the ground, that a red line for us is we start seeing a whole bunch of chemical weapons moving around or being utilized. That would change my calculus. That would change my equation.
>
> ... We have communicated in no uncertain terms with every player in the region that that's a red line for us and that there would be enormous consequences if we start seeing movement on the chemical weapons front or the use of chemical weapons. That would change my calculations significantly.

The American president had issued an ultimatum, but he also set himself up. If the Syrian regime used the weapons, or if it were made to look like they did, he would have to act whether that was a good idea or not.

On August 21, 2013, a large-scale chemical weapons attack at the suburbs of the Ghouta region occurred. It was estimated that there were more than 1,000 victims.

The UN pledged to investigate and the OPCW (Organization for the Prohibition of Chemical Weapons) was to assist them. The regime agreed to allow them in.

The U.S. government claimed proof, but an August 30, 2013, CBS News article asserted that:

> No tangible evidence has been offered by either the U.S. or Britain to demonstrate what lead to the conclusion that Assad's forces must have been behind the previous suspected chemical attacks, and the UN inspection team—which had its original plans derailed by the unexpected attacks in Ghouta—has not reached any other sites. Much like the Ghouta attacks, the intelligence behind the accusations that Assad's regime was involved in previous chemical weapons incidents has remained secret.

The United States, purporting to be sure of its evidence, contemplated action, but something happened. The president had second thoughts and wanted to explore other options. President Obama would go to Congress and seek authorization. According to a July 19, 2016, *Politico* article by Derek Chollet:

> What transpired over the next month was one of the most controversial and revealing episodes in eight years of Obama's foreign policy. Despite the administration's strong advocacy and support from a small minority of hawkish politicians, Congress and the American people proved strongly opposed to the use of force.

Of course, why wouldn't the citizenry look askance at this new adventure? Bush's Iraq war was rightly called "dumb" by the man ready to throw bombs. The Libya project had made a mess of another country. The plebs were rightfully skeptical of their betters in government, and the solons were not enthusiastic.

What to do?

It would be refreshing for an administration to have to work to get the people on board, especially without lies about incubators or pumping up WMD that did not exist, but without scare tactics the people were not going to get on the train.

Obama had done the congressional thing, but it looked like he had to do the war thing on his own.

It did not look good, but a way out appeared.

At a press conference in London on September 9, 2013, Secretary of State, John Kerry was asked what the Syrian president could do to avoid bombing, he replied admit he had the weapons and give them up. Kerry opined, "he isn't about to do it and it can't be done."

Soon after exiting the stage, Sergei Lavrov, the Russian foreign minister, called. Though what Kerry said was not a policy statement, Lavrov wanted to discuss the "initiative."

Moscow would put pressure on Assad to get rid of the chemistry. The Syrians admitted finally they actually had the stuff. They pledged to give them up.

Thanks to the Russian government we got an out. President Obama received criticism from hawks that he wimped out.

Some of us might like to say that the same man who called the Iraq invasion less than genius came to the fore. It would be nice if he had, but he was still on board with Assad needing to go.

But Assad was not going to go quietly and his allies have been there for him. His army retrained with Russian help into a more effective force. Over the last several years they have retaken land and, using diplomacy, allowed some rebels to reconcile and others to leave for Idlib before an all-out battle with government forces in some future.

When Obama's administration ended, Trump became president. There was a glimmer of hope that we would have a sane policy as regards Syria. During his campaign, he noted that Syria is better off with Assad than with whatever might come after him. In a debate with Hillary Clinton Trump said, "I don't like Assad at all, but Assad is killing ISIS," Trump said during his second debate with Clinton. "Russia is killing ISIS. And Iran is killing ISIS.... I think you have to knock out ISIS." In the quotes, it might appear that he grudgingly saw Assad as part of the solution. He made other statements that signaled a desire not to get involved deeply in Syria.

So, what changed?

Donald Trump was an enigma.

Sultan Mehmet II, the conqueror of Constantinople, who was known to keep his own counsel, supposedly said that "If a hair of my beard knew (his thoughts), I would pluck it out and burn it." Maybe Trump is a cagey fellow who knows how to use indirection to achieve results. After all, he did become president against all odds.

Or, maybe even he didn't know what he was doing until he was doing it. Maybe not even then.

Nevertheless, he turned a hawk, and acted as such. On April 7, 2017, the United States fired 59 Tomahawk cruise missiles at the Syrian Shayrat Airbase in response to the Khan Shaykun chemical attack. The Syrian government denied it. The Russian ally had been notified and casualties were light.

Trump, constantly reviled by the media, got some wonderful press for the effort to be tough.

Not many people noticed the *Associated Press* headline of February 2, 2018, that the "US has no evidence of Syrian use of sarin gas, Mattis says." Still claiming they used them, the Secretary of Defense said, "We have other reports from the battlefield from people who claim it's been used," Mattis told reporters at the Pentagon. "We do not have evidence of it."

Media outlets hardly disputed the claims before the bombing, so it was kind of a bombing on spec. Try not to let it shake your faith in the Fourth Estate or the due diligence of your government.

Another day, another chemical attack. On April 13, 2018, the president would order a strike in reaction to a chemical hit that took place in rebel-held Douma. The president called the attacks mindless and tweeted that "President Putin, Russia, and Iran are responsible for backing Animal Assad. Big price to pay."

So off went the planes and cruise missiles. President Trump announced "mission accomplished" and Pentagon officials claimed a "very serious blow" at "the heart of the Syrian chemical weapons program." Not everyone agreed with that assessment. The Russians claimed the Syrians had shot down 70 missiles. Who was right? Who knows?

Shortly before the incident that led to the bombing, President Trump had pushed the generals as to when we could get out of Syria. He agreed the troops could stay until ISIS was defeated. ISIS, no longer possessing much conventional force, is a guerrilla entity, which means U.S. forces looked to be in Syria for quite a while.

In an article on his blog, *Sic Semper Tyrannis*, Colonel Patrick Lang opined that Trump had been "rolled" by the generals to keep troops in Afghanistan. That is as good an analysis as any as there is no reason to be there. It is not unreasonable to think the flag rankers did the same as regards Syria.

Well, we shall have troops in Syria for a long time as well. Can we blame the generals for that? They might or might not be for a mission there, but our other regional friends, Saudi Arabia, Qatar, Israel, Turkey, etc., have no love for the Assad regime and would want us to stay. Heck, they would love us to destroy the regime.

Other than petroleum as supplied by Saudis and Gulfies, there is little reason for us to be in the region, but then again, as Afghanistan proves, having no reason is not necessarily going to cause us to leave.

Indeed, we are in deep. When he was National Security Advisor, John Bolton imagining that the Syrians might use chemical weapons, threatened more strikes. Assad, on the verge of victory, hardly needs the chemicals to win as he gets ready to clear the last refuge of his enemy, Idlib. Bolton and others were crying crocodile tears, as they never show any concern for the victims of the Saudis' brutal if not genocidal war in Yemen as we refuel their bombers.

Having troops in Syria also means possible interaction with Russia that could go badly. Why do we need that?

On balance, even considering our need for Saudi and Gulf oil, there is no true compelling reason to keep troops there.

Yet it appears we shall be there for some time.

The Guardian reported in January of 2018 that then Secretary of State Rex Tillerson had announced in a speech at Stanford, "an open-ended military presence in Syria, not only to fight ISIS and al-Qaida but also to provide a bulwark against Iranian influence, ensure the departure of the Assad regime and create conditions for the return of refugees."

That does have the ring of open-endedness, if not a quest that would be eternal.

However, the president did say he was looking to get out of Syria after that. Then, in September of 2018, *The Washington Post* reported the new strategy of indefinitely extending the military presence coupled with a diplomatic push.

For what?

Assad is not going anywhere. A good guess is that opposing Iran is the big reason, but who knows?

In December 2018, President Trump again announced his intention to bug out of Syria. A chorus went up calling it the worst move ever. Everyone centered on how bad it would be for the United States if the troops in Syria left.

Actually, no one did that. Mostly, they were worried about the Kurds. Lindsay Graham was terribly upset, according to *The Hill*:

> Sen. Lindsey Graham (R-S.C.) is warning of a "major disaster" if Syrian Kurdish forces align with President Bashar Assad following President Trump's decision to withdraw U.S. troops from Syria.
>
> "If reports accurate about Kurds aligning with Assad, major disaster in the making," Graham tweeted Friday. "Nightmare for Turkey and eventually Israel. Big winners are Russia, Iran/Assad & ISIS."
>
> "New conflicts between regional powers take pressure off ISIS," Graham added in a second tweet."

Senator Graham did not mention the country whose senate he serves in.

Bolton and Secretary of State Pompeo were holding onto the Syrian deployment for dear life.

And, then in mid-January of 2019, a suicide bomber killed four Americans as well as Syrian nationals. Hardly had the smoke cleared than the call went up that we had to stay, as this bombing proved ISIS was still alive and kicking.

One could say this actually proves we should leave. After all, if the troops were gone and a suicide vest was detonated, the probability of our soldiers being killed gets as close to zero as anything can.

Writing in *The American Conservative*, Scott Ritter claims the bombing was purposely done to keep us in Syria. ISIS knows that if we leave, the Assad government comes back and life won't go that well for them as in not at all.

One does not have to believe that Trump is a deep thinker to see that in this instance, instinct works. If he had followed that rather than his advisers, we'd all be better off instead of sitting on the oil fields.

31

Iran

The Trump Administration seemed out to get Iran. Is Iran out to get the United States?

Supposedly Iran still has rallies wherein participants shout "Death to America." No one would argue that the Persians love the Yanks.

Maybe that is not completely true. Rick Steeves's travel show features happy interactions with Iranians and their families. Then again, his shows rarely show any other types of interactions.

What is true is that the governments as currently configured are not going steady.

Administration functionaries as well as many in the media are always pointing out that Iran is "the leading state sponsor of terrorism."

If that is correct, our government should evaluate its position versus that country insofar as they threaten us.

But, is that true?

For Americans, there are Iranian actions that stick in our collective craw. The seizure of the hostages from our embassy is hard to forget, as is the Iranian national who drove the truck bomb that killed the Marines in Beirut. The author remembers the incident with no little resentment.

What do the Iranians remember? It would be expected they pay attention to events and know of the coup that removed the elected government of Mohammad Mosaddegh as orchestrated by the CIA. That they remember as a proxy war their almost eight-year-long conflict with Iraq cannot have failed to breed resentment.

Both sides can point out the crimes of the other. The important question is, is Iran an existential threat to the United States or is it the other way around?

George W. Bush contemplated going to war against Iran to stop them from obtaining nuclear weapons until analysts from the National Intelligence Estimate informed him that Iran had ceased working on nukes some years before.

Clearly, we are a threat to them, even though we couch it in terms such as a desire for "regime change" to bring about "democracy" as sacred terms even though our success in pursuing that dream has led to few impressive results.

Are they a threat to us as a leading sponsor of terror? Not according to a group known as Veteran Intelligence Professionals for Sanity (VIPS). Granted, the name could be considered an affront. Is there a mirror image organization that is for insanity, or does the crazy inhere in the profession? An exhaustive treatment of the question is for another time.

According to the VIPS, a bipartisan lie that is "being pushed on the public with the enthusiastic help of a largely pliant media is that Iran is the prime sponsor of terrorism in the world today."

The VIPS further point out, "While Iran is guilty of having used terrorism as a national policy tool, the Iran of 2017 is not the Iran of 1981. In the early days of the Islamic Republic, Iranian operatives routinely carried out car bombings, kidnappings and assassinations of dissidents and of American citizens. That has not been the case for many years."

The car bombings overseas are done now, but that doesn't mean the United States doesn't see "terrorism." Of course they do. On November 9, 2018, NPR's *Morning Edition* host Steve Inskeep spoke with State Department adviser on Iran, Brian Hook. Brian claims the Persians are still big in the terrorism business. "This is a revolutionary regime that does not invest in its own people. It does invest in violent misadventures in Syria, Iraq, Yemen, Lebanon, terrorism in Europe. And so we are trying to get this regime to start behaving like a normal country, and the Iranian people are asking for the same thing."

The quote is the usual boilerplate heard or written by functionaries and the "pliant media." Never is a proven incident mentioned. As has been noted elsewhere, in Yemen, Iran is probably assisting the Houthis, but they are hardly the instigators, and whatever they are doing pales in comparison to the terror and famine being spread by the Saudis.

As to Hezbollah, another bête noire:

> *Iran's relationship with Hezbollah also has evolved radically. In the early years of the Islamic Republic, Hezbollah was often a proxy and sub-contractor for Iran. However, during the last 20 years Hezbollah has become an entity and political force in its own right. It fought Israel to a standstill in 2006 in southern Lebanon, which was a watershed moment in establishing Hezbollah's transformation into a conventional army. In the intervening years, Hezbollah, which is now part of the Lebanese government, also has turned away from the radical, religious driven violence that is the hallmark of the Sunni extremists, like ISIS.*

What we see is that terms like terrorism, extremism, and "normal country" have definitions that are somewhat fluid. We define the terms to our liking. Iranian support for the Syrian regime seen in context of a Sunni and Turkish push to get rid of a government not to their liking is a natural alliance. The fall of Syria would be to the disadvantage of Tehran. Why would they not support Assad?

Mr. Hook also mentioned the Revolutionary Guards. The Islamic Revolutionary Guard Corps (IRGC) is organized conventionally and fights that way. Granted, it is in the service of the Islamic Republic and is designated as a terrorist organization by Saudi Arabia and Bahrain.

That could be construed as the pot calling the kettle black. If we are going to look at what that makes the definition of terrorist, it is effectively any group that spreads terror whether organized conventionally or as guerrillas or lone wolves. Just about any army, air force, or navy could be so defined, other than the Papal Swiss Guard.

NPR was speaking with Hook ostensibly about sanctions though the discussion was wide ranging. The most interesting part of the discussion occurred when Hook pontificated about what the Iranian people wanted:

> The Iranian people have been working at trying to achieve a representative government since 1905, and it has had peaks and valleys. And we very much stand with the Iranian people. So much of the things that they ask for are the same things we're asking for. This is a revolutionary regime that does not invest in its own people. It does invest in violent misadventures in Syria, Iraq, Yemen, Lebanon, terrorism in Europe. And so, we are trying to get this regime to start behaving like a normal country, and the Iranian people are asking for the same thing.

Putting aside the chutzpah of an American State Department adviser speaking for the Iranian people, Hook left something out. Mr. Inskeep called him on it.

Some people who know the history of Iran will be shouting at their radios at some point because you alluded to the history, that one of the valleys of Iranian democracy was a U.S.-backed coup in 1953. There was then this revolution in 1979. And they've had elections but not what we would recognize as full democracy ever since. What is the mechanism by which you think the current regime would be overthrown?

That little coup where we stood with the Iranian people—not. Though we have been bugging the Islamic Republic for all of the Trump administration since it began, Hook had to make sure we understood what he meant with the precise level of obfuscation.

We're not talking about regime change. The future of this regime is up to the Iranian people. What we have been looking for is a change in their behavior, and we are very hopeful that our campaign of maximum economic pressure on this regime is going to help accelerate the path to reform that not only we want but the Iranian people want.

"Not only we want but the Iranian people want." It was radio, so we couldn't see if he said that with a straight face.

The story of American sanctions to promote good government and healthy living has been examined elsewhere. The policy, as applied to Iran may or may not bring about what we purport to want.

The Trump administration began to re-impose sanctions after most of them were lifted due to an agreement between Iran and the P5+1 countries (i.e., members of the UN Security Council plus Germany). The agreement, the Joint Comprehensive Plan of Action (JCPOA) called for Iran to cease and/or limit certain nuclear related actions in return for the curbing of sanctions.

Why did the United States leave the JCPOA? On May 8, 2018, the president spoke about the reasons. A *Washington Post* article the next day by Salvador Rizzo and Meg Kelly quoted President Trump:

> In fact, the deal allowed Iran to continue enriching uranium and – over time – reach the brink of a nuclear breakout. ...
>
> The agreement was so poorly negotiated that even if Iran fully complies, the regime can still be on the verge of a nuclear breakout in just a short period of time. The deal's sunset provisions are totally unacceptable. ...

If we do nothing, we know exactly what will happen. In just a short period of time, the world's leading state sponsor of terror will be on the cusp of acquiring the world's most dangerous weapons.

Salvador and Kelly looked at the pros and cons of Trump's action. There is at least a case that Iran, despite the agreement, is working toward nuclear weapons, but there is also the argument that Iranian progress in that endeavor has been stopped for a considerable time.

The other parties to the JCPOA are much closer to Iran than to the United States. They would have much more to fear from the development of ballistic missiles that could carry a nuclear warhead, but they completely support the agreement.

In the same neighborhood as Iran, Pakistan has atomic weapons and its rival, India, does as well. The stability of Pakistan is questionable on a good day. That Iran could want a weapon to counter those two might be understandable. That would we fear a Persian bomb more than the extant supply of the not so level-headed Pakistanis is a question not asked. Maybe it should be? Pakistan, supposedly an ally, understandably serves only its own agenda no matter what they get from us. They are also much dependent on the largesse of the Saudis.

In abandoning JCPOA, because the administration believed Iran wasworking on nuclear weapons, we were back to the point where Bush contemplated war. Though there is speculation that Trump wished to do that, the reimposition of sanctions, as Mr. Hook was called on to make the case for, was the action taken.

Mr. Hook pointed out the effect the sanctions were having on the oil business, the Islamic Republic's big money earner. Will they bring Iran to its knees the way it didn't Saddam? Time will tell.

Hook did not opine on how it will affect the average walking-around Iranian he cares so much about.

Will sanctions ever bring about whatever it is we want in Iran? There will certainly be some pain to the people, if not the rulers. The Iranians have been under sanctions before and have not cracked. They are resourceful and will not just roll over.

They may even have gotten some help from unlikely places, according to what the agricultural news website, *AgFax*, reported on October 9, 2018:

> *Thanks to Friday's data from the U.S. Census Bureau, we now know that U.S. soybean exports were up again in August, to 123.7 mb in 2018 from 109.9 mb a year ago. If you thought it was odd that Egypt was the number one buyer of soybeans in July, you might want to sit down. The top buyer of U.S. soybeans in August 2018 was Iran.*

Do the Iranians have an insatiable appetite for American legumes and are gaming the sanctions to satisfy their craving? Judgment on the Persians' desire for our beans is not to be made here. It does appear that they had something else up their sleeve.

Soybeans are exempt from sanctions for "humanitarian" reasons. Whether we feel for the Iranian people or the farmer is for others to answer. Chinese purchases had dried up and who wants the beans to rot? They were sold at bargain prices to the Iranians.

The author of the *AgFax* piece, Todd Hultman, speculates on the possibility that "Iran is sweetening the pot for China to keep buying oil by also throwing U.S. soybeans in the deal?"

Mr. Hultman makes it plain he has no proof. "Again, I am not interested in spreading rumors—the world has enough of those and, as I said earlier, the evidence is lacking. But, as far as U.S. soybean demand is concerned, I must point out for the second month in a row that the market has found ways to make up for the loss of China's direct participation."

Are the Iranians still playing the market? No proof of anything, but don't think that Les Perses won't utilize a lot of fancy footwork to stay afloat.

According to Al Jazeera, Iran signed a free trade agreement with Iraq. Iraqi President Barham Salih announced the agreement less than two weeks after the reimposition of sanctions.

Iranian President Rouhani hopes the pact will increase trade between the two countries from $12 billion to $20 billion. Maybe not that huge in the big scheme of things, but it is something.

As we kind of broke Iraq and have thus sort of bought it, as in Colin Powell's Pottery Barn analogy, we have to let some things slide.

In that invasion of 2003, where we did Iran the favor and got rid of Saddam, evidence tends to suggest the Persians did better out of that war. The free trade pact seems to say the winning continues. Not enough to offset the sanctions completely but enough to suggest those sanctions are hardly, as someone else once said in relation to Iraq, "a slam dunk."

The Iraqis are importing Iranian oil with our permission. Even though they have lots of crude under their soil, they are not producing enough gas to keep the lights on. According to a December 5, 2018, headline on CNBC, "US likely to continue Iran sanctions waivers for Iraq, but neutering Tehran's influence is a long-term goal."

Will that goal happen? Who knows? We do know that the campaign to isolate Iran is not popular in the greater world.

In the end, is it all worth it? Does the United States have a real problem with Iran or are we doing all this at the behest of regional players who are using us for their advantage?

No longer confronting Iran and bringing the forces home leaves us impervious to Iranian attack other than terrorism. Would the Islamic Republic feel the need to hit us with pinpricks after we left? Maybe, but there would be retaliation.

Keep in mind, there has been terrorism inflicted on Iran. Scientists have been assassinated and we support the MEK (People's Mujahedin of Iran). MEK was officially designated as a terrorist organization by the State Department until they became useful.

As an update to the question of continued Iranian sponsored terrorism, in August of 2018 two Iranians were arrested in Chicago as agents of Iran, monitoring Americans and a Chicago Jewish center. Anyone monitoring a Jewish center is not probably doing it with goodwill, unless they are Jewish.

The two men deny the charges. The lawyer for Ahmadreza Mohammadi Doostdar stated that accusations "wouldn't even make sense in a B-rated spy novel." He claimed the men were innocent. "They took pictures all over Chicago and all over the University of Chicago that had nothing to do with anything," said Doostdar's lawyer. "The government is trying to play geopolitics here, somehow suggesting he had some ax to grind with members of the Jewish faith is ridiculous."

The pair is accused of surveilling targets in America, but not American government targets. They are also accused in the plot of targeting the MEK. The case has since been resolved. Per the U.S. Department of Justice:

> *Ahmadreza Mohammadi-Doostdar, 39, a dual U.S.-Iranian citizen, and Majid Ghorbani, 60, an Iranian citizen and resident of California, have been sentenced to prison terms of 38 months and 30 months, respectively, for their criminal convictions relating to their conduct conducting surveillance of and collecting identifying information about American citizens and U.S. nationals who are members of the group Mujahedin-e Khalq (MEK).*
>
> *On Jan. 15, 2020, the Honorable Paul L. Friedman sentenced Doostdar to a prison term of 38 months, 36 months of supervised release, and a fine of $14,153. Ghorbani was sentenced to a prison term of 30 months and 36 months of supervised release.*

Nothing about targeting places of worship, just pics of a terrorist org.

That they see MEK in the United States as fair game is understandable. We do, however, as a nation have an obligation to see that no foreign state ever carries out operations on our soil, something we botched on September 11, 2001.

If we stop playing games with them, maybe they will leave us alone. True, maybe they won't and will continue to see their eternal mission as jihad against The Great Satan.

If we left their neighborhood, they would be, in all likelihood, in a much stronger regional position than before. There would still be area rivalries they would have to deal with. Turkey and the Saudis as well as others would not go away. That would keep them busy enough.

Also, we might note, they have no capability of raising a fleet, air force, or an army capable of sailing out of the Gulf and around Africa and crossing the Atlantic to invade our homeland. The lads and lasses at the think tanks may not have noticed that.

32

Russia

In the second half of the twentieth century, the United States was engaged in what was the Cold War. Our rivalry was with an entity known as the Soviet Union. With the demise of the Communist Bloc and its transformation into successor states, the hope was for a more peaceful world.

Unfortunately, we find ourselves in a new cold war with the Russian State that remains of the old union. What happened?

With the breakup of the Soviet Union into the various independent states, the remainder went into a tailspin that some might have thought fatal. Amongst the pessimists (or depending on point of view, optimists) was Jeffrey Tayler who penned an article in the May 2001 issue of The Atlantic, "Russia is finished."

Mr. Tayler thought he was seeing, "The unstoppable descent of a once great power into social catastrophe and strategic irrelevance." Who knows, in the long run, he may be right. What he chronicled at the time was a country well down on its luck:

> Average Russians continue to suffer abuse daily at the hands of the militia, the traffic police, and corrupt bureaucrats. The state may try them more than once for a crime. They may be detained without charges for seventy-two hours or held in a tuberculosis-ridden pre-

trial detention center for years. Opening a business involves as much paperwork and bribery as ever. The mafiya still extracts dan' from entrepreneurs. The countrywide decay that began during the Yeltsin years continues, with television towers catching fire, nuclear submarines sinking, military aircraft crashing to earth, apartment buildings exploding from leaks in decrepit gas pipes, and entire regions of the country going without heat and electricity in winter months.

He further called Russia "Zaire With Permafrost."

Although the Kremlin's superpower pretensions may preclude it from becoming a loyal partner of the West, the country's economic failings, to say nothing of its shrinking population, will eventually prevent Russia from posing a significant threat abroad. Given that Russia is surviving on human, material, and military reserves accrued during the Soviet years, and that Putin has put forward plans that will only worsen his country's plight, we can draw but one conclusion: Russia is following the path of Mobutu's Zaire, becoming a sparsely populated yet gigantic land of natural resources exploited by an authoritarian elite as the citizenry sinks into poverty, disease, and despair.

So how is that working for the Russians? More to the point of this book, how is it working for us?

Is Russia out for the count as Mr. Tayler predicted?

It kind of looked like it at the time. Then, economically, the country started coming back.

Tayler was writing in 2001 after Russia had suffered from the Asian currency crisis and had had to devalue the Ruble. Maybe he was missing something because Russia was growing as he spoke. According to *Investopedia*, "A significantly depreciated ruble helped stimulate domestic production leading to a spurt of economic growth over the next few years with real GDP growth reaching 8.3% in 2000 and approximately 5% in 2001."

The *Investopedia* article's author credits the new president with reforms to simplify taxes and regulations that help set the country to recover and grow. Putin's popularity would increase as well. Matthew Johnston, the *Investopedia* writer, does note that the "unprecedented growth" did take place during an era of rising energy prices.

The energy sector had been privatized in the '90s and the Russian state under Putin determined to get that which was taken at fire sale prices back. Yukos was renationalized, and when hydrocarbon values were increasing, that helped.

Russia was hit by the global financial crisis that occurred in 2008, but prices would recover. Since then, with the Ukraine conflict and the imposition of sanctions, there have been problems, but the apocalypse as predicted by Mr. Tayler has not taken place.

It may not be all hunky dory for the Russians economically, but there may be reason to take all of those westerners who were celebrating the end is nigh of our Slavic friends with a grain of salt, or at least some grain.

Growing up in the '50s and '60s in the United States we heard Nikita Khrushchev tell us that the Soviets were going to bury us. At that time, his USSR had to buy grain overseas. How could his system be all that great if it couldn't raise enough food to feed itself? All this while the United States was setting records for farm exports year upon year.

That was then.

> *Russia has captured more than half of the world's wheat market in recent years, becoming the world's biggest exporter of grain, thanks to bumper harvests and attractive pricing. In 2016, Russia became the world*

leader in wheat exports. Since the early 2000s, its share of the world wheat market has quadrupled.

This is now.

Granted, this quote is from RT, which we are always reminded is a television station owned by the Russian state, but this is a somewhat mundane fact that is probably true enough. Anyway, we might admit that mass starvation is not more a problem in Russia than homelessness is here.

While we are working with "biased sources," Sputnik, another Russian state-owned news agency, reports that Russia would post a budget surplus about 2.1% of GDP for 2018. On January 29, 2019, Bloomberg Quint (owned neither by the U.S. government nor the Russian state as far as one can tell) had the headline, "U.S. Treasury Set to Borrow $1Trillion for a Second Year to Finance the Deficit."

Make what you will of either datum. The Zaire-as-permafrost business would be reformulated by the late Senator McCain as "Russia is a gas station masquerading as a country." McCain would say that in 2014 when he was doing his best to stir up trouble. It was one of the many things he was wrong about.

One might conclude that Les Russes are probably not on the verge of sinking below the waves in the near future.

Russia's Wars
The Struggle with the Caucasians

In *The Gulag Archipelago* Aleksandr Solzhenitsyn recounts how the Russian people as well as other nationalities were rounded up and caged by the Soviet system. It may have not been easy to get all the prisoners into the camps, but with a system it was doable.

Why was it that the subjects of the USSR were so pliable? Eventually, we learn in the third volume of Solzhenitsyn's work.

They weren't Chechens.

This is not to say there were no Chechens in the Gulag, but a whole Soviet Union of them would have been impossible to corral.

Solzhenitsyn was a Russian nationalist, but if there were any people for whom he had respect, it was the Chechens. He made plain who and what they were as contrasted to more cosmopolitan Soviets by the behavior of the Chechens when a Gulag escapee is apprehended. The Chechens tried to help the recaptured "Zek" with compassion and generosity in the face of the authorities' brutality.

Of the Russians and other groups:

> *If it had been on a station platform in Moscow, Leningrad, or Kiev, or any other flourishing city, everybody would have passed by the gray-headed old man, kneeling and manacled, like a figure in a Repin picture, without noticing him or turning around to look—publishing executives, progressive film producers, lecturers on humanism, army officers, not to mention trade union and Party officials. And all ordinary, undistinguished citizens occupying no position worth mentioning would also have tried to go by without noticing, in case the guard asked their names and made a note of them—because if you have a residence permit for Moscow, where the shops are so good, you must not take risks... (Easy enough to understand in 1949—but would it have been any different in 1965? Would our educated youngsters have stopped to intercede with his escort for the gray-haired old man in handcuffs and on his knees?)*

As Kris Kristofferson put it, "freedom's just another word for nothing left to lose," and this was a people who had to be threatened with losing. The Chechens, who had suffered much at the hands of the state, could find heart to defy the agents of repression on behalf of another sufferer.

In our politically correct age, would people in our country go out of their way for somebody a bit outré being apprehended with extreme prejudice or would it just be move along, let's not be late or make a scene?

Chechnya, considered part of the Russian Federation, was not to get its own independent nationhood in the Soviet breakup. No matter, the Chechens were going to give it the old college try with great reserves of tenacity and courage.

In the mid '90s there was a picture that appeared on the then relatively new Internet of a mustachioed man with a Soviet air force cap. He was Dzhokhar Dudayev, a former officer with a distinguished career in the USSR's service and now was president of the Chechen Republic. In other pictures of the man, he looked distinguished, but there was something about him that suggested that he would have been a dashing raider out of the mountains in another century. Whatever else, it was the face of a serious man.

As the USSR deteriorated, Dudayev, as president of the breakaway state, declared its independence in November of 1991. This was not recognized by any other country other than Georgia.

Russia would not countenance the separation but didn't do too much to oppose with force at first. Meanwhile, the Chechens engaged in intramurals. President Dudayev was not without opposition at home. The breakup took its toll on Chechnya as other nationals, important in infrastructure, left feeling not welcome, and the economy was having the same problems as elsewhere.

The opposition to Dudayev was fierce and even bloody at times, but one point of unity among the population was the desire for independence.

Russia supported internal opposition, and air operations over Chechnya began. Opposition forces launched unsuccessful attacks on the capitol, Grozny, in which Russian personnel were captured.

When Boris Yeltsin called on the warring factions to disarm, the Chechen government refused. In late 1994, the Russian army was sent in.

The Russians bombarded Grozny from the air and with artillery causing large large-scale death and displacement. The Chechens fought back causing many casualties among the invaders. There was a reason for all the Russian death and wounded, according to GlobalSecurity.org:,

> Troops who were sent to Chechnya had in many cases only just arrived for their mandatory conscription service. As a result, they had only been through about half of what U.S. soldiers would consider basic training. Since Russian planners wanted to conserve their "good stuff"— the 6,000 tanks that they considered to be combat worthy against the West—older models were pulled out of depot storage and issued to troops. As a result, few tankers were trained on any of the systems they would have to fight in, and even trained ones were assigned to the wrong tanks. Trained T-72 drivers wound up in T-80BV tanks, and T-80 tankers in T-72As. Crews were thrown together and had to train and become familiar with each other during the road march to Grozny.

Among the setbacks:

"The result was an unmitigated disaster, highlighted by the nearly complete destruction of the 131st Independent

"Maykop" Motorized Rifle Brigade and the 81st Guards Motorized Rifle Regiment on New Year's Eve 1994–95."

Death and destruction were not about to stop a war machine that had in its last world war seen even worse and longer brutalization. Not much was left of the capital, but the Russians finally had it.

There was still territory for the Chechens to defend and use for guerrilla warfare and they made use of it with all the skill they could muster.

A ceasefire was announced, some elections were held and prisoners exchanged, and Russian Federation forces were able to kill Dudayev. Thus, a dirty little war ended, more or less.

Round Two

The official end of the First Chechen War was the Khasavyurt ceasefire. This was negotiated by Russian general Alexander Lebed and Aslan Maskhadov. Maskhadov would become president of Chechnya.

The peace that would come about would not be one of absolute stability. Chechnya was in horrible shape and there wasn't much of an economy to provide stable income for the Chechens.

Kidnapping became a major source of income in the countryside, and opposition to the Chechen government was widespread. Wahhabi Islam was promoted by Saudi influence in the region and this led to conflicts within Chechnya.

Attacks on Russian border posts were also taking place and were taken seriously in the Kremlin.

A series of apartment bombings that killed almost 300 occurred in Moscow and other Russian cities in September of 1999. They were blamed on Chechens.

The trigger for the second war was the invasion of Dagestan in August of 1999. The men, Wahhabists, led by Shamil

Basayev, attacked the neighboring republic. In September, they would be pushed back into Chechnya, and the war was on.

The Russians united behind the man who was becoming their leader, Vladimir Putin, and the always fractious Chechens would put that aside and mostly come together behind President Maskhadov.

The Russian siege of Grozny, as described by Brian Glyn Williams in his *Inferno in Chechnya*, was brutal and effective. His description of Russian terror weaponry is beyond horror.

Despite that and the Russian desire to avoid close contact with the use of standoff weapons, it would not be possible to avoid having to mix it up with Chechen fighters. They would use their knowledge of the tunnels and sewers to emerge and inflict casualties on the Russians.

The resistance was tough and tenacious, but in all probability doomed. The Sufi Mufti and other non-Wahabi Chechens threw in their lot with the Russians. The exact Sufi/Wahabi fault lines are for others to discuss, but they did exist.

The Chechens who did not give over fought on and still had victories against the Russians attacking Grozny. The time would come, however, when it would be necessary to leave the city. The fighters would have to attempt a breakout through a minefield around February of 2000. The indomitable Shamil Basayev, who was wounded in the escape, led the way with Aslanbek Ismailov and the mayor, Lecha Dudayev. Basayev would lose his foot, but keep on with the struggle.

As for others, many men were lost, but most made it to the southern mountains to continue the fight. It was a defeat for the Russian forces.

Atrocities

From all accounts, the Russians were making much of Chechnya a free fire zone with aerial, artillery, and rocket fire. They were not overly worried about discriminating between combatants and others.

If Chechens were not killed outright, they might get caught in the filtration camp system. The internment and torture has been compared to Abu Ghraib, with the Iraq prison looking comparatively benign.

If any people were not inclined to take this lying down, that would be the Chechens. The second war was more brutal anyway. Brian Glyn Williams saw a change: "While the rebels, especially Basayev, had established a policy of publicly releasing captured conscripts to their mothers during the first war, they were known to be in a less forgiving mood now that it was widely known that the Russians were killing tens of thousands of Chechens in indiscriminate bombardments, zachistkas, filtration camps, and "disappearances" throughout the country."

It would be trite to quote General Sherman on the nature of war at this point.

Basayev would be the most famous avenging angel, but there would be others. The war was one of desperation for the resistors and thus, having nothing to lose, they would be up for anything.

They would carry the fight into Russia, sometimes deeply. It would start with a Chechen Black Widow suicide bombing but became famous with the hostage-taking at Dubrovka Theater that caught the world's attention. Armed Chechens took the stage and told the audience they were hostages. They made their demands and released some of the playgoers from the Moscow Theater.

Vladimir Putin was as implacable as the terrorists and was not about to give in and an operation went forward. Gas was pumped into the theater and then Russian Alpha forces attacked. The Chechens were subdued and hostages taken to hospital.

Over two hundred of the hostages were killed by the chemicals used against the Chechens.

Basayev was behind the incident and would lose all his positions with the official Chechen government, but he was not done. He would set in motion the Beslan School hostage-taking and it too would see many of hostages killed—but no wavering by Putin.

And so it would go. The Chechens would continue to resist and the Russians would continue to not give in. This would go on, but the Chechens could not win.

Other Chechens would succeed to the leadership of the Chechen government as a Russian republic. Since 2007, the Republic has been under the leadership of Ramzan Kadyrov. It is seen as corrupt but its reconstruction has been going on steadily, and appears stable.

In the long struggle, both sides learned from mistakes. The Russians had a lot to study and correct. They would face more wars and would have more to learn and apply.

Why didn't Russians just say the heck with it and leave? If all that Chechnya had was a brave and troublesome populace, why not just say au revoir. There could be any number of reasons, but there is something people can often find to fight over and that is energy.

In an article posted at LSE online, James Hughes writes:

The most important political economy factor, undoubtedly, is its strategic location on Russia's main transshipment pipeline for the billions of tonnes of extractable reserves in the Caspian Basin. If Russia is to be a key player in the Caspian oil business it must control

Chechnya or at least peacefully coexist with it or risk losing its position as the key strategic actor in the Caucasus. An independent Chechnya could pose a threat to Russian economic interests in the Caspian, particularly if ruled by an uncooperative leader and not a client of Moscow.

In light of the renewed cold war that was going on, one might wonder if there was any interference from the West during the Chechen conflict.

Vladimir Putin seems to think so. We learn of this from a BBC article from 2015 about a Russian documentary. The Russian President made his comments in a state-run television film marking his 15 years in power. The documentary gives considerable time to the conflict in the North Caucasus, a battle for independence that mutated into an Islamist insurgency. Mr. Putin accuses the West of trying to tear Russia apart by supporting terrorists. "Our security services recorded direct contact between North Caucasus fighters and representatives of U.S. intelligence in Azerbaijan," Mr. Putin discloses in the lengthy film. Once informed, he says, President George W. Bush promised to "kick ass." But he claims U.S. intelligence then wrote to their Russian counterparts, proclaiming a right to support all "opposition forces" in the country."

Is Putin telling the truth? According to much of the American Mainstream Media, as Mary McCarthy said of Lillian Hellman, every word "is a lie, including 'and' and 'the.'" Putin would probably return the favor.

Georgia

If ever one were to ask, "What were they thinking?" the Georgian attack on South Ossetia would be an obvious occasion. Much could be explained by the fact that the

Georgian president, Mikheil Saakashvili, was and probably is not a terribly stable fellow.

Georgia wasn't completely to blame and Russia has its share. Each side had reasons for conflict, but Russia came off the better.

Russia didn't get a good feeling over the 2008 recognition of Kosovo independence. The 2008 NATO Bucharest Summit wherein Ukraine and Georgia were promised eventual membership was even less likely to cause joy in the Kremlin. Moscow could have no illusions as to the expansionist policy of the alliance.

Russia was not going to happily acquiesce to Georgia in NATO. Who would expect them to? After the breaking of the "not one inch eastward" pledge, they had to have no illusions. According to Michael Kofman in a post for *War on the Rocks*:

> *By 2008, Russia had fleshed out plans for a military operation to impose its will on Georgia. The strategic aim was to give Moscow plausible deniability when it came to whom to blame for the conflict while preventing Georgia from being able to choose its own strategic direction. Moscow actively sought the war, and hoped it might result in regime change in Tbilisi.*

Mr. Saakashvili, after becoming president in a landslide, was becoming a bit heavy handed and his popularity was on the decline. His government was pursuing enlargement and modernization of its forces. It was the "most rapidly expanding military in the former Soviet space, a force capable of not only seizing Georgia's breakaway regions, but potentially deterring Russia from intervention." Huge acquisitions of equipment were made.

Something had to give. Again, according to Mr. Kofman:

> *Russia set up Georgia's leader, Mikheil Saakashvili, into initiating hostilities against its proxy forces in South*

Ossetia, and then crushed the Georgian military in a brief conventional conflict. Saakashvili walked down that path, despite U.S. warnings, because of his own ambitions. Yet Moscow was also surprised by the timing of the Georgian attack, which somewhat pre-empted Russian plans. NATO's declaration added a broader geostrategic dimension to a war that was already well on its way to happening given Georgia's ambitions to retake lost territory, and Russia's intent to deal Saakashvili a major defeat. Putin was not going to let Saakashvili take the territories back, but after NATO's declaration at the Bucharest Summit he resolved to teach the West a lesson about Russia's ability to veto further NATO expansion eastward. Indeed, as I discuss later in this article, the indicators were there in advance in Russian statements that this was going to happen. It was meant as a clear warning to other governments about integrating with NATO. Even today Russia's Prime Minister Medvedev warns that bringing Georgia into the alliance "could provoke a horrible conflict."

The United States underestimates Putin. Despite all the advantages economically and militarily we have, Vlad has been able to oppose us effectively everywhere. We forget that he was selected and not elected at first.

The American president is elected in a contest to see how glib he or she is. It is important that they seem somewhat plausible to a majority of those who can bestir themselves to vote.

In the old Soviet Union, smarter brains could not start a business like high tech entrepreneurs in the US. They would gravitate to something else, like maybe the KGB. Now, according to no less an authority than Hillary Clinton, that proves evil. In 2016, She said Putin "was a KGB agent. By definition, he doesn't have a soul," and then went on to compare him to Hitler in the 1930s.

Maybe she is right. The man prosecuted the Chechen war with no little brutality. Other than a defense of "we meant well," what can Hillary say about her tenure at state and its debacles? Putin sent a signal that he was keeping Russia together.

In Georgia, he sent the signal that he would not let affronts to Russia in the "Near Abroad" go unchallenged. In the process, he cleaned Saakashvili's and Georgia's clock.

As to Mr. Saakashvili, after losing the war, his party would lose and he would serve out his term. Then, like not a few American politicians, Sash would score a teaching gig at an American college (Tufts).

Later, he was invited to the Ukraine and as he was not going back to Georgia to face charges that had been filed, that was where he went. The Poroshenko government in 2015 gave him citizenship and a regional governorship. In a bite the hand move he would accuse Poroshenko of corruption, quit and start a party. He would lose his citizenship and become a kind of political vagabond. As a Georgian success, the lad was no Josef Stalin.

Saakashvili reentered Ukraine through Poland but was arrested in February 2018 and deported from whence he came. He moved to the Netherlands, where his wife had citizenship, and found a job as a lecturer. In 2018, Georgian courts sentenced him in absentia to three years and six years in prison in two separate trials.

The Georgia saga does not want to go away. On March 25, 2019, NATO Secretary-General Jens Stoltenberg said Georgia would eventually join NATO and Russia can't stop it happening. Is this a good idea? You have all those prosperous euro countries who won't pony up their fair share for the alliance and does anyone think those Caucasians are going to be quick to reach in their pocket? By the way, how does this increase the security of anyone in the alliance?

Ukraine

There is probably no one who would have expected Ukraine to become a shining city on a hill and thus everyone's expectations were met. For a time there it was going its own way and hardly noticed by the world but not by much.

In the 2010 presidential election, the incumbent, Viktor Yushchenko, was trounced by his opponents. Yushchenko, in his previous successful election campaign had a mysterious disfiguring condition the cause of which is still controversial. You've got to be tough to run for president in Ukraine.

Yushchenko, on his way out the door, rehabilitated the Ultra-Nationalist World War II leader Stepan Bandera. Maybe not as bad as if Germany nominated Goebbels for a Nobel for contributions to advertising, but there was no little understandable disgust.

In the runoff, Viktor Yanukovych would be elected president. He too was going to end up unpopular, and would be run out of office.

Money problems started the ball rolling. The Ukrainians needed a lot and the IMF was holding out the carrot with the stick. According to a March 5, 2014, *CounterPunch* article, "Chronology of the Ukrainian Coup" by Renee Parsons, quoting the *Kiev Post* on April 11, 2011:

> "*Ukraine Hopes to Get $1.5 Billion from IMF in June.*" *The article states that the loan is dependent on pension cuts while* "*maintaining cooperation with the IMF, since it influences the country's interaction with other international financial institutions and private investors*" *and further that the* "*attraction of $850*

million from the World Bank in 2011, depended on cooperation with the IMF.

Well, that about says it all—if Ukraine played ball. *Then* the loan money would pour in.

In late 2013, Yanukovych would get a better offer from Putin. The Russians would buy $15 billion of Ukrainian government bonds and would cut the price of gas.

This was not going to be taken lying down. Behind the scenes machinations would begin. According to *CounterPunch*:

Anonymous Ukraine hackers released a series of emails from a Lithuanian government advisor to opposition leader and former boxer Vitaly Klitschko regarding plans to destabilize Ukraine; for example:

> *"Our American friends promise to pay a visit in the coming days, we may even see Nuland or someone from the Congress." 12/7/2013*
>
> *"Your colleague has arrived …. his services may be required even after the country is destabilized." 12/14/2013*
>
> *"I think we've paved the way for more radical escalation of the situation. Isn't it time to proceed with more decisive action?" 1/9/2014"*

So, it appears, if CP is correct, the game was afoot. On November 29, protestors were on Kiev streets when the European Commission President Jose Manual Barroso announced that the EU would "not accept Russia's veto" of the Agreement.

American fingerprints were all over the Ukrainian upheaval as *CounterPunch* further reported:

> *December 13, 2013 – As if intent on providing incontrovertible evidence of U.S. involvement in*

Ukraine, Assistant U.S. Secretary of State for Europe and Eurasia Victoria Nuland proudly told a meeting of the International Business Conference sponsored by the U.S.-Ukrainian Foundation that the U.S. had "invested" more than $5 billion and "five years' worth of work and preparation" in achieving what she called Ukraine's "European aspirations." Having just returned from her third trip to Ukraine in five weeks, Nuland boasted of her 'coordinated high level diplomacy' and a more than two-hour "tough conversation" with Yanukovych. Already familiar with Nuland as former Secretary Clinton's spokesperson at State, one can imagine her discourteous tone and manner when she says she made it "absolutely clear" to Yanukovych that the U.S. required "immediate steps" ...to "get back into conversation with Europe and the IMF." While Western media have portrayed Yanukovych as a "weak" leader, Nuland's description of a "tough" meeting can only mean that he resisted her threats and intimidations. In what must have been a touching moment, Nuland spoke about a show of force by government police on demonstrators who "sang hymns and prayed for peace."

At about the same time in Kiev, the late Senator McCain, who seems to have never seen an anti-Russian campaign he didn't love, was hanging out with Connecticut Senator Chris Murphy as progressive as any American solon gets except when he is burnishing his neocon credentials. The Democrat and Republican had no problem sharing a stage with Oleh Tyahnybok, head of the neo-Nazi Svoboda Party.

Protests began and were ongoing and who were in the streets? The Western press has it as opponents to the corrupt regime. CounterPunch disagrees:

> January 24, 2014 – President Yanukovych identified foreign elements participating in Kiev protests warning that armed radicals were a danger to peaceful citizens. Independent news agencies also reported that "not all of Kiev's population backs opposition rule, which depends mainly on a group from the former Polish town of Lvov, which holds sway over Kiev downtown—but not the rest of the city.

The archived Department of State media notes of January 30, 2014 give an extensive itinerary of an upcoming trip that the Assistant Secretary of State Victoria Nuland would be taking. The last item:

> In Kyiv, Assistant Secretary Nuland will meet with government officials, opposition leaders, civil society and business leaders to encourage agreement on a new government and plan of action that can put Ukraine back on track toward fulfilling the aspirations of the Ukrainian people for democracy, respect for human rights, European integration and economic growth.

What that meant was that, as *CounterPunch* explained, "In other words, almost a month before President Yanukovych was ousted, the U.S. was planning to rid the world of another independently elected president."

None of it is anything we can be proud of, but the worst bit is our Ambassador Pyatt and Assistant Secretary of State Victoria Nuland deciding the fate of the Ukrainian government after we had helped riot oust an elected, if corrupt, president. The pair were recorded doing just that and the foul, heavy-handed discussion went viral. As of this writing, it is still extant at https://www.youtube.com/watch?v=WV9J6sxCs5k.

Rioting would occur on February 19, 2014. The peaceful protestors were not all that peaceful and their ranks included armed men who would shoot people protesting and the police as part of the strategy to oust the president.

Any attempt to blame the incumbent fell apart due to a leaked phone call between EU foreign affairs chief Catherine Ashton and the Estonian foreign minister Urmas Paet. *The Guardian* reported that the phone call "discussed a conspiracy theory that blamed the killing of civilian protesters in the Ukrainian capital, Kiev, on the opposition rather than the ousted government." The paper didn't call into question the reality of the leaked call, but a conspiracy is not tenable.

At the end of the article, the newspaper quotes a U.S. State Department spokesman about his thoughts on another leak making an escape: "As I said around the last unfortunate case, this is just another example of the kind of Russian tradecraft that we have concerns about."

He should have concerns about the Russkies outclassing him, but more important would-be concerns about who the United States is backing and what it says about our policy.

The EU reacted to what Putin had offered by laying on sanctions on February 21, due to U.S. pressure. After some more machinations in Kiev, Yanukovych fled for his life.

So the coup was accomplished and as it was being done, Renee Parsons wrote, "March 1, 2014 – During a conversation initiated by the vice president, Biden delivered his 'atta boy' with a phone call to newly installed prime minister Arseniy Yatsenyuk reaffirming U.S. support for Ukraine's 'territorial integrity.'"

The Biden family would do well out of the coup. In May, it would be announced Joe's son, Hunter, received an appointment as a director of a Ukrainian oil and gas company. Talent will out, nepotism doesn't hurt either.

Sometimes, it's necessary to call on dear old dad. And, sometimes dear old dad doesn't know when to shut up.

According to John Solomon's Hill article of April 1, 2019, "Joe Biden's 2020 Ukrainian nightmare: A closed probe is revived":

> Two years after leaving office, Joe Biden couldn't resist the temptation last year to brag to an audience of foreign policy specialists about the time as vice president that he strong-armed Ukraine into firing its top prosecutor.
>
> In his own words, with video cameras rolling, Biden described how he threatened Ukrainian President Petro Poroshenko in March 2016 that the Obama administration would pull $1 billion in U.S. loan guarantees, sending the former Soviet republic toward insolvency, if it didn't immediately fire Prosecutor General Viktor Shokin.
>
> "I said, 'You're not getting the billion.' I'm going to be leaving here in, I think it was about six hours. I looked at them and said: "I'm leaving in six hours. If the prosecutor is not fired, you're not getting the money," Biden recalled telling Poroshenko.
>
> Well, son of a bitch, he got fired. And they put in place someone who was solid at the time," Biden told the Council on Foreign Relations event, insisting that President Obama was in on the threat.

There was something missing from Joe's not-so-humble brag:

> But Ukrainian officials tell me there was one crucial piece of information that Biden must have known but didn't mention to his audience: The prosecutor he got fired was leading a wide-ranging corruption probe into the natural gas firm Burisma Holdings that employed Biden's younger son, Hunter, as a board member.

At least Joe didn't try to hug Poroshenko or smell his hair. The probe Biden short-circuited in 2018 may come back to haunt the former veep.

> Note: The Hill has labeled Solomon's piece "opinion" after attacks that were either partisan or pure as the driven snow. No matter, Joe's words might live forever on YouTube.

After the Coup

Ukraine is not a country made up of one ethnicity. People of several nationalities are inhabitants. The two largest are Ukrainians who are over 75% and Russians who are less than 20%. The Russians in the eastern part of the country and Crimea, which is a peninsula almost an island, did not favor the coup. The exact reasons may be in dispute, but they did oppose the new regime and that government wished to enforce state power in the region.

The people of Crimea voted overwhelmingly to return to being part of Russia and the peninsula was taken into the Russian Federation. Whether one agrees or disagrees with Putin on the subject, it is impossible not to understand his concern with what was going on in Ukraine and the West's machinations.

More trouble was brewing. On May 2, 2014, 42 pro-Russians were killed in Odessa during a demonstration at the Trade Union House while six had been shot earlier in the day.

The ethnic Russians in eastern Ukraine held referendums in Donetsk and Luhansk, declaring "People's Republics" on May 11, 2014. The Ukrainian government did not recognize the secession and began efforts to suppress it.

On July 17, 2014, Malaysian Airlines Flight MH17 was shot down with the loss of 298 passengers. A joint investigation team concluded the BUK missile was fired from rebel-controlled territory.

With sanctions laid and skirmishes ongoing, a peace deal was attempted in Minsk. It did not go well. In January, the Ukrainians were beaten by the separatists at the Donetsk airport, and the next day, January 23, 2015, a rebel leader announced an offensive.

While U.S. Secretary of State John Kerry was running around accomplishing nothing, the Germans and French were working with the Russians and the Ukrainians to secure a peace agreement. It would be agreed upon in Minsk in February 2015.

The situation may not be completely precarious, but neither is it great in what has, according to one commentator, settled into not-war.

Now and again there is a flare up. Most recently, as this was being written, was the Kerch Strait Incident. On November 25, Russian coast guard vessels intercepted Ukrainian gunboats attempting to pass through the strait to the Ukrainian port of Mariupol.

There are disagreements and accusations from both sides concerning who did not follow correct protocol. The Black Sea is not the Pacific Ocean, and who has a right to do what is dictated by a 2003 agreement between Russia and the Ukraine. There are news articles taking the case of either side.

What was predictable was the imposition of sanctions, this time on Russian officials blamed for the incident. President Poroshenko called for enacting a state of emergency though some have opined that that may have been due to a desire to postpone an election he is sure to lose.

Needless to say, our own government was quick to see the nefarious hand of Russia doing nefarious Russian stuff. General Curtis Scaparrotti, who is the commander of NATO forces in Europe, wants to, as reported by Al Jazeera, "bolster

Ukraine's defenses against Russia's "increasingly aggressive" posture in the east of the country and the Black Sea."

It's not as if we haven't been arming the Ukrainians for some time, but can there ever be enough?

Of course not. Also from Al Jazeera: "In the past year, the United States has already sold Javelin anti-tank missiles to Ukraine but there are 'other systems, snipers systems, ammunition' that Washington could provide to strengthen Kiev's forces, Scaparrotti told the U.S. Congress."

The general also thinks we may have to help on the water as well due to the Kerch Incident, of course. U.S. ships have a history in the Black Sea. Around August 2008, Coast Guard ships were patrolling off the coast of Georgia, as they should be. If a mayday call happens off of Savannah, they can quickly respond.

Except it was the wrong Georgia. Surely, there was a reason and no doubt a good one. As there is now.

Al Jazeera continued with the general, "Five years after Russia annexed the Crimean peninsula, Moscow 'continues to arm, train' and even 'fight alongside anti-government forces in eastern Ukraine,' said Scaparrotti, calling Moscow's activities a breach of a 2015 agreement designed to end the conflict."

"The conflict in eastern Ukraine remains hot, with numerous ceasefire violations reported weekly..."

Russia may be completely in the wrong, but they seem to be doing what we are doing, other than the fighting alongside and maybe Scaparrotti has proof. It does kind of sound like a question of motes and beams that may apply to both sides.

Or maybe it's all just a joke. On March 12, 2019, Secretary of State Michael Pompeo was the keynote speaker at CERAWeek, an annual energy conference held in Houston, Texas. Prior conferences have had U.S. presidents, secretaries of state, and energy industry leaders. Whether or not previous speakers have said anything of note is hard to say. Secretary of State Pompeo did.

> *And we all know the story in Russia. It invaded Ukraine to gain access to oil and gas reserves. It in turn deprived Ukraine of the possibility of developing those resources for itself and using its pipelines and its networks to bring energy to its own people. Rather, it uses those pipelines to put pressure—political pressure—on the people of Ukraine.*

Ukraine does have some energy resources including shale reserves, but it is more a consumer. The secretary's remarks are so off base that any conclusions one can make are not to his credit.

That Russia might in some ways be assisting the separatists is possible and understandable. To imply an all-out invasion embarrasses a man who is beyond embarrassment. Whatever was done, it was hardly another Operation Bagration.

Our whole involvement in the Ukraine as some noble action is not believable. There may be people in government who do think the mission is necessary for the security of the United States as a nation. How they contort their mind for that is something to wonder about, but then again there are still people who believe we have to be in Afghanistan.

Pompeo then goes on to speak even more bizarrely:

> *The story isn't too terribly different in Syria. Assad covets the oil fields to the east of the Euphrates River in the eastern part of the country. He wants those resources, he wants that wealth to continue to impoverish the people of Syria, and use those resources for himself and the cronies who are around him.*

The sovereign Syrian state is involved in a civil war and the eastern part of the country is recognized internationally as part of Syria. The Syrian forces have been making progress to retake all of the territory from rebels who are for the most part Islamic radicals. That they cannot take back some territory east of the Euphrates is due to our presence and support of the Kurds. The Kurds have their reasons for being in the field, but that doesn't mean they are our reasons. Pompeo was speaking at an energy group and, if anything, projecting.

But discussing Syria is a digression. Suffice it to say, there is no reason to be involved in Ukraine and a crucial reason to leave it to the locals. Russia is a nuclear state with some very powerful weapons. The leadership has not had a bad run in Syria and saw the Chechen war to settlement. They dispatched Georgia quickly while none of our adventures have had successful outcomes. Vladimir Putin will not be in charge forever, but playing nuclear poker against him and expecting him to fold at our bluff does not seem like a smart bet.

As an aside to the Ukrainians, we might look at a note from Gallup posted on March 21, 2019:

> WASHINGTON, D.C. -- *In the lead-up to the presidential election on March 31, Ukrainians go to the polls with less faith in their government than is true for any other electorate in the world. Just 9% of residents have confidence in the national government, the lowest confidence level in the world for the second straight year. This is far below the regional median for former Soviet states (48%) as well as the global average (56%) in 2018.*

Clearly, the United States and NATO don't seem to have worked wonders for the Ukrainian Nation judging from a measure of satisfaction. Of course, Ukrainians being Ukrainians, they might have still told Putin to take a hike even if they had known the outcome.

As to the recent Mueller investigation and the idea that Russia came close to deciding if not actually electing a president. That is beyond the scope of this work, more or less. Still, the drumbeat over the two years has been reminiscent of the run-up to the Iraq war when the American press and punditocracy, with few exceptions disgraced itself. Why would anyone think it is trustworthy now?

Amongst the exceptions, Professor Stephen Cohen has been stalwart. His book, *War With Russia: From Putin & Ukraine To Trump & Russiagate* is the chronology of the events of what he has referred to as Intelgate as opposed to using the term Russiagate. That members of the intel establishment were active in promoting a false narrative might be worth looking at should have occurred to the American media. It has not.

Professor Cohen has pointed out that Russia and the United States have been interfering in each other's elections for a long while. If we can catch them at it, great. Let's just not pretend we're not sinners as well.

In 2017, reporter Luke Harding's book *Collusion: Secret Meetings, Dirty Money, and How Russia Helped Donald Trump Win* came out to no little praise. The mainstream press loved it, from the gushing Michelle Goldberg in the *Times* to Terry Gross's kiss on NPR's Fresh Air, it looked like a big nail in the Trump coffin until Harding ran into a journalist as opposed to a stenographer.

Aaron Maté of the Real News Network had Mr. Harding on for an interview. He was not unfair or in any sense impolite. The problem for Harding was that he was undergoing a unique experience. Someone was asking him questions for which his pat answers were in no way sufficient. Harding seemed genuinely pained that the follow-ups were actual inquiries instead of praise.

Mr. Maté's work was so skillful that the networks immediately engaged in a bidding war for his services. Just kidding. The Real News Network is a small enterprise without a huge audience. Maté's work is off in the same ghettoized corner as Glenn Greenwald and other critics of the accepted narrative.

It is possible that Donald Trump is hand in glove with the Kremlin for some nefarious reason. Whether or not this is true, the American media is not the place to look for the truth other than by accident.

If Russiagate is the mirage its critics claim, we have lost precious time when instead of trying to make the Ukraine safe for Biden's kid we might have sought rapprochement with a nuclear power.

To this point, Professor Cohen ends his March 27, 2019, *Nation* article, "The Real Costs of Russiagate," with the following that says it all:

> *Finally, but potentially not least, the new Cold War with Russia has itself become an institution pervading American political, economic, media, and cultural life. Russiagate has made it more dangerous, more fraught with actual war, than the Cold War we survived, as I explain in War with Russia? Recall only that Russiagate allegations further demonized "Putin's Russia," thwarted Trump's necessary attempts to "cooperate with Russia" as somehow "treasonous," criminalized détente thinking and "inappropriate contacts with Russia"—in short, policies and practices that previously helped to avert nuclear war. Meanwhile, the Russiagate spectacle has caused many ordinary Russians who once admired America to now be "derisive and scornful" toward our political life.*

33

China

Up until the late 1960s the United States and The People's Republic of China (PRC) had no official or acknowledged relations. The communist regime on the mainland had been anathema to the U.S. government after they had ousted the American supported Nationalists to the offshore island of Taiwan.

China, and the other large communist state, the USSR, were drifting apart. In 1969, the two would fight along their common border. China's disdain for the capitalist running dogs of the West paled against the distrust of its ideological soul brother.

The change happened quickly and President Richard Nixon, hitherto considered a hawk on China, and his administration did not do too much to prepare the American public for the about face.

The first signal that change was in the wind was an invitation in April of 1971 from the Chinese ping-pong team. This was an understandable place to start. They didn't play our sports like football and baseball and nor would they match us in basketball. Neither of us were soccer powers. They were good at ping-pong and we didn't care about it at all, so they could get all the bragging rights and our feelings couldn't get hurt.

In July, Secretary of State Henry Kissinger would make a secret visit to China. Not long after, the United Nations would switch recognition from the Nationalist government on Taiwan and transfer the permanent Security Council seat to the People's Republic.

In February of 1972, President Nixon, the arch cold warrior and anti-communist, visited the PRC. Things had moved fast but were not going to go at the speed of light. Though relations would grow, formal recognition would not occur until 1979. There would have to be some diplomatic acrobatics, as we would still be allied with Taiwan without recognizing them.

The Reagan administration would continue the One China policy while still providing support for the Nationalists. Reagan would visit China and allow the PRC to purchase U.S. military equipment.

The climate suffered an abrupt change in 1989 with the Tiananmen Square massacre. A large number of students demonstrated in Beijing Square demanding reform and an end to corruption. The PRC government was hardly about to devolve authority to the youngsters. Mao's dictum about the origin of power was not lost on the leadership.

Troops were sent in to clear the square resulting in hundreds of deaths. The United States suspended arms sales and relations cooled.

No one should have been shocked. In Orwell's 1984, the party man, O'Brien, says the party "seeks power entirely for its own sake." Does the Chinese Communist Party as well? Maybe not, but they clearly understand what power is and the consequences of losing it.

Our next contretemps with the PRC occurred far away from China, and for that matter, the United States. It was in Serbia during the Kosovo War bombing campaign. American aircraft destroyed the Chinese embassy in Belgrade in May of 1999. Both NATO and the Clinton administration apologized for the mistake, but was it that? An October 16, 1999, *Guardian* article would call it deliberate. "According to senior military and intelligence sources in Europe and the United States, the Chinese embassy was removed from a prohibited targets list after NATO electronic intelligence (Elint) detected it sending army signals to Milosevic's forces."

Whether or not that is true, taking into consideration the denials, is an open question. How hard is it to know the location of diplomatic missions and avoid them is another, but related, question.

Despite the embassy bombing, trade relations normalized in October of 2000 as President Clinton signed the U.S.-China Relations Act of 2000. The act granted the PRC permanent normal trade with the United States. Bilateral trade would grow quickly and China would surpass Mexico as our second-biggest trading partner in 2006. The trade is big, and to get a measure of it, look at the label on your clothes.

All was not perfect. The next year, 2001, an American reconnaissance aircraft would collide with a Chinese fighter. Our plane would have to make an emergency landing on Hainan Island and would be detained over twelve days. The standoff would end with the release of the crew and President Bush expressing regret for the death of the Chinese pilot.

Other than that, relations did not seem to be going horribly even with blips. In 2007, China began increasing military spending. This occasioned then Vice President Cheney to say the buildup was "not consistent" with the country's stated goal of a "peaceful rise." True, the Chinese spending would not cause it to come near exceeding that of the United States, and would not stop China from becoming the largest creditor of the United States in 2008.

Further, in August of 2010, *Bloomberg* would report that "China surpassed Japan as the world's second-largest economy last quarter, capping the nation's three-decade rise from communist isolation to emerging superpower." Considering where it was when Nixon's opening to China occurred, the economic rise may not have been a miracle, but it was as impressive as any advance in the modern era.

As our wonderfully successful adventures in the Middle East continued, we began what became known as the "Pivot to Asia" as articulated by Hillary Clinton in 2011. It was a call for "increased investment—diplomatic, economic, strategic, and otherwise—in the Asia-Pacific region" and was seen as a move in opposition to China. As time went on, our trade deficit with the Middle Kingdom continued to grow and the United States would find that worrisome. Trade questions would continue to bother the two countries' relations more and more. Another area of contention would be the theft of technology by Chinese enterprises.

Maybe because it's called the South China Sea, China wants much of it. They have taken to doing land reclamation and building artificial islands to get as much as they can. Other countries in the region are not at all happy about the development. American surveillance in the region asserts that the Chinese are placing military equipment on the islands. In 2015, Defense Secretary Ash Carter called on the Chinese to call a halt to the land reclamation.

In April of 2017, the new U.S. administration seemed to be getting off to a good start with the Chinese regime. Donald Trump would host President Xi at his Mar-a-Lago resort. The lovefest would not continue without some bumps. The United States and China have not resolved their disagreements on trade and technological piracy.

In late 2018, the Canadian government arrested an executive of the Chinese company Huawei. The arrest was made at the request of the U.S. Justice Department. The accusation was that the executive and the company violated sanctions on Iran and committed fraud. In retaliation, China detained a couple of Canadians. China demanded the executive's release while the U.S. claimed it was an honest legal process.

The controversy is ongoing as of this writing.

The true question is, must we be confronting China? One might ask if it is not so that they are confronting us?

All nations want trade that is beneficial. True, different population segments might view it differently. Industrialists want it to benefit their enterprises; workers don't want it to cause the loss of jobs. If there is to be trade, all sides, at the very least, must get something.

America's trade with the Saudis has symbiosis in that we have access to oil and they are protected from other nations. Granted, it is not that simple, but if we went away, the Saudis would need a new friend soon.

With China, it is a bit different. When the Nixon administration opened China, we wanted a counterbalance to the Soviets and they did too. They also needed to change their economy. For us, there is no chamber of commerce member with a soul so dead that the word trade does not start him or her salivating.

Alternate history may not be a useful exercise, but sometimes it might have minimal value. Had Nixon not decided to engage China, what might have happened?

It is doubtful that the outcome in Vietnam would have been otherwise. China's economic rise might have been altered. Who knows? If there had not been a Sino-American warm-up, possibly China would have collapsed, but in any case, its rise would have been slower.

As it stands, its economy has gone from zilch to enormous. There is no choice but to consider how we deal with the Asian behemoth. The day when we can have it all our own way is long gone.

Tariffs are a two-edged sword and accommodation by both sides would be a wiser policy. Is that possible? Maybe it isn't, but if there can be no fair play with the Middle Kingdom, one would hope it would not lead to war.

China is embarking on what is called the "One Belt One Road" initiative. There are many reasons for it, but it should result in greater trade and infrastructure as well as communications all across the Eurasian landmass.

What's in it for us? Funny you should ask. Former ambassador and diplomat Charles W. Freeman, Jr. addressed the same question in a speech in 2016. The "One Belt One Road" initiative might crash and burn, but it might also become the greatest trade route in history since the Silk Road—and with an ambition to exceed it.

Freeman begins his piece by quoting Alexander the Great and citing President Eisenhower on the importance of logistics. He notes that the Chinese have exceeded our interstate system as well as rapidly building up rail transport and airports—all this within a short time span.

Freeman asks if we want to be left out. The short answer is maybe. Does America want to play if it can't run the show? Not since the end of the Soviet Union anyway.

As Mr. Freeman notes:

> *Any aspiration for indefinite U.S. global supremacy is, of course, delusional. This is not just because of the reemergence of China as the world's largest economy, though that is part of it. China's industrial economy (as opposed to "services" like financial engineering, health care, retailing, entertainment, and the like) is already almost half-again larger than that of the United States. The European Union's industrial production is about one and one-third times ours. Japan's manufacturing sector is about two-fifths the size of that here in the United States, Brazil's one-fifth, and India's one-ninth, but gaining. America is still a very large factor in global*

manufacturing but we are no longer either dominant or even remotely self-sufficient.

Do we continue to, as the cliché has it, be the world's policeman, or should we work with another bloc?

Freeman asks, "To my nationalistic American mind, a more important question is: What's in it for us? If it's going to happen anyway, how can Americans leverage it to our advantage?"

China is not a country most Americans who value such things as the First Amendment would like to live in. Their desire to control the Internet and interactions with Google have been reported in our press.

When another country doesn't share our values, problems arise—for them. Witness Iraq, Libya, and currently, Venezuela. As we confront North Korea, charging in the front door with the flash bangs and the swat team is not readily contemplated. This is due to at least some of the DPRK's weaponry being rated in kilotons.

If we are a tad circumspect as regards the North Koreans, we must be more so as regards the PRC. They have nukes, there are a lot more of them and we owe them money.

Even countries with good relationships will occasionally confront each other.

The Israeli historian, Martin Van Creveld, has written a short survey of strategy through the ages. His review of the Chinese approach to the subject is interesting. True, we must remember that they have had low points over time, but they have also had eras that could be described as golden ages.

Over the last several decades, the Chinese sage, Sun Tzu, has been read in the West. How much we get out of it may be questionable, but surely he is studied more closely in his homeland. Van Creveld notes other military authorities as well.

The Israeli scholar in discussing the archaic Chinese texts asserts reasonably that they "cannot be understood without bearing in mind the underlying way in which Chinese Culture approaches war."

> *War was neither a means in the hands of policy nor was it an end in itself. Instead it was regarded as an evil; albeit one that was sometimes made necessary by the imperfection of the world. "Weapons are instruments of ill omen," said Sun Tzu, the oldest and most famous general of all who may or may not have been a historical figure. 'However vast the state, he who takes pleasure in the military will perish' added Sun Pin, reputed to have lived a century or so after Sun Tzu and to have been the latter's direct descendant. As Wu Tzu told the Marquis of Wei in their first interview, "a ruler might not have a liking for military affairs. Still not to prepare for war was to fail in his duty—when the dead lie stiff and you grieve for them, you have not attained righteousness."*

"War is of vital importance for the state," said Sun Tzu. Therefore, "military affairs cannot be but investigated," Sun Pin concluded.

The words of Trotsky come to mind: "You may not be interested in war, but war is interested in you."

> *To the Chinese, war was both a necessary evil and a temporary departure from "cosmic harmony," or dao. By definition, dao can only be restored by dao. Hence the war will be won by the side possessing the greatest Virtue, Virtue itself being but another translation of dao. "You should cultivate your Virtue... and observe the dao of heaven says Ta'i Kung in his Opening Instructions. In general, warfare is a question of Heaven, material resources, and excellence," says Ssu-ma Ch'ien. "Appraise it [war] in terms of the five fundamental factors," says Sun Tzu. "The first of these factors is moral influence ... by moral influence I mean that which causes*

the people to be in harmony with their leaders, so that they will accompany them in life and unto death without fear of mortal peril." In the words of Sun Pin, *"engaging in a battle without righteousness, no one under heaven would be able to be solid and strong."*

Keeping in mind that the Chinese Communist Party came to power espousing Marxist doctrine, there is a question of how much ideology affected the strategic mindset of the leadership and how much of the ancient knowledge is part of their worldview.

Since 1949, after the civil war, the party has maintained itself in power over state, the army, and the people. This has required no little skill. It has known when to change, if not perfectly, well enough to maintain its position.

China is run by a communist party and government, but it is not a communist country. That a Marxist-Leninist party can do that shows an ability to rule and understand power that is second to none, or a pragmatism with ancient roots.

What is China's strategy against us? This was addressed by foreign policy analyst Michael Horton in the November/December 2018 issue of *The American Conservative*. The title of his article says it all, "Is China Waiting Us Out?"

Mr. Horton begins by stating, "The one constant in recent U.S. foreign policy—regardless of which party occupies the White House or controls Congress—is that it prioritizes military intervention, both covert and overt to advance its interests overseas. Now, this is not a surprise to anyone who has been following American affairs since before this century.

His article avers that the Chinese are taking a different tack, that is, they are doing what the title suggests. It is a policy not without wisdom, as Horton observes.

> *The election of Donald Trump gave the international community pause: Trump appeared unpredictable, eschewed tradition, and flouted convention. He might well have followed through on his promise to move the U.S. away from its long embrace of forever war. China's government in particular must have worried about such a move. If the U.S. focused on its internal problems and instead pursued a restrained foreign policy that was constructive rather than destructive, it might pose more of an impediment to China's rise to global power status.*
>
> *But the Chinese need not have worried. With a continued troop presence in Afghanistan and Syria, a looming conflict with Iran, and even talk of an intervention in Venezuela, Trump is keeping the U.S. on its perpetual wartime footing.*

Our need to be everywhere all the time running the universe is a short-term activity, but as long term policy might leave something to be desired.

The Chinese strategy, by contrast, as it were, has taken a different stance:

> *This is good news for Beijing, whose own foreign policy could not be more different. Rather than embracing a reactive and shortsighted approach that all too often ignores second- and third-order consequences, the Chinese strategy appears cautious and long-ranging. Its policymakers and technocrats think and plan in terms of decades, not months. And those plans, for now, are focused more on building than bombing.*

Is prioritizing next week over next decade wisdom? The great rise of the United States took place in the nineteenth century, an era without a huge investment in war and related war making capacity, except for the unpleasantness between the states. Granted, we did not at that time possess a government with a dirigiste policy other than tariffs. Internal improvements did happen, but they weren't considered on a grand scale as was the inter-state highway system under Eisenhower.

Now, the infrastructure deteriorates, but there are troops in hundreds of countries.

A Yemeni ex-official might not be the go to guy to quote as that country has its problems, but what he has to relate is interesting:

> A senior aide to Yemen's former minister of foreign affairs, Abu Bakr al-Qirbi, told this author just before Yemen descended into war in 2015 (that the U.S. is deeply involved in), "the Chinese think so differently than Americans. They're patient. Their first foreign policy objective is to not make too many enemies."
>
> He pointed out that the Chinese diplomats traveled around Yemen's capital and throughout the country without bodyguards. Conversely, U.S. diplomats rarely left the American embassy, and when they did, it was only in a convoy of armored vehicles with Yemeni and American bodyguards in tow.
>
> The diplomat went on to argue that China's "second objective is to learn. They have people in their embassy who know more about what is going on in parts of this country than I do. Only after learning, do they act on their third objective, which is to tie countries into their economy: resources and access in exchange for their imports and aid." He added, "it's their patience, their superior understanding of time, that will allow the Chinese to replace the U.S. as the world's superpower."

It might happen, or it might not. China has a lot of debt, and one big market. Maybe they will have internal problems and so addressing them could push their bigger goals off the timetable, or maybe our practice of short-termism leaves them in the dust?

Covid-19

Whatever governments and intelligence agencies knew about the Covid-19 virus, for the general population of the United States, it is, to use a popular term, a "black swan." Completely unpredictable, it has changed everything in this country, and one might assume, the world.

It's impact on United States/China relations is unfolding and may not be predictable, but history never ends.

There are many in American public life who want to punish China for actions and maybe lack of action that have resulted in the present situation.

The question is, what is the wisest course?

The English statesman, Lord Palmerston, opined that "Nations have no permanent friends or allies, they only have permanent interests." It is not certain whether or not the United States understands that, but the Chinese probably do. That does not mean perpetual war, but does mean pursuing what is best for the country.

Do the elite of this country have any concept of what is good for the nation as a whole? The Communist Party in China seems to have a better grasp of what serves the party and they might take that to mean the nation and state.

China is not our friend. Does that mean we have to go to war with them? That depends on what one means by war.

> As I have stated elsewhere I now consider the CCP and the Chinese government to be enemies of the U.S. that are

> engaged in an undeclared war against the Unites States. The present pandemic is merely one theater of that war.
>
> It is apparent that the CCP has sought to nurture the creation and/or development of the COVID-19 virus. To that end they used their money to infiltrate American and Canadian research facilities to enhance the capabilities of their own research facilities. Some Americans in their worship of money above all aided that infiltration.

So wrote Colonel Patrick Lang on his intel blog, *Sic Semper Tyrannis*, on April 14, 2020. Lest you think this hyperbole, it appears that on January 28, 2020, Charles Lieber, then chairman of the Department of Chemistry and Chemical Biology at Harvard University in Cambridge, Massachusetts, was arrested.

According to the colonel:

> A criminal complaint was filed supported by an affidavit. Lieber had an arrangement with the Wuhan University of Technology in Wuhan, China. The large city of around 10 million people or more is in current news stories about the SARS-CoV-2 virus. The affidavit contains considerable detail about alleged false statements Lieber made to the Department of Defense (DoD) on 24 April 2018, and to the National Institutes of Health (NIH) through Harvard on 10 January 2019–"

Further:

> "Zaosong Zheng came into the U.S. through the "J" nonimmigrant visa category, often called a J-1 visa. He had a medical degree from China, and was working in cancer research in a lab at the Harvard Medical School teaching hospital, Beth Israel Deaconess Medical Center. One of its labs is the Wenyi Wei Laboratory, where Zheng

was working. As he was preparing to leave the U.S. at Boston Logan airport, 21 vials were discovered hidden in a sock in his checked bags. He admitted that he had stolen 8 of them from the teaching hospital lab. He was first charged by a complaint supported by an affidavit, and later was formally charged by an indictment with making a false statement and trying to send material out of the country that was not properly declared and packaged—"

Also:

Yanqing Ye is a Chinese national who on 14 October 2017 entered the U.S. using a nonimmigrant J-1 visa to do research at the Department of Physics, Chemistry, and Biomedical Engineering, Center of Polymer Studies, at Boston University. It turned out that some of her research was for the People's Liberation Army (the Chinese military). She was a lieutenant in the Chinese military and a member of the Chinese Communist Party.

On 20 April 2019, she was interviewed at the Boston Logan airport by the FBI and Customs. However, she apparently was allowed to leave the country, since the Justice Department says she is in China. A criminal indictment was filed against her on 28 January 2020—"

So, the Chinese are spying on us. That should not be any surprise. We do our share of cloak and dagger stuff. What is particularly galling about this is that the U.S. intelligence agencies, and Harvard and BU were more than lackadaisical regarding the vetting process. Then again, the cool folks in Cambridge and just over the river all seem to be singing "We are the World" with some naiveté.

If we believe that we are the arbiters of world behavior, well then, enforcing good conduct on the foreign nations is inevitable. If we believe also that there is no reason to insist that American born, including those whose people who have been here a couple of generations or more, should advance in our institutions of higher learning and those who are loyal to another country should be favored, we may not expect a world shattering disease, but we cannot expect anything good.

We don't have to be seeking war across the world, but we do have to start to act like a nation that knows what its real interests are.

34

Africom

United States Africa Command (Africom)

There is a problem with Africa and China. Well, a problem with China in Africa. Is that Africom's reason for being?

It is not all that easy to discern. At the official website, there are sections and subsections, but one must search for a raison d'être such as a mission statement. After googling "Mission Statement," it was found in the "What We Do" subsection. That statement is below:

AFRICOM Mission Statement

> United States Africa Command, in concert with interagency and international partners, builds defense capabilities, responds to crisis, and deters and defeats transnational threats in order to advance U.S. national interests and promote regional security, stability, and prosperity.

"U.S. national interests" is an open-ended term that can mean many things. If it means thwarting an invasion of the homeland, well, we probably don't need a command base over there, and in fact, we really don't, as it's headquartered in Stuttgart, Germany.

Africom provides a "posture statement," a perfectly bureaucratic term that has a definition. The U.S. Army's own posture statement is defined as:

> The annual Army Posture Statement is an unclassified summary of Army roles, missions, accomplishments, plans, and programs. Designed to reinforce the Secretary and Chief of Staff of the Army posture and budget testimony before Congress, the APS serves a broad audience as a basic reference on the state of the Army.

The Africom posture statement includes:

> U.S. Africa Command Strategic Approach
>
> The successful advancement of U.S. interests in Africa is best achieved with stable nations on the continent. Accountable governments, well-trained and disciplined militaries with a respect for the rule of law and human rights, and growing economies are cornerstones to this stability. Over the past year, consistent with the updated national strategies, U.S. Africa Command revised our strategic approach to effectively strengthen our African partners by evolving our security cooperation from a focus on crisis response to capability and capacity building against our new strategic priorities: state fragility, increased involvement of China and Russia, VEO expansion, and threats to U.S. access and influence.

The statement does not emphasize China over other priorities, but on March 7, 2019, in a *Stars and Stripes* article by John Vandiver we learn:

> The United States needs higher level political engagement in Africa to counter China's growing influence even as the military cuts back troop levels on the continent, U.S. Africa Command's commander told lawmakers Thursday.

Marine Corps Gen. Thomas Waldhauser was speaking. He had more to say about China.

> *"But now as the military shifts priorities to counter powers such as Russia and China, the United States will need to elevate its political profile in Africa, where China routinely deploys high-level delegations,"* Waldhauser said.

The article continues:

> *In recent years, much of the United States focus in Africa has centered on countering violent extremism in places such as Niger, a country that military leaders have long acknowledged there is no immediate threat to the United States. Meanwhile, Beijing has invested billions to finance mineral extraction ventures, telecommunication projects, port and infrastructure deals in Africa.*

In Niger, we lost four soldiers in 2017, a place the article noted was of "no immediate threat to the United States."

So, if there is no African threat to America, the threat must be China. Indeed, that does seem to be the case, judging from a Council on Foreign Relations "Backgrounder" by Stephanie Hanson from 2007:

> *In February 2007, President Bush announced the creation of a unified military command for Africa. This puts the continent on par, in the Pentagon's eyes and command structure, with the Pacific Rim (Pacific Command), Europe (European Command), Latin America (Southern Command), the Middle East (Central Command), and North America (Northern Command). The Pentagon and many military analysts argue the continent's growing strategic importance necessitates a dedicated regional command. But some experts suggest the command's creation was motivated by more specific*

concerns: *China and oil. With Soviet influence gone and France's traditional presence much diminished, China has poured money into the continent in recent years as it jockeys for access to natural resources. And the United States is projected to import at least 25 percent of its oil from Africa by 2015, according to the National Intelligence Council.*

The Backgrounder's prediction of 25% did not come close to happening.

One assumes the Chinese are paying for the resources, or at least giving some value (e.g. building infrastructure, providing jobs, etc.) that the African nations find attractive. Is all we are doing just a military presence?

It would appear so from a February 20, 2018, New York Times piece, "'An Endless War': Why 4 U.S. Soldiers Died in a Remote African Desert." The first part of the headline, "An Endless War" is more than apt. The "Why 4 U.S. Soldiers Died in a Remote African Desert" does not give a sense of the "Why."

The article does tell us a lot about the lives of the soldiers who gave their lives. All of them come off as excellent men thus making the whole African adventure, absent a true reason for deployment, an absurd tragedy.

Actually, there is a why from the discussion and it's that the blank check of authorization for use of military force, or A.U.M.F., that said Congress authorizes the president to use "all necessary and appropriate force" against the nations, organizations or people that "he determines planned, authorized, committed, or aided" the terrorist attacks on Sept. 11 "to prevent any future acts of international terrorism against the United States by such nations, organizations, or persons."

Passed with only the dissent of Rep. Barbara Lee. The A.U.M.F. may not have been meant as the blank check by many of those who have voted for it, but is has become that.

In Africa, the A.U.M.F. is reduced to absurdity. If China is why we should be in Africa, Congress should debate that. It should be recognized that the authorization has been extended beyond a reasonable shelf life.

As to the China in Africa debate, opposing another nation just because they are there is not really a reason to have a presence on another continent, let alone to see our soldiers get killed.

35

Venezuela

It's beginning to look like regime change time in the Caribbean region. Two countries that border on that sea, Venezuela and Nicaragua, appear to be in play. One island country, Cuba, may be a possibility as time goes on

Most in the American news lately is Venezuela. The tone of the coverage is that there is a horrible government in that nation, that it should be removed, and that action is called for. In the mainstream media, that is the basic theme. It is so prevalent that a Web search has to be willing to drill down before there is much depth of coverage on Venezuela.

We have had problems with the current Venezuelan system even before Maduro became president. In 1998, Hugo Chavez was elected. He was, what else but, a reformer. As the leader of the "Bolivarian Revolution" his party instituted many reforms and alienated the United States by his choice of foreign friends.

Not all his plans worked well and his popularity plummeted. When bloodshed occurred during a protest in 2002, he was taken into custody and replaced. The chosen successor, Pedro Carmora, quickly overplayed his hand and Chavez would, after a few twists and turns, be returned to office.

It would come to light that the U.S. had its fingerprints on the action. According to a *Guardian* article on April 17, 2002:

> The White House yesterday confirmed that a few weeks before the coup attempt, administration officials met Pedro Carmona, the business leader who took over the interim government after President Hugo Chavez was arrested on Friday. But the White House press secretary, Ari Fleischer, denied that the U.S. had offered any support for a putsch.
>
> The U.S. defense department also confirmed that the Venezuelan army's chief of staff, General Lucas Romero Rincon, visited the Pentagon in December and met the assistant secretary of defense for western hemispheric affairs, Roger Pardo-Maurer.

One might fairly ask what did we know and when did we know it, but we at least knew. U.S. officials claim they were not at all supporting a coup, but, "in the conversations they had they explicitly told opposition leaders the United States would not support a coup," he added. "However, a defense department official quoted by *The New York Times* yesterday said: 'We were not discouraging people.' We were sending informal, subtle signals that we don't like this guy. We didn't say, 'No, don't you dare' and we weren't advocates saying, 'Here's some arms; we'll help you overthrow this guy.'"

Clearly, some people were being cute.

Chavez was no stranger to coups; he had led one, unsuccessfully, years before that had led to his successful election.

In mid-2019, Venezuela was still on the boil and in then National Security Advisor John Bolton's gun sights. Bolton had been a busy fellow, trying to get everyone in that country to abandon President Maduro. True, mismanaging a valuable resource (Petroleum) doesn't speak well for the Maduro administration. The popularity of the incumbent took a beating. Of course, that justifies the United States imposing sanctions and calling for the ouster of Maduro because of incompetence, just like Venezuela imposed them on us, and called for regime change here during the great recession in 2008. Well, no, they minded their own business.

Maybe what Bolton was trying to achieve is justified by the brutal police crackdown on protesters that had been going on for several months. Actually, that had been happening in France, a nation sans crude. The American press has been stalwart in its non-reporting of the yellow vest struggle among the Gauls.

Which brings us to the real point about Bolton. In a previous administration, the press was happy to criticize him. Versus Maduro, the media was happy to be his enabler. Anyone who has been following U.S. politics in this century knew that Bolton's was always gonna Bolton. There is nothing about him that has changed. The press that used to make fun of the man may not have praised him, but neither was he held to the same scrutiny he once was.

Is this the convergence of team neocon and team neoliberal? It may be, to judge by the headline from a FAIR (Fairness & Accuracy in Reporting) posting on April 30 of 2019: "Zero Percent of Elite Commentators Oppose Regime Change in Venezuela." This includes *The New York Times* and *The Washington Post*. Both papers have been more than vocal in their disdain for the administration, except on issues of foreign intervention. They never seem to mention that Maduro is the legally elected president.

Still, the unanimity is impressive. The Soviet Union needed the threat of the Gulag to enforce journalistic conformity.

At the end of the day, is meddling in an independent country in this hemisphere really going to do any good? The internal dynamics of South American countries are a mystery to all but a tiny segment of the American public. There are questions of race and class in Venezuela just as there are here. We are not close to solving them.

Whatever Maduro's faults, he is hardly the Hitler du jour. There may be reasons to cancel a vacation on Venezuela's Caribbean beaches, but there is no reason for the United States to bug the Bolivarians.

36

NATO

In looking at NATO, it might be useful to think of it in terms of if/then. If everything we, or the Soviets, believed about the other side was true, then the Cold War had to be "fought." Some, maybe more on the left, think that we might have avoided the Cold War and come to an accommodation with the Soviet Union. Others, that opposition was all that saved Europe from the yoke of totalitarian Marxism.

With current search engines, one can use resources that might find the answer to the question of necessity or choice. Failing that, at least a partisan source or sources to back up any position, pro or con.

Putting that aside, we will assume that the Cold War was inevitable whether it was necessary or not. The question is now, in the so-called post–Cold War world, is the North Atlantic Treaty Organization necessary.

Eventually, by "containing the Soviet Union" we were able to see it collapse. Now that should have been victory. We should have said to our NATO buddies, "Okay, boys and girls, we're taking of. You have a few years to work out your modus vivendi for the next millennium, but, you're on your own." How naive such a sentiment is. No, with all those bureaucrats out of work, Pentagon planners with nothing to plan, and a president who could no longer refer to himself as "Leader of the Free World" (granted, it doesn't have the ring of Dux et Imperator, but we do still pretend to be a republic; it will take a while before even "Princeps" appears). So, we had our Cold War commitment, without a cold war.

The perpetuation of the Cold War might not have happened if the United States and NATO had honored a commitment given to Mikhail Gorbachev. The Western honchos promised the Soviet leader that the alliance would not move "one inch closer" to Russia.

And, of course they kept their word. NATO did not move "one inch"; it moved millions of inches. After all, Russia was finished and done for.

What about that pledge given to Gorbachev?

This has been denied by Western leaders and others. In a 2014 Brooking Institution article by Steven Pifer, Gorbachev, the promisee himself, is quoted as buttressing the denial and making it clear what was actually given.

Time moves on and in 2017 declassified documents would come to light to show that Western leaders did promise the former general secretary that the alliance would not move the inch. In a posting at the National Security Archive website, several documents are displayed that detail what was given the last Soviet leader by everyone including George Bush the elder, James Baker, Hans-Dietrich Genscher, Helmut Kohl, Robert Gates, François Mitterrand, Margaret Thatcher, Douglas Hurd, John Major, and Manfred Woerner.

Clearly, with the way things were going, Gorbachev needed some assuring formula. The archives bear that out. If the Soviet Union had remained a going concern, at least in some form, there may have been an inclination to restrain the migration eastward.

As it was, the feeling of having Russia on the run was too difficult to resist. That might have worked if history had actually ended.

That it became apparent it had not was evinced with the passing of authority from Yeltsin to Putin. Yeltsin could end the Soviet Union, but someone else would be needed to rebuild Russia.

That man is Vladimir Putin. So far, his stewardship of Russia has seen him sail the ship of state through some choppy seas. We'll leave it to others to issue the definitive report card. Suffice it to say, the new world order was not to be ordered completely along lines dictated from near the Potomac.

The new cold war is not the same as the old face off. Maybe we could give it a new name, such as the Cold Non-Peace. Does it have to happen?

Enrolling former Warsaw pact countries up to and past the borders of the old Soviet Union can only be considered provocative to the Kremlin. The question for us in the West is, why shouldn't we also think of this as provocative?. Even more so, should we not ask, not just should NATO have added members, but should NATO still exist at all and should the United States not withdraw?

One could posit a world where membership in NATO is an absolute necessity. Vladimir Putin is portrayed in the American media as a bit of an evil superman even to possibly controlling our elections. What could happen if the United States withdrew from NATO?

Let us look at a worst-case scenario. The Russian president tells Sergey Shoygu, the minister of defense, to get to work with the battle plan to end any threat to the Russian nation forever. The chiefs of staff of all services work together to come up with a plan.

The strategy to be executed will have the Russian tank steamroller head west and drive hard in a surprise attack. The European defenses are a joke, as they were without the United State providing the backbone. The tanks are taking a southerly route, but that is a ruse.

Just as they reach the Franco-German border they head north and meet the fleet at the channel ports and in a deft maneuver cross over and seize the British Navy as they are also taking the French ships.

The planning has been flawless so far, but the worst is yet to happen. Russia has been training far more sailors than necessary for peacetime duty. Their course of study has been on how to use French or British ships. Boarding the captured vessels, the Atlantic is crossed in record time and landfall is made on Cape Cod, Cape Ann, and Cape May. Pausing only to gorge themselves on fried clams, they move West after every clam shack is out of product.

It has all been a shock and the collapse of the U.S. Army is complete.

Now, no one other than Rachel Maddow is capable of believing in the possibility of this scenario. Assuming the logistics were not impossible, a big if, nuclear weapons would have been unleashed at the very least tactically.

NATO has been aggressive by enrolling new members eastward, but we should be aware, that if pushed too far, Russia would see no choice but to respond with such weapons as well.

Is there a more reasonable scenario should the United States retreat across the water from the Old World?

Maybe nothing happens. Without the largesse of Uncle Sam, accession of Georgia and Ukraine would not be considered all that smart, not that it really is anyway. Hydrocarbons would be a factor in the desirability of getting along with Russia. Moderation of all parties works for everyone.

It would make sense in light of the history of the twentieth century. In a perfect world, that would be true. History may not actually repeat, but it seems so as the lessons of the past are often forgotten by another generation.

Historians suggest Russia, with few natural boundaries, seeks security by dominating other countries. Is that true and unique? Russia dominated much of Poland in centuries past. Was it the result of a conquering army crushing a nation?

Not exactly. True, there was some military activity, but Poland and Lithuania were carved up in partitions with two other accreting powers, Austria and Prussia.

The Baltic states were incorporated, but they weren't about to be free in the same way most other Europeans from smaller states were not such as the Slovenes and Croats, Bohemians and Slovaks, Catalans and Basques. The Brits took over all of the area of the islands until the Irish got back less than they deserved by their own efforts.

Need one mention Manifest Destiny? Maybe dominating neighbors is a Russian thing, but it is at least arguable that it is in the same way for others. After all, the Soviet domination of Poland came after a German conquest.

One can make many cases for Uncle Sam being the watchdog on Russia, but aren't most rationalizations for us doing what we want to do and Europe wanting us to do it?

In *The Nation*, James Carden, of the American Committee for East-West Accord, wrote of a warning not heeded:

> In an open letter to the Clinton administration in June 1997, dozens of high-ranking former policy-makers and diplomats, including Senators Bill Bradley, Gary Hart, and Sam Nunn; Paul H. Nitze, Ambassador Jack Matlock, and Defense Secretary Robert McNamara, warned that "NATO expansion is neither necessary nor desirable and that this ill-conceived policy can and should be put on hold."

Carden further notes:

> The diplomat-scholar George F. Kennan also foresaw trouble. Writing just after the New Year in 1997, Kennan

predicted that "the Russians will not react wisely and moderately to the decision of NATO to extend its boundaries to the Russian frontiers' For Kennan, the decision was 'the greatest mistake of the entire post–Cold War period."

"Time has proven the skeptics correct."

Carden ends his article by deeming NATO expansion as "largely responsible" for the dangerous situation.

Who can disagree? We had a passel of buffer states and now there is permanent confrontation.

We got into a century of trouble when Woodrow Wilson joined the Great War. We should declare World War I over and leave the Old World to the Old World.

There is an even bigger reason to just say au revoir to NATO, if political analyst Gilbert Doctorow is right. The alliance is... meaningless.

According to Doctorow, at its seventieth birthday NATO is militarily America's fifth wheel. He makes the case that NATO is so far behind the United States in technological capability that it is irrelevant. According to Doctorow:

> The real gap is a technological gap which the United States has opened up and continues to widen at present, leaving the Europeans to understand that they all are nothing more than a 'fifth wheel' militarily, or, at best, a tool kit to be used to pick up additional competences in variable geography alliances to confront challenges that the United States defines unilaterally and without consultation. This is so, because the cutting-edge technologies which the United States is developing for its war machine are so far ahead of anything Europe has or will have that the underlying military principle of the Alliance these past 70 years, interoperability of the forces

from the various national entities, is no longer feasible across the board.

The writer quotes a USN officer as to what this might mean:

A big problem is at the operational level. There is too big a gap. As one U.S. Rear Admiral remarked back in 1998, if a friend or ally is operating without the specific tactical communications link, they get in the way and may be shot down by friendly fire.

So, if the Europeans are just in the way, what happens then?

We are in the age of Great Power politics, when there are only three Sovereign States in the world capable of conducting independent foreign and military policies, namely the United States, Russia and China. On their own, and even in combination with the United States, the European member states of NATO count for nothing. It is interesting to see that here in Belgium at the very heart of the NATO organization that reality is now spoken about in public by professionals who know the score.

The United States, Russia, and China sounds a lot like Oceania, Eurasia, and Eastasia in a book submitted to the publisher in 1948 that came out in 1949. It caused a bit of a splash for several decades. Nevertheless, only three superpowers have some relevance currently.

Europe in NATO could still start a war they might not want, though at this point in time, the United States seems more likely to find a war to drag the allies into. Yes, leaving NATO means they might have to come to terms with Russia not from a position of great strength. But that should not be our problem.

37

The Press and the Punditocracy

The American press has a long history of cheerleading for war. The rise of mass media would see support for foreign adventures. Famous are the words of William Randolph Hearst when his man in Cuba, Frederic Remington, found too much tranquility to promote conflict. Hearst told him, "You furnish the pictures and I'll furnish the war."

Sometimes the working press just doesn't do much work. Those who came of age and were aware before the First Gulf War may remember the testimony of Nayirah before the Congressional Human Rights Caucus. The young lady told a tale of how the Iraqi invaders of Kuwait took babies out of incubators in a Kuwaiti hospital and then stole the incubators while leaving the babies to die.

It was emotional and compelling testimony and a lie.

Nayirah, it turned out, was the daughter of the Kuwaiti ambassador and part of a PR campaign orchestrated by the firm of Hill and Knowlton. The credulous media didn't ask too many questions and the assertion was widely disseminated, being cited by the president several times.

That the press didn't get overly excited about Nayirah and the expensive firm that was pushing for war shouldn't surprise anyone. The Fourth Estate has a record to uphold of being propagandist for one crusade or another.

After September 11, 2001, it would be easy for a president to ask for and receive authorization for any action to go after the perpetrators of the crime of that day. Though there is no proof that the Taliban played a part, they sheltered the man who claimed credit. Whether or not destroying the Taliban state in Afghanistan was the wisest course of action, it was understandable.

The Second Gulf War was another matter entirely. If ever there were a time to push for a war of choice, a couple of years after the destruction of the Twin Towers would be it. The president, by having, so it seemed, successfully removed the Taliban from Afghanistan, had a lot of political capital to spend.

Still, the case for an invasion was nowhere near a "slam dunk" as George Tennant put it. Fortunately, for the administration of Bush *fils*, there was a corps of intellectuals, journalists, and hacks willing and eager to push for war.

The cheerleaders would be willing to abase themselves, but no one would outdo David Frum. He came up with the phrase "Axis of Evil" to condemn Iraq, Iran, and North Korea. Though there may have been arms trade and oil sales between Iran and North Korea, there was hardly a strategic alliance. Iran and Iraq had fought a long war and there was no love lost.

Frum's little turn of phrase is in a league by itself for misleading State of the Union rhetoric. One would think he would have taken to a hermitage, but no, he still writes and more surprising, *The Atlantic* publishes him. Well, maybe that is not so surprising.

The war would come and the reasons for it turned out to be wrong. The members of the chorus should have been completely disgraced. That, however, did not happen. The term that best describes what became of the stalwarts who promoted the invasion of Iraq is "failing upwards." Many of them still infest the airwaves and overthink in foundations and what should only laughingly be referred to as "think" tanks. It almost seems that to have been wrong about Iraq was a good career move.

Is there no humility amongst the wrong thinkers? There is, but not much.

Peter Beinart stands out for suggesting that maybe there was something to answer for. Beinart is a widely published journalist and author. He was an ardent supporter of the invasion of Iraq, but came to see it as a tragic mistake. In this he was much earlier than most as he arrived at the conclusion by 2006.

In a June 18, 2014, *Atlantic* article, "Even Iraq's Sinners Deserve to Be Heard," Beinart opines the war hawks do need to come clean,

> *Doves are right that when offering their views on the foreign-policy topic du jour, pundits should be confronted with the views they offered in the past, especially when discussing the same country. Simply knowing such questions were coming, I suspect, would make folks like Kristol, Paul Wolfowitz, Paul Bremer, and Dick Cheney—all of whom have publicly criticized Obama's Mideast policies in recent weeks—think twice before accepting interview requests. It's certainly had that effect on me.*

Mr. Beinart's stance is fair and correct, and oddly for the scrivener class, humble. The questions need to be severe as what happened in Iraq cost the lives of American soldiers and Iraqi citizens and made a mess of the country. It also made the position of Iran much stronger. Iran is the current worst country we can think of, as more than a few pundits are happy to go on about.

Never have so many been so wrong about so much.

So, of whom should we ask questions? It is not enough that they have already said they are sorry. They have to tell us why they made the mistake and why should the public think their current reasoning is better.

There are many more than the quartet mentioned by Mr. Beinart. George Will comes to mind. Always measured in what he writes or says, Will gives the appearance of gravitas in print or on TV. That does not mean he wasn't ridiculous.

He was a cheerleader for the war, albeit with the dignified voice of a sage. Somber tones did not make his remarks in any way meaningful and hindsight reveals a propagandist. His "Iraq War May Save Lives" commentary at ABC News of March 16, 2003, easily makes that point. Citing Walter Russell Mead, a less famous deep thinker, he agrees that containment would cost more Iraqi lives than war. It had the flavor of "let's run this up the flagpole and see if anyone salutes."

That is not Will at his worst. In an October 8, 2002, interview with Charlie Rose, Will's words betray either a deep naiveté or a man who is an active shill,

> I think the answer is that we believe, with reason, that democracy's infectious. We've seen it. We saw it happen in Eastern Europe. It's just—people reached a critical mass of mendacity under those regimes of the East bloc, and it exploded. And I do believe that you will see [in the Middle East] a ripple effect, a happy domino effect, if you will, of democracy knocking over these medieval tyrannies . . . Condoleezza Rice is quite right. She says there is an enormous condescension in saying that somehow the Arab world is just not up to democracy. And there's an enormous ahistorical error when people say, "Well, we can't go into war with Iraq until we know what postwar Iraq's going to look like." In 1942, a year after Pearl Harbor, did we have a clear idea what we were going to do with postwar Germany? With postwar Japan? Of course not. We made it up as we went along, and we did a very good job.

Leaving aside that comparing Japan and Eastern Europe with Iraq was a stretch, Will was calling for war on spec that we could do well by the Iraqi people because that is what we did elsewhere. It was cute and wrong.

Since, Will, who is well able to tell which way the wind is blowing, has seen the light. Not one to defend an untenable position, the man is happy to point out the war was a mistake, and some of his writings about the error seem dead on. Illuminating the problem now that a bright light is shining is not hard to do.

Will is happy to not mention how he was able to be so wrong. This should give us all pause when he pontificates about foreign policy, which would seem impossible for him to not do.

Like Beinart, he should be ready to answer.

There are some targets so easy that one almost feels bad pointing them out. Sean Hannity was a fervent backer of the war. On his February 19, 2003, show with Alan Colmes he was confident "We're going to find all the weapons of mass destruction."

One can only admire Hannity. He doesn't shrink from proclaiming that we did the right thing even now. On his radio show, as recently as September 7, 2016, Sean tells us, "I was a real believer in the Iraq War. I still am to this day. I still feel that there were probably weapons of mass destruction. I do believe they were likely moved to Syria in the long lead-up to the war."

Using the word "feel" is probably as appropriate as he can get, as there is no evidence to back up the position. Unlike OJ promising to spend the rest of his life looking for Nicole's killer, Sean has not vowed to find WMD to back up his perception. After all, even his fellow warmongers have abandoned that position.

His now-departed mate at Fox, Bill O'Reilly, also wanted war. In the afternoons, while he still had his ill-fated radio program, one could hear him promote it at length. The man did say he would apologize if the casus belli were not found.

To his credit, O'Reilly proved as good as his word. When confronted on *Good Morning America* by host Charles Gibson, he said, "Well, my analysis was wrong and I'm sorry." Bill also came to the conclusion, "I am much more skeptical of the Bush administration now than I was at the time."

O'Reilly called out the intelligence community: "I don't think there's any doubt about that George W. Bush wanted to remove Saddam. And in history, I believe that will be a good thing. ... But I think every American should be very concerned, for their families and themselves, that our intelligence isn't as good as it should be."

How Mr. Beinart would rate the mea culpa is hard to say, but for a right-of-center talker, it wasn't bad.

One of the cheerleaders has survived and though an object of scorn to many did get back into government for a mercifully short time. John Bolton seems a caricature not merely for his mustache that supposedly put Trump off.

The man is well rounded, that is, if having been in think tanks and on radio as well as government qualifies. One spot the proponent of war avoided was actual service in the regular army. During Vietnam, he joined the National Guard rather than be drafted writing later, "I confess I had no desire to die in a Southeast Asian rice paddy. I considered the war in Vietnam already lost."

Bolton was ahead of his time considering his desire for an Iraqi invasion went back to 1998. He was a signatory on a letter from the Neocon group Project for a New American Century urging President Clinton to attack Saddam.

He supported the Iraq War from inside the government, as Under Secretary of State for Arms Control and International

Security Affairs from May 11, 2001, until July 31, 2005. Bolton supported the contention that Saddam Hussein sought uranium in Africa. "We are confident that Saddam Hussein has hidden weapons of mass destruction and production facilities in Iraq."

Though proven wrong about WMD he has not changed his opinion of the war, "I still think the decision to overthrow Saddam was correct …. You can't assume if he had stayed in power, sweetness and light would prevail in the Middle East today."

As if anyone was suggesting sweetness and light would prevail, but what's a strawman among neocons now and again.

The man has done well in his failing upward. He would become ambassador to the United Nations and after that was a Fox contributor, and was part of the Trump administration as National Security Advisor. If there was ever an American to whom Talleyrand's words about the Bourbons apply, it is Bolton: "They learn nothing, and they forget nothing." Well, at least the first part.

Not all the cheerleaders were to the right. Bill Keller was a columnist and editor for *The New York Times*. That usually means a standard liberal, and it did. Nevertheless, *les gens à gauche* can be pro-war too as Keller noted when he wrote, "I christened an imaginary association of pundits the I-Can't-Believe-I'm-a-Hawk Club, made up of liberals for whom 9/11 had stirred a fresh willingness to employ American might."

The quote above is from a column, "My Unfinished 9/11 Business," where Mr. Keller looks back at the decade of war and his part in it all. It's not bad.

The article is wide ranging and goes over where he should have known better, even if that was not always what he meant. As an honest account, and it seems so, it does allow one to ask, would Keller allow himself to be snookered again.

One of Keller's hawk list members was Richard Cohen of *The Washington Post*. He got on the bandwagon with gusto.

After Secretary of State Colin Powell's UN speech in New York, Cohen wrote:

> The evidence he presented to the United Nations—some of it circumstantial, some of it absolutely bone-chilling in its detail—had to prove to anyone that Iraq not only hasn't accounted for its weapons of mass destruction but without a doubt still retains them. Only a fool—or possibly a Frenchman—could conclude otherwise.

Cohen bought it all.

He would later say more about his reasons for supporting the invasion

> We are a good country, attempting to do a good thing. In a post-Sept. 11 world, I thought the prudent use of violence could be therapeutic. The United States had the power to change things for the better, and those who would do the changing—the fighting—were, after all, volunteers. This mattered to me.

Richard, next time you need therapy, book a session.

He now thinks the average GI has a right to feel duped by Bush, Vice President Cheney, and others. "The exaggerations are particularly repellent. To fool someone into sacrificing his life to battle a chimera is a hideous abuse of the public trust."

Well, Richard, you too were an easy dupe.

Another member of the hawk club was Andrew Sullivan. Sullivan is kind of all over the place. Once an editor at *The New Republic*, he is a self-described conservative. The man is published in all the correct outlets.

In the run-up to the Iraq war, Sullivan fell hard for the hoax. When anthrax was delivered to Senator Daschle's office,

Sullivan said it meant "a refusal to extend the war to Iraq is not even an option."

Those of the author's demographic are generally skeptical and tend toward outright cynicism where the pronouncements and policies of government are concerned. They know they are the governed.

Keller, and the others, are men of influence and used to having their phone calls returned by important people. Though not officially part of the government, it is not called the Fourth Estate for nothing. When he is swayed, or allows himself to be swayed, he takes a lot of folks with him.

Hard to classify as liberal or conservative, Robert Kaplan is an imperialist and sees that as benign, if not beneficent.

Kaplan had his part in the biggest U.S. failure of the new millennium to date. He "participated in a secret meeting convened by then Deputy Secretary of Defense Paul Wolfowitz," and "helped draft an internal government document advocating the invasion of Iraq."

To his credit, Kaplan admitted to the error and to deep remorse. That has not led to anyone thinking maybe Bob's not the heavy hitter we thought. He is still published in *The Atlantic* and was Chief Geopolitical Analyst at Stratfor, which if past is prologue, meant the guy in charge of getting it wrong.

Like Bolton, he too is Bourbonesque. In 2014, it was as if he wanted to show the world what he had not learned.

In a July 9 piece that year that appeared originally at *Stratfor*, we learned that Robert Kaplan was worried about Moldova. He didn't come out and say it, but it almost felt like he was going to do a full-on McCain and claim "We're all Moldovans now."

The place sounds like a mess. The article "Why Moldova Urgently Matters" certainly makes one think that the denizens of that god-awful spot, as Kaplan describes it, have a reason to care. Bob didn't really tell us why the United States should.

He opened by quoting Iulian Fota, Romania's presidential national security adviser, that "NATO's Article 5 offers little protection against Vladimir Putin's Russia." Well, that's worrisome. After all, Romania is a NATO member. Was Putin, fresh from not invading Ukraine, about to send his divisions to Bucharest? Not to worry, it is a subversion the Dacians have to fret. You know, the stuff Victoria Nuland was caught doing red handed.

And, what is that subversive threat Mr. Kaplan was worried about? Why it's "intelligence activities, the running of criminal networks, the buying-up of banks and other strategic assets, and indirect control of media organs to undermine public opinion." That's the usual stuff big powers engage in. Ah, but those sinister Russkies take it a step further: "Article 5 does not protect Eastern Europe against reliance on Russian energy." Romania itself has hydrocarbons, but somehow, it's a problem to worry about.

Yeah, but wasn't this about Moldova? Sure, but let's let Bob finish up with the Romanians. They know just how evil Vlad the non-Impaler is: "Putin's Russia will not fight conventionally for territory in the former satellite states, but unconventionally for hearts and minds." What a dirty fighter.

He did get to Moldova and was convinced that it's a wreck. So, what to do? Can Bob guide us? From what he wrote, one should not be confident: "I am not here providing a fully fleshed-out policy toward Moldova or the other states facing Russia. I am saying only that there are incalculable human costs to Western inaction. And Western action must mean a whole-of-government approach—political, intelligence, economics and so forth—in order to counter what the Russians are doing."

Should we listen to Bob? He made a big splash in a 1994 *Atlantic* article, "The Coming Anarchy." Kaplan's writes well and convincingly. The article starts off by telling us that Africa is going to hell in a handbasket. Twenty years on, the Dark Continent still has problems, but hasn't rotted on any schedule a reader of the article would have anticipated. Your man has made a cottage industry of books and articles about sad places.

Still contributing to the *Atlantic*, his April 2014 "In Defense of Empire" waxes poetic about being under an Imperium: "Throughout history, governance and relative safety have most often been provided by empires." Bob does not mention the most salient fact about empires: they all die. Notice we don't currently exchange ambassadors with Imperial Rome or the Sublime Porte.

Robert Kaplan has written other essays and his "Art of Avoiding War" in 2015 is an improvement. Still, his willingness to suggest we get involved in the nowheresville of Moldova causes us to ask what he learned from Iraq.

Transition is a popular term these days. One of the more well-known Iraq war proponents has transitioned away from conservatism. Actually, he has never been what could be called a conservative. Max Boot was a neoconservative and kind of still is, in that much of the Democratic Party is looking at some common enemies.

Boot was a huge supporter of the Iraq war even before we had chased Osama out of Afghanistan. He wrote "The Case for American Empire" in *The Weekly Standard* on October 15, 2001, that:

> Once Afghanistan has been dealt with, America should turn its attention to Iraq. It will probably not be possible to remove Saddam quickly without a U.S. invasion and occupation—though it will hardly require half a million men, since Saddam's army is much diminished since the Gulf War, and we will probably have plenty of help from Iraqis, once they trust that we intend to finish the job this time. Once we have deposed Saddam, we can impose an

American-led, international regency in Baghdad, to go along with the one in Kabul. With American seriousness and credibility thus restored, we will enjoy fruitful cooperation from the region's many opportunists, who will show a newfound eagerness to be helpful in our larger task of rolling up the international terror network that threatens us. Over the years, America has earned opprobrium in the Arab world for its realpolitik backing of repressive dictators like Hosni Mubarak and the Saudi royal family. This could be the chance to right the scales, to establish the first Arab democracy, and to show the Arab people that America is as committed to freedom for them as we were for the people of Eastern Europe. To turn Iraq into a beacon of hope for the oppressed peoples of the Middle East: Now that would be a historic war aim. Is this an ambitious agenda? Without a doubt.

It was not only ambitious, it was wrong. Did Boot repent and realize where he went wrong? No and yes.

Boot did not try to do a Bolton and claim that the WMD went to Syria, but would not admit error readily.

In a December 2011 Council on Foreign Relations "expert roundup" titled "Was the Iraq War Worth It?" he gave his opinion that there was hope, but regretted not leaving troops there.

In *Commentary* of March 2013, he boldly published "No Need to Repent for Support of Iraq War."

With the rise of Trump, Boot has become a new man, or a different man or something. He seems to be against most of what he had been previously ardent for. He now regrets Iraq and his part in it. Of course, the question is, why did it take you so long? There is an answer.

Had Jeb been nominated and gracefully lost to Hillary, Max would probably still be on Team Conservative. It is his Trump hatred that fuels flight away from the Republican Party.

Whether or not his old adversaries will love him, he will not have to get on the peace train. Sooner or later, when the push for war with Russia gets going, he can jump on board from his perch at *The Washington Post.*

Boot has much to answer for but after his day late and a dollar short conversion, he should never be taken seriously.

An interesting aspect of those who passionately wanted war is that few of them have actually served. Not only that, their offspring usually go to the right schools, and basic training isn't part of it.

One exception among them is Bill Kristol. No, he did not serve. Can anyone ever think it possible that he would enjoy breaking bread in an enlisted mess? Unless commissioned a colonel at the outset and lecturing at a war college, it would not be his style.

However, rare among the chattering class, his son, Joseph, is a Marine veteran having served in Afghanistan. He stands out from that crowd, at least for that.

There are many more, left and right that caught war fever. It would be tiresome to go over the complete list and excess to name such media stars like Ann Coulter and Rush Limbaugh and their part. Suffice it to say that in a time when a major newspaper has the legend Democracy Dies in Darkness on its masthead, it might reflect on its own role in not spreading light along with the rest of the media and pundits in the run-up to the Iraq War.

As the phenomenon of failing upward is verifiable just by turning on the TV and seeing the same old talkers who got it so wrong all the time, could there be something called succeeding downward?

It happened to Scott Ritter. Ritter, a complicated man, was right on the Iraq war. Much of Ritter's descent was due to his prosecution. Ritter would serve time for crimes for which he has steadfastly denied guilt.

In much of the New England region, one can receive the broadcasts of several NPR stations. The coverage seems much more in depth than most commercial radio. Nevertheless, in the buildup to Iraq, though sounding less strident, it was not off message.

The exception was WAMC in upstate New York. To his credit, Alan Chartock, the man who has long been at the station's helm, would have Ritter on the air warning against the rush to war. This took some courage as his guest's legal problems had become known.

Since the war on Iraq, Ritter has published articles and books. He is not seen as much as others in big media, and one could explain that as due to his arrests and convictions, but it can also be because he is not on the team. He is neither for the next war on Iran nor does he see the Russia bogeyman. Able to see the emperor has no clothes, whatever else he does.

WAMC has been a bit of a disappointment since their Iraq stance. Monitoring the station, not too much so we may be in error, one hears little skepticism about the current neocon policies. Whether or not that was due to the fervent opposition to President Trump or the feeling of why beat a dead horse is anyone's guess. The new president is hardly gotten on a peace train. It is good to have an alternative to what thinks of itself as an alternative. The silence on the matter is a loss.

Most of the groups that oppose the interventionist foreign policy, Antiwar.com, *Democracy Now*, and the few others, are small potatoes and out in the wilderness. Even so, there is little real support for our robust foreign policy despite the pervasive worry about how Russia is supposedly rampaging in Ukraine and the menace of an Iran constantly on the verge of becoming a nuclear power.

The support is declining possibly because the bankruptcy of the policy is becoming obvious. To quote William S. Lind of *traditionalRIGHT*:

> Both the U.S. Army and the Marine Corps are failing to meet their recruiting and end-strength goals. One obvious reason is the hot economy, which offers plenty of jobs. A less obvious cause, mentioned to me by a friend in the National Guard, is the effect on recruiting of the endless television ads about "wounded warriors." These ads bring home to young men the unpleasant reality that joining the military can lead to life-changing injuries.

All too many know of someone walking with skill on an artificial limb. Lind then notes:

> A third cause is the endless, pointless wars we continue to pursue in the Middle East and Afghanistan. Whatever the initial rationale for these conflicts was, most people have since forgotten it, including both the decision-makers in Washington and the young men in the recruiting pool. Who wants to sign up to fight halfway around the world for a cause no one can remember?

Ask the next person you meet, How is an American soldier in Afghanistan keeping us free? Like as not, even a supporter will draw a blank.

L'état has not given up on war even if there are less willing potential enlistees to take the shilling. A good economy and a dwindling pool of recruits mean more creativity in finding new troops. *The Washington Times* of July 18, 2019, reports "Military eyes 16-year-olds as ranks and candidates dwindle." A couple of days later, the same paper headlined, "'Hyperfit' women intrigue U.S. military." Helen Reddy can only be considered a prophetess.

Are the people getting it? One might think so. After all the propaganda to sell Iraq, that anyone would believe the mainstream media without question should be a shock.

This is a problem as far as a man who was one of the most ardent Iraq hawks is concerned. That we don't want to be the world's cop doesn't smell right to David Brooks. His July 14, 2019, column at *The New York Times*, "Voters, Your Foreign Policy Views Stinks!", drips with elite condescension. He starts off with:

> Most of human history has been marked by war. Between 1500 and 1945, scarcely a year went by without some great power fighting another great power. Then, in 1945 that stopped. The number of battlefield deaths has plummeted to the lowest levels in history. The world has experienced the greatest reduction in poverty in history, as well as the greatest spread of democracy and freedom.

True, but it leaves out some other facts. It has not been an era of peace. The spread of democracy and freedom has a number of misfires including the Korean War, the Vietnam War, two Gulf wars, the Afghanistan War, and side shows such as Panama and Grenada. The bombing of Serbia was in there somewhere. Two wars are ongoing and we have troops uninvited in a sovereign country (Syria) doing something murky. Our fingerprints are on the mess that is Libya.

The foul scent emanating from Mr. Brooks's foreign policy is one of war and more war. If we bug out, there may be war, but if we don't bug out there will be war.

Brooks has a gig on NPR where he does an Alphonse and Gaston act with E.J Dionne or Mark Shields. Dionne or Shields is the progressive and Brooks is the neocon kind of mostly agreeing with E.J. or Mark. What's the point?

Not all the media people supporting our zombie foreign policy are elite stars. Some make the effort locally. In Western

Massachusetts, radio station WHMP is, like most of the Pioneer Valley, to the left. Bill Newman fits in and has a program. He also does a weekly "Civil Liberties Minute." Below is a transcript of May 14, 2019 broadcast:

> *For listeners who may be squeamish about violence you should turn off this civil liberties moment now, really right now. Because today we are focusing on systemic horrifying violations of international law inflicted by the Syrian dictator its president Bashar al Assad. Assad's imprisonment and torture system has thrown hundreds of thousands maybe a million people suspected of insufficient political loyalty into prisons to be tortured and denigrated and killed. Some examples, a protester a teenager was detained by the Syrian security forces and thrown into prison. Where he was doused with fuel and set on fire. The boy languished for days and then died. A civil rights attorney who cited the Syrian law about a fair trial to a judge was thrown behind bars blindfolded, handcuffed, stripped naked, not allowed to sleep, deprived of water for days and forced to drink his urine. Prisoners are hung from cell walls. A prisoner who complains of hunger is dragged to a toilet and then his mouth is stuffed with excrement. And women are routinely raped and then thrown into cells only large enough for them to stand up, a cell without a toilet. These kinds of stories from Syria are not new, but they have recently been reported again on the front page of the New York Times and on PBS and yet and still governments are complacent and complicit and the world sleeps. The civil liberties minute is made possible by the ACLU, because freedom can't protect itself.*

His delivery was dramatic, but again, what was the point? Was he campaigning for greater involvement in the war in

Syria? Was he supporting the rebels, and if they won did he expect all governmental mistreatment of citizens to end?

Another question is, Why did he trust his sources? His speech did seem to depend on a May 11, 2019, *New York Times* article by Anne Barnard, "Inside Syria's Secret Torture Prisons: How Bashar al-Assad Crushed Dissent." Anne relies heavily on the Syrian Network for Human Rights (SNHR). The organization portrays itself as independent and neutral.

That may not be so. Not to question all the shoe leather expended in Syria by Ms. Barnard, but according to the *Grayzone*'s Max Blumenthal on June 14 of the same year, "the Syrian Network for Human Rights is far from the impartial arbiter that it has been sold as. In reality, it is a key player in the Syrian opposition. Currently based in Qatar, SNHR is funded by foreign governments and staffed by top opposition leaders."

Blumenthal and *Grayzone* are not at all portraying Assad as a gentle nice guy. They don't survive in the Middle East. The question is, What is the agenda of the SNHR and how honest is their reporting?

According to *Grayzone*:

> In a typically slanted report in 2017, SNHR claimed that the Syrian government was responsible for over 92 percent of all deaths during the conflict. Meanwhile, the group reported that "extremist Islamic groups" like ISIS and al-Qaeda's local franchise were responsible for less than two percent of those killed. As usual, the organization provided nothing to back up its absurd numbers other than a cartoon graph.

Who knows? Maybe Max and the *Grayzone* are absolutely wrong, but what is obvious is there is another side to the story, and as Newman did little more than distill the *Times* piece without even mentioning the possibility. Thus, his minute (actually a minute and a half) was little more than shouted stenography.

It is no fun to pick on Newman. He has been championing Edward Snowden and many progressives haven't been much on the radar in the cause of privacy. Still, one wishes he had not been so credulous.

To finish off the discussion, we have a man who has provided no little entertainment. Max Fisher at Vox, which is reliably left and pitched to those who think themselves youngish and cool, seemed to be on the Russia/Putin beat. It may have been a case of misreading the man, but it could be assumed he was not pro-Russia judging by the headlines of his pieces that started in 2014. It is hard not to consider that Russia is almost a Fourth Reich from his article titles:

"Why Putin is doomed to fail in Syria" – October 1, 2015

"Russia is invading Ukraine. How do we know? Russian troops' selfies, among other things" – June 17, 2015

"Is Russia about to invade Ukraine?" – May 28, 2015

"This quote about Putin's machismo from Angela Merkel is just devastating" – May 20, 2015

"Former Russian general: Russia will defend eastern Ukraine, even if it means taking Kiev" – May 7, 2015

"US troops just paraded along the Russian border. Is that as insane as it sounds? – February 26, 2015

"The Ukraine peace deal is great news for Putin and a disaster for Ukraine" – February 13, 2015

"Russia is starting to use the same line on Baltic countries that it used to invade Ukraine" – October 1, 2014

"Everything you need to know about the Ukraine crisis" – September 3, 2014

"A complete guide to Russia's war with Ukraine" – September 3, 2014

"Why Russia is invading Ukraine, in 2 minutes" – September 2, 2014

"Russia's army gets even more brazen about Ukraine" – August 30, 2014

"Why no one will call Russia's invasion an invasion" – August 30, 2014

"How Putin backed himself into invading Ukraine" – August 29, 2014

"The cold, crazy logic of Putin's Ukraine invasion" – August 29, 2014

"The very scary word in Putin's Ukraine statement" – August 28, 2014

"Video shows Russian tanks in Ukraine" – August 28, 2014

"Satellite images show Russia invading Ukraine" – August 28, 2014

"Let's be clear on this: Russia is invading Ukraine" – August 27, 2014

Not sure the list is all-inclusive, but over-the-top would not be amiss as a theme. Still, we should be generous. One has to wonder if *Vox* required him to be constantly anti-Russian as some of the above articles plumbed the depth of silliness.

If a prize were to be given out for the dizziest example, the trophy would be: "This quote about Putin's machismo from Angela Merkel is just devastating" from May 20, 2015.

Despite the date of the article, the reported incident occurred in 2007. Meeting Merkel in Sochi, "Putin, surely aware of Merkel's well-known fear of dogs, waited until the press gathered in the room, then called for his black Labrador to be sent in. The Russian president watched in unconcealed glee as the dog sniffed at Merkel, who sat frozen in fear."

According to Max, Merkel would get her own back. "Later, in discussing the incident with a group of reporters, Merkel attempted an explanation of Putin's behavior. Her quote, reported in George Packer's December 2014 profile of Merkel in *The New Yorker*, is one of the most pithily succinct insights into Putin and the psychology of his 14-year reign that I have read."

Angela said: "I understand why he has to do this—to prove he's a man," Merkel said. "He's afraid of his own weakness. Russia has nothing, no successful politics or economy. All they have is this."

Oh, no. No mere human being, let alone head of state could recover from such devastation. Junior high schools are now middle schools, but back in the day, such banal repartee was par for the course and we all got over it.

If this is an example of what the reporter considers "devastation," and "pithily succinct," we must wonder if he was in school in the eighth grade.

Putin was so discombobulated by the event, he entered an Orthodox monastery to hide from the world. Well, no. He has been soldiering on not without some success.

Junior High is not a bad description of most of the media.

Alternative Press

Are there any voices of a real alternative press? Yes, but they have some problems being heard. Libertarians who are true to their faith, such as Ron Paul, do speak out against foreign intervention consistently.

SHE SEARCHES FOR MONSTERS TO DESTROY

One of Paul's associates was banned from Twitter for calling out Sean Hannity for wearing a CIA pin while challenging the deep state. Supposedly, the word was "retarded." This is not to say Mr. Hannity is that, or whatever more correct term is politically okay.

McAdams pointed out that the offending word is used often on Twitter without penalty. Maybe he was too effective.

The late Justin Raimondo was the wild-eyed crazy guy at the antiwar.com website and was always ready for the fight. Unfortunately, he recently died of the lung cancer. May his unbelieving shade find rest in another dimension.

Antiwar.com, which Raimondo co-founded with Eric Garris, continues the battle. If someone has intelligently written against intervention, it will be aggregated there.

There are people to the left who have pushed back against the hysteria. One of them even does a video show that is posted on YouTube called Pushback, oddly enough.

Aaron Maté does the show on the *Grayzone*, but is probably best known for a video he did on The Real News Network. It was an interview with Luke Harding about his book *Collusion*. Nowadays, when the word collusion is mentioned, it is most associated with the idea that Trump, or someone associated with him, was colluding with Russia. Mr. Harding probably thought he was going to get a kiss, much like his interview on NPR's *Fresh Air*.

As things got going, Mr. Harding was getting questions he was not prepared for and was annoyed that he was having to come up with answers that were not quite adding up. It may have been where they came up with the name Pushback, because Aaron was doing quite a bit of it that day.

The founder of the *Grayzone* is Max Blumenthal. He is the son of Sidney Blumenthal, most known for being a Clinton loyalist.

If one follows Max, he is not replicating his father's politics. He is solidly anti-interventionist. That he is not hot for conflict with Russia got him called out as a useful idiot in a *New York Times* piece titled surprisingly "Useful Idiots."

"Useful Idiots" was written by Slawomir Sierakowski, whose many writings give the appearance of a man who has no love for Russia. As a Pole, this is understandable. Useful Idiots seems to have the underlying tone that if you want to get along with the Russians, you are naive at best. His sinecure is *Krytyka Polityczna (Political Critique)* magazine and a think tank.

Also, visit Syria and get called names. Blumenthal went there for *The Grayzone*. What is a reporter to do? Probably stay away from controversy and just do stenography.

Certainly, don't write a book. Blumenthal's *The Management of Savagery: How America's National Security State Fueled the Rise of Al Qaeda, ISIS, and Donald Trump* gives us a history going back to before the beginning of the so-called war on terror to the American machinations in Afghanistan. It covers a lot as our country pursues what the former Brit home secretary Reginald Maudling referred to as an "acceptable level of violence."

Another man of the left pilloried in the same *Times* April 28, 2014, article was the late Stephen Frand Cohen. Cohen, a longtime writer for *The Nation* and Professor Emeritus at Princeton and NYU, could often be heard on John Batchelor's radio show where his analysis was refreshing.

Cohen was also part of a group that wants us to get along with countries that are disliked by the establishment. The American Committee for East-West Accord (ACEWA) seems to be opposed by a grand ad hoc coalition that could be called the American Committee against East-West Accord. ACEWA aggregates articles that are not party line.

Consortium News is another alternative voice. It was founded by the late Robert Parry, one of reporters who broke the Iran-Contra story.

As part of the reason he gave for founding CN, he "was distressed by the silliness and propaganda that had come to pervade American journalism. I feared, too, that the decline of the U.S. press foreshadowed disasters that would come when journalists failed to alert the public about impending dangers."

He might have put it that the press is much of the danger.

Colonel Patrick Lang's *Sic Semper Tyrannis* committee of correspondence serves as a corrective for much of mainstream hysteria.

There are other sites out there and individuals who provide dissent and it is an injustice not to name them all. True, some might not be as responsible as others, but the major outlets have much more to answer for.

The alternative voices are voices crying in the wilderness, but are in this day and age needed more than ever. Almost all of them are just ignored, which begs the question, is there ever really a truly free press or does the media just bind itself to power and merely pretend to act as tribunes?

38

Finance, Sanctions, Bankruptcy

If one pays too much attention to the media, it often seems that a day does not pass without the United States announcing sanctions against another country or one of its agencies or an individual. The United States does this because of some transgression against an American policy or action in the world. As a tool to bend the world to its will, it has not always been successful.

Indeed, sanctions get a bad press, most famously when Madeline Albright was called on to defend it in a *60 Minutes* interview while she was ambassador to the UN.

Lesley Stahl (of CBS News): "We have heard that half a million children have died. I mean, that's more children than died in Hiroshima. And, you know, is the price worth it?"

Madeleine Albright: "I think this is a very hard choice, but the price—we think the price is worth it."

The statement is an admission that your country can be as heartless as it wishes in pursuit of its foreign policy goals.

To be fair to Madeline, who would become the first woman Secretary of State, it was a hard question to answer. Obviously, a more practiced diplomat would have obfuscated by saying, "We disagree with those figures. Our research differs and had I known of this line of questioning, I would have had the facts with me."

The magazine, *Pacific Standard*, published an article disputing the half million figure in 2013. They pointed out that the author of the research that led to the large figure had retracted it.

It doesn't matter. Albright has later said how stupid her statement was, but even so. She is on record that lots of deaths are okay cause you gotta do what ya gotta do.

It is worth noting that whatever sanctions did to Iraq and its people regime change only came about by invasion.

Is the constant imposing of sanctions a worthwhile tool? Probably not, as one hears mostly of them being promulgated, but rarely is it announced that they are being lifted due to their achieving the desired end. Indeed, they might be coming to the end of any useful life.

On his website, *As I Please*, Martin van Creveld has a guest post by Karsten Riise. Mr. Riise is former senior Vice President Chief Financial Officer (CFO) of Mercedes-Benz in Denmark and Sweden. Currently he conducts research and management of major changes with Change News and Change Management.

The title of the article, posted on September 27, 2018, is "US Sanctions reach a Turning Point." At the top of the article is a cartoon of a pooped Uncle Sam pulling a rickshaw with what looks like the Chinese president reading a newspaper with the headline, U.S. MUST BORROW $1.75 TRILLION.

Mr. Riise starts out by noting that the EU would usually acquiesce in whatever the United States was imposing. "But now, 'secondary sanctions' regarding Iran also hit hard at strategic EU companies and financial institutions and negatively affect EU global strategic interests in energy from the Persian Gulf. US sanctions in effect attack the liberty, security and sovereignty of its biggest group of friends, the EU."

Mr. Riise pointed out that the U.S. economy is declining steadily. The rest of the world will collude with each other against the sanctions regime because of parallel interests.

> *The US economy is already less than a quarter of the world's GDP in USD dollars, and in 2023 it will fall to only just about one fifth of the world (source: IMF). The non-US part, the four fifths of the world economy (now including the EU and China), constitute an increasingly advanced group, and they are about to collude against the US sanctions regime. Collusion is the result of parallel interests, and the EU may not actually (or at least not publicly) coordinate all its counter-sanctions with other major power center.*

Clearly, Europe is not ecstatic that the United States has left the nuclear deal with Iran. They would love to do business with the Persians. Germany and others in Europe want to buy petrochemicals from a Russian pipeline rather than ship it expensively from the United States.

Now, have the Europeans told us to go fry ice? Not yet. There is something they get from us that they don't wish to let go of: NATO. We are the guarantor of their independence from Russia. If that is not exactly it, the alliance keeps them from needing to spend a lot on their militaries. Thus, they can have free college and other social programs that we argue about.

Mr. Riise sees things going sour for the United States in several areas sooner or later. Let's look at some of them below.

Finance

In this area, Mr. Riise posits something that should be scary if he is right.

> *Looking at the long-term trend, the US financial industry has become really the ONLY big growth*

industry, which drives upwards the USA economy. No other sector in the US economy has the combination of size and growth, which finance has (weapons are a bit the same, but finance is unique in size)—so this will be very hard for the USA.

Not being an economist, it is impossible for me to say if this is true. If it is, and it were to be impaired, that would be a bad thing for the United States. Even if it isn't the only big growth industry, it is to the advantage of the United States to be the payment-transfer agent of the world. If we were to lose this, we are less prosperous and less scary to the rest of the world.

"Everybody outside the USA will be reluctant to let their money be touched by US financial institutions, or let their money touch US shores even for a millisecond. And of course, the EU and China know how to engineer legal and technical solutions for this."

Riise sees growth of U.S. credit cards slowing down as China and the EU take market share. No surprise there. Russia kicked out U.S. credit companies, so it can be done.

"New global IT money transfer system regimes, which counteract US influence on SWIFT, will erode US political influence. The SWIFT system is based in Brussels, but under heavy US political influence. Russia has already built itself an alternative to that. The EU can no longer accept that the US might be able to hurt EU companies on their SWIFT transfers. The EU will therefore have to take actions either to liberate SWIFT from US control, or to create a parallel EU-system."

That would be the logical path for other parties to follow if it is true the U.S. regime has too heavy a hand.

De-dollarization

Riise continues:

> The EU now will shift trade of energy from dollars to Euro – this trend will also diminish dollars in other international trade. Trillions of international dollars flowing around in trade may come back "home" to the USA – risking inflation and economic crisis. Gold is according to unconfirmed reports being speedily bought up by governments, not only by Russia and China, but even Turkey, recently also hit by U.S. sanctions.

This might be big. Again, not an economist, but, I have read it bruited about that one of the reasons Saddam and Gaddafi were taken out was attempts to substitute gold for the dollar in oil sales. Whether or not that is true, the primacy of the dollar is important. It would be a great loss if it became just another currency.

Should we be doing things that make others want to not do business with us?

Collusion Against the USA

Riise sees the other world entities and states colluding with each other against our interests.

"With aggressive, unilateral trade-war, started by the US, all the rest of the world will now have even more motives to coordinate their counter-strategies to the US sanctions regime." He sees the EU doing it because it has to and will.

Whether that does happen, it could and would be the result of the sanctions that we so blithely inflict on other powers. If the reaction was successful, the sanctions weapon would be gone.

Once we lose the power to inflict effective sanctions, it won't be coming back. What coercive weapons would be left?

Interesting Times

The United States spends a lot on defense. We often hear that the U.S. defense budget is greater than the cost of the next several countries combined. How do we pay for that? We don't, at least not right away. We do what all countries do: we borrow the money. Though it is paid back over time, more is constantly being borrowed for new planes and tanks and guns and other toys for the boys and more and more, the girls. One would think that this is the way of the world and has been going on long enough to be of little concern. Is it so?

According to the *New York Times*' economics reporter, Nelson D. Schwartz, "The federal government could soon pay more in interest on its debt than it spends on the military, Medicaid or children's programs." He wrote this for the paper on September 25, 2018, that this could happen by 2023.

Granted, in legislative circles 2023 is a lifetime away and hardly to be worried about now. When the time comes, there will be a lot of different reps and senators with another election looming. Anything could happen.

Schwartz makes the case that the trajectory is valid and he is not hysterical in his reporting. He maintains that we are not going the way of Greece and their recent problems.

However, can this go on forever? Anyone who has lived in this country long enough has seen their share of recessions, the most recent one noted for a severity not experienced in a long time. Would another downturn of similar proportions with the deficit problems noted by the reporter be too much?

It probably won't be the straw that breaks the financial camel's back, but with sufficient severity, painful decisions may have to be made. Will a bloated defense budget that pretends to be keeping us safe be on the block? As usual, not if the MIC (Military-Industrial Complex can help it.

According to other sources, the end of the world has already happened; we just haven't noticed it.

The progressive website, *CounterPunch*, headlines a piece by John Whitehead with "War Spending Will Bankrupt America." Mr. Whitehead then outsources to an *American Conservative* article, "America is Bankrupt and Republicans Couldn't Care Less." It is a strange tag team, but if you're on a ship heading into an iceberg, political outlook should not prevent you from seeing what's ahead.

Both articles give us a litany of over-spending and over-extension and they are right, but does that mean there will be a day of reckoning? Maybe, but we know neither the day nor the hour.

Whitehead quotes investigative journalist Uri Friedman stating, "For more than 15 years now, the United States has been fighting terrorism with a credit card, "essentially bankrolling the wars with debt, in the form of purchases of U.S. Treasury bonds by U.S.-based entities like pension funds and state and local governments, and by countries like China and Japan."

Friedman is not the first to use the credit card analogy, but if one listens to the ads on radio offering ways to get out from under the crushing burden of credit card debt, it may be a problem.

One point Whitehead makes is that "The glaring economic truth is that at the end of the day, it's the military industrial complex—and not the sick, the elderly or the poor—that is pushing America towards bankruptcy."

Maybe a close study of the United States might come to a different conclusion, but it is hard to argue that the MIC is not catered to. Meanwhile, we go along as if this can last forever. It is not fun to watch, or, as we all are, be a part of.

Sanctions as a Plague and the Plague

It has been noticed elsewhere that sanctions oppress the average citizen of the sanctioned country rather than the leadership. State might intone how they are only doing it to bring the pleasures of American-style democracy to the benighted plebs of the enemy du jour. There may be some rationale in another dimension that makes sense, but in this world, it hardly does.

The Covid-19 virus has struck far and wide and one can look up all the countries that are afflicted. Iran has been especially hard hit. In this devastation, the United States has seen an opportunity to inflict more sanctions. Other hard hit countries that we have been sanctioning for years are re-sanctioned.

This is not to suggest Iran, Nicaragua, Cuba, and Venezuela are shining cities on a hill, but they come off far better than the country that is waging a genocidal war in Yemen that is our ally.

We have institutionalized Madeline Albright's philosophy of worth.

39

Force Structure

In a November/December 2013 article in *The American Conservative*, Andrew Bacevich notes that we have two sets of the one percent. According to Bacevich, the sets are "the one percent whose members get sent to fight seemingly endless wars and that other one percent whose members demonstrate a knack for enriching themselves in 'wartime.'"

It might seem a symbiotic relationship and may be, but Bacevich further notices, "Needless to say the two one percents neither intersect or overlap. Few of the very rich send their sons or daughters to fight. Few of those leaving the military's ranks find their way into the plutocracy."

As a popular way of talking would have it, what's not to like? The 98% don't have to worry about fighting, nor do the people who do well out of it. Bacevich does excoriate the apathy of the general public and surely a class who will just toss off the obligatory "thank you for your service" deserves to be castigated.

Maybe this is a good thing and overseas small wars are America's business in the same way Calvin Coolidge was quoted as saying, "The business of America is business."

As one would expect, there are some cheerleaders out there for eternal amnesia to go with the eternal war. Max Boot, who supports U.S. wars overseas for probably any reason, likes it. Bacevich quotes Boot, "'Public apathy' he argues, "presents a potential opportunity," making it possible to prolong 'indefinitely' conflicts in which citizens are not invested."

Boot, in arguing for indefinite war, speaks for a constituency that may not be broad, but it is deep. The Military-Industrial Complex is more than what Eisenhower was talking about. It could easily be expanded to the Military-Intelligence-Industrial-Congressional-Think Tank-Educational-Media Complex or just call it The Grand Complex. With some effort, other members of that blob might be found. That he rejoices should not be unexpected. Max is a part of a class that promotes and profits off war and could only do so if the rest of the nation sleeps.

A question to consider is, How asleep are the people? When President Trump announced in early 2019 that he intended to take the troops in Syria out of that country, the war class, which had by that time become a mix of liberals and conservatives, began bleating that it was a horrible decision. The press served as their echo chamber.

The way they spoke one might have thought that a whole nation agreed with them. Despite the wall-to-wall "leaving one centimeter of MENA (Middle East and North Africa) is dumb" coverage, more Americans agreed with Trump according to a YouGov and Charles Koch Institute poll. It may not be that Americans don't have an opinion, but that the constant one-sided news makes them feel not so much apathy as what's the point? Real discontent doesn't show up until it gets beyond that. Witness the *gilets jaunes* (the Yellow Vests of France).

Putting that aside, is forever war really a good idea? There is much testimony in history to suggest it is ruinous to the nation and its freedom. Sun Tzu said, "There is no instance of a country having benefited from prolonged warfare." Our own James Madison told us, "Of all the enemies of public liberty, war is perhaps the most to be dreaded, because it comprises and develops the germ of every other."

If you don't think our country is less free today, then maybe Madison was wrong. Possibly, we might not be taking our shoes off before flying if we had never sent troops to the Middle East or had just let the Soviets figure out Afghanistan without Zbig's help.

But we digress. For those who might believe a non-interventionist policy is wiser, what would a U.S. military look like after the forces come home, and what does such a force need to accomplish?

The first obligation of any state is maintaining its territory. Not getting conquered is the goal, . As important for us, is to not get into wars of choice that aren't vital to the nation.

An armed force is necessary, even without the inclination for overseas wars. The Costa Rican example of abolishing the military is not really an option for us.

Having been able to end their army and establish a stable government in a short, bloody civil war, Costa Rica has been fortunate, but it isn't a relevant example. Central American armies have historically been mostly a danger to their own people, and when theirs was abolished it changed little externally and much for the better internally.

Considering that, after insuring the nation's safety from foreign invasion, armed forces should not get into unnecessary wars. Not bugging the citizenry either should at least be a third pillar.

Central America as well as most South American standing armies have been sinks of monetary waste and of no real use. To be honest, that sink of monetary waste thingee is not unknown here. Our Founding Fathers warned us of the dangers of a standing army for such reasons.

Assuming a country can avoid civil war, what should the military look like? For most of the nineteenth century, other than during the intramural unpleasantness, we didn't have much of one, and that was used against the indigenous people who were comparatively small and poor and at a horrible geopolitical disadvantage. It didn't matter what skill and courage they displayed because the outcome was inevitable.

We were able to get away with that, as the oceans on either side were larger then and the technology to shrink them was not as developed. In the last century, a sizeable navy was necessary. Those oceans are still there and though easier to cross in this day and age, the investment to get here is huge.

So, we have to have a navy, and as hemispheric defense would be the most important task, it is the more important arm. It should not be near as large as one tasked to be everywhere controlling everything. As of now, there is no foreign power anywhere capable of building a fleet to quickly invade the continental United States. It would take, in all probability, a few decades to do that and could not be hidden once started.

Going back to the wars against the Barbary States, thought must be given as to what would be our nation's role in keeping open sea lanes against piracy. Recent times have seen raiders such as the Somali pirates and supposedly corsairs off of other coasts.

How much of a navy would need to be dedicated to patrolling is a question to be answered if the United States were to concentrate on continental defense instead of being the world hegemon. It would have to be done in cooperation with other countries.

An air force would have essentially the same mission as a navy, continental defense. As it too would be tasked with making sure an enemy did not reach our shores, a USAF would also be more important than the army.

Back to the question of an army. The most radical proposal, and the one the author favors, is universal service with no exceptions. This would have to be different from the last conscription regime we had. As someone who had to register during the Vietnam War, I knew few who had to serve if they did not want to. Educational "opportunities" expanded to meet the needs of those who wanted knowledge or at least a deferment. The institutional expansion from back then is still with us and the question of whether that truly serves the needs of the nation or is a misapplication of resources can be answered elsewhere.

This is not to say the draft didn't catch up many young men. The less well connected did get taken far more than others.

Our military, as it is now structured, means never-ending war. Author C.J. Chivers in an NPR interview put it succinctly that without a draft, that is, a "blood lottery" there isn't much incentive to end the wars. Certainly, the Grand Complex would not take the lead in that.

A truly fair system would see everyone go, without exception. The most important advantage would be that the plutocrat one percent might be less inclined to go to war if Brent might have to share a Bradley Fighting Vehicle with DeShawn or Billy Bob or Miguel while under fire.

Now, in the current social and political environment, there is absolutely no chance of such a system being put into place. This would be so even if we went over to a non-interventionist foreign policy.

But, it is important to think of some advantages. The abovementioned one percent's progeny would get to spend some time, at least in initial training, with the other one percent and the rest of the nation's youth. That those who look down from the heights would have to spend some time in the depths might be of some benefit to all classes. That may not be so and an abiding hate could arise. If that is true, maybe there is no purpose in our calling ourselves a nation.

Done wisely, we would have the benefits of a force that could be activated quickly without the hazards of a huge standing army.

That there is a rising a military caste, as we are witnessing, in the nation may not be a good thing. Madeleine Albright's obtuse question to Colin Powell, "What's the point of having this superb military you're always talking about if we can't use it?" has been answered. We use it for everything and nothing.

The weeping and gnashing of teeth that accompanied Trump announcing a Syria withdrawal and a partial withdraw from Afghanistan tells us that no other president would attempt what he has. Sadly, as on some issues, he retreated from a sensible idea.

If we accept that eternal war is not desirable, a system of universal service should mean everyone would be mobilized. This would be the biggest brake on foreign adventure. It would have to be a very popular cause or the people would not stand for it.

Would a system of total participation work? Switzerland has that system. The question was asked on a blog as to whether the Swiss would not put up a good fight considering that they have not been tested and have no recent history of war other than constant training and received the following reply.

> *Switzerland's forces would fight for a while in prepared defensive positions but when things got really tough they would fold up. They have no context in their individual or collective experience for the great stress they would be under. The transition to becoming a real soldier is made through repeated stress that gradually transforms. If you have not experienced that you probably won't believe what I just wrote. Perceptive writers like Stephen Crane (The Red Badge of Courage) and James Jones (The Thin Red Line) have captured that psychological process. I*

would think that the Swiss forces have no offensive value whatever. Orchestrating attacks is a stage of military individual and group development for which they have no real preparation at all. BTW, some people are incapable of making this transition either from a lack of natural inclination to the warrior's trade or because of poor leadership. These unfortunates usually break down mentally and become a burden often for life. Yes, I am talking about what is now called PTSD.

The last armed conflict among the Swiss was a short mid-nineteenth century civil war that wasn't overtly violent. The Swiss were once the bad boys of Europe. At one time, most sovereigns had an elite Swiss Guard and one still does. In Hamlet, Claudius called for his Switzers.

When Western Europe had fallen to the Third Reich, Switzerland was alone. The chief of the military, General Guisan, addressed the army's commanders. They were to fight to the end if invaded. Should they hear a surrender broadcast, they were to regard it as enemy lies.

Though prepped to never give up, the Swiss were able to maintain neutrality. Did their posture of "¡No pasarán!" affect Axis calculations?

The point that a static defense posture would not augur well over the long term in battle must be considered. The Swiss are not thinking of destroying an enemy, merely stopping him. An enemy would probably be doing the opposite.

At the beginning of most large conflicts, other than the professional core, everyone is raw, and over a usually short time, the armies learn to be better at what they have to do, unless they are swiftly defeated. As the United States is not a small country surrounded by mountains, the levée en masse should come up to speed as quickly as the enemy.

We have had forces in the field since early in the twenty-first century and there is no dearth of returned soldiers suffering PTSD.

An additional benefit of adopting the Swiss system would be that the Second Amendment debate would go away. If someone were considered sane enough for military service and then qualified via training to be issued a weapon to keep and maintain in the Swiss manner, who could object to possession? Too crazy for military service? No gun.

What about the Marines?

Historically, with not much of an army, the United States used the Marine Corps to project force elsewhere. All too often, as famously pointed out by Major General Smedley Butler, the Marines were not executing a wise national policy but enforcing the will of subsidized bankers and businessmen.

Generally, the USMC has been used in intra-hemispheric events that served economic interests of a few. Could a force structure that included the Marines not see the Corps providing enforcement of the private concerns of bankers?

So, the question becomes, should there be a Marine Corps at all, seeing as it has often been the servant of the bad neighbor policy? If there is to be one, how do we insure that it is only used against real enemies of the nation and not enemies of the plutocracy?

There are few flyover Americans or inner city denizens who do not know someone who has served in the Corps. Going through exurban neighborhoods, sooner or later will be seen a Marine flag, no doubt flown by someone who fondly remembers his service. Many have been deployed in the War on Terror. It will be a ready-made and formidable lobby.

Like most political questions, the probability is that it will not be answered on what is best for the nation but on who has the more effective advocates.

When and if the country realizes that running the world or being the global cop or whatever we are always doing must stop, we shall have to think about the configuration of the military.

We have to think about the Marines and how to use them for only truly necessary missions as well as consider what type of army we want. A standing military will eventually come up against an even ditzier Madeleine Albright.

Universal military service would be fair and a brake on the impetus to war. The willingness of the people to participate in such an institution would truly make us a nation. It is also the least likely outcome.

There is something not being proposed in these pages and that is non-military national service, which is now and again suggested. Most recently, the presidential candidacy of billionaire Tom Steyer came up with the plan. At this point, while calling for a huge program, he wasn't suggesting it be compulsory, though incrementalism is never far behind such proposals.

It would probably have benefits for certain classes. The children of Ivanka and Chelsea would probably do well enough. For kids from down-market neighborhoods, it will be different. The sons and daughters of the Ivy League will feel important and the lesser folk will be told to get the mop.

One other aspect of American defense needs to stop and it is the use of mercenaries, officially known as contractors. Edward Snowden, in the chapter "Homo Contractus" from his book, *Permanent Record*, puts it well:

> *By the time I arrived, the sincerity of public service had given way to the greed of the private sector, and the sacred compact of the soldier, officer, and career civil servant was being replaced by the unholy bargain of Homo contractus, the primary species of US Government 2.0. This creature was not a sworn servant but a*

transient worker, whose patriotism was incentivized by a better paycheck and for whom the federal government was less the ultimate authority than the ultimate client. During the American Revolution, it had made sense for the Continental Congress to hire privateers and mercenaries to protect the independence of what was then barely a functioning republic. But for third-millennium hyperpower America to rely on privatized forces for the national defense struck me as strange and vaguely sinister. Indeed, today contracting is most often associated with its major failures, such as the fighting-for-hire work of Blackwater (which changed its name to Xe Services after its employees were convicted of killing fourteen Iraqi civilians, and then changed its name again to Academi after it was acquired by a group of private investors), or the torture-for-hire work of CACI and Titan (both of which supplied personnel who terrorized prisoners at Abu Ghraib).

Outsourcing the military is an expedient for a state that is doing too much, but relying on a mercenary army is not a long-term solution for a nation whose people like to say, "it's a free country."

Bringing everyone home and saying goodbye to the bloated overseas commitments is the first and most necessary step. What is done next after America comes home is almost as crucial.

Though not optimistic, one lives in hope. The system is horrible and will catch its one percent until it can't. Remember John Kerry's botched joke?

"You know, education, if you make the most of it, if you study hard and you do your homework, and you make an effort to be smart, you can do well. If you don't, you get stuck in Iraq."

Yeah, it was contemptuous of the men serving, but it revealed a truth we all know. As George Carlin said, "It's a big club, and you ain't in it."

Kerry is not the brightest bulb, but he is part of that big club. He wasn't intending to tell the lower orders a truth, but if anyone wants to get it, it's there.

Max Blumenthal was even more to the point. Kerry, part of the Democratic Party elite (and a man who actually served) is of a party whose membership had been usually less hawkish, that is, up until Trump and their anti-Russia hysteria.

Blumenthal attended a College Young Republican convention in 2007 and asked the kids why they were such gung-ho war supporters while being, shall we say, gun shy. The Young GOPers were not going to get "stuck in Iraq" no matter how much they believed.

Let's expand the club of those who get to wear the uniform of their country beyond the other one percent to all the percents.

In Conclusion

The word "zombie" is much in popular use nowadays. It is appended adjectively to another word to mean something that has little life, but will not die. There are zombie malls with some stores shuttered and others with few shoppers. One could argue that we have a zombie foreign policy.

We lurched from one course enunciated by the former president to another seemingly opposite in Syria. Are we staying? Are we leaving? The nightmare (mostly for others) of our involvement may be coming to an end, or is it?

Barack Obama, who correctly called Iraq a dumb war, managed to involve the country in two of them with the help of a secretary of state. Libya is an ongoing mess. Syria is a sovereign country we have troops in for some vague reason, as we have not accomplished our original goal of overthrowing the internationally recognized government. President Trump once stated his desire to keep and exploit Syrian oil, as legally dubious an idea as having soldiers in that country.

In late 2019, the United States is involved in a zombie war in Afghanistan. There is no reason to be there, but rationales are constantly invented. How long will this go on?

As realistic a prediction about how it will all play out for the foreseeable future was given by author C.J. Chivers, mentioned in a previous chapter, on NPR's *All Things Considered*. He was being interviewed on August 13, 2018 by Mary Louise Kelly about his new book, *The Fighters: Americans in Combat in Afghanistan and Iraq*. Chivers has no little experience as a war correspondent. Late in the discussion, she asked him:

> KELLY: So, what are the options now? I mean, I guess this is the eternal David Petraeus question. Tell me how this ends? Is there anything that gives you hope that 17 years from now, you and I would not be sitting here having a somewhat similar conversation?

> CHIVERS: As long as we don't have a draft, as long as we don't have American households hooked up to the blood lottery that is war where any parent might have to worry about their child being called off to serve, I think that we will have a Pentagon that's not quite fully supervised because the public doesn't really feel a stake here. And until the country invests more fully intellectually in the war, I think that we're bound to keep having conversations like this year after year.

Mr. Chivers is right. There is nothing to get members of the public to look at our war effort with much seriousness unless (or until) a family has been affected by loss. One is reminded of what Adam Smith said of the general population and war:

> In great empires the people who live in the capital, and in the provinces remote from the scene of action, feel, many of them scarce any inconveniency from the war; but enjoy, at their ease, the amusement of reading in the newspapers the exploits of their own fleets and armies. To them this amusement compensates the small difference between the taxes which they pay on account of the war, and those which they have been accustomed to pay in time of peace. They are commonly dissatisfied with the return of peace, which puts an end to their amusement, and to a thousand visionary hopes of

conquest and national glory, from a longer continuance of the war.

As the people don't really know or understand the true cost of the military, the current situation can continue indefinitely.

It is hard to say what will get the full attention of the American people to the folly of the path we are on. Maybe a Dien Bien Phu in Afghanistan, maybe not even that. But, there are those who still insist we must be in Afghanistan, not because of national security. No thinking person is buying that.

Now, the establishment has to be a bit more inventive, and they are. On February 2, 2019, NPR's Scott Simon kind of agreed that the war was more or less pointless except that we can never leave as all the gains woman have made will vanish. He is okay with American servicemen and women facing possible death at the hands of people who will probably never give up and will only sign a treaty the way the North Vietnamese did, one that will allow them to take it all in the fullness of time.

So, we may have to be there for a millennium or so to protect women's rights, not that we can secure their lives from IEDs and other death-dealing innovations. As there is no wonderful deal for women in Afghanistan in real terms, it would be something to know if there is another reason for the absurd policy?

Though no one uses national security as the excuse for Afghanistan, it is still in use elsewhere. For politicians and functionaries and others, national security is a mantra.

Regarding national security concerns of the Trump administration, national security was invoked by Lieutenant Colonel Vindman as a reason for his concern regarding the president's phone call with his Ukrainian counterpart. According to Vindman, as reported by *Politico* on October 28, 2919: "I realized that if Ukraine pursued an investigation into the Bidens and Burisma, it would likely be interpreted as a partisan play which would undoubtedly result in Ukraine losing the bipartisan support it has thus far maintained," Vindman said. (Burisma is a Ukrainian energy company of which Hunter Biden was a board member.) "This would all undermine U.S. national security," Vindman added.

So, if support for Ukraine deteriorates as a supposedly corrupt deal is investigated and our "national security" is undermined the implications are enormous. Maybe a little bit of a stretch, actually, maybe a huge stretch. The idea that Trump seeking dirt on the Bidens in exchange for arms will lead to the nation's collapse is laughable.

Lieut. Col. Vindman is hardly the only one to make use of a mantra. One of the older and sillier incantations came up in the hearings.

Former NSC official Tim Morrison opened his testimony with the following:

> *I continue to believe Ukraine is on the front lines of a strategic competition between the West and Vladimir Putin's revanchist Russia. Russia is a failing power, but it is still a dangerous one. The United States aids Ukraine and her people so they can fight Russia over there and we don't have to fight Russia here.*

This is a variation of what was repeated at the beginning of what was and may still be called the War on Terror, that is, we have to fight them over there so we don't have to fight them over there. The idea of sending sizeable forces overseas so that an invasion of terrorists would not occur was as foolish as the belief that the Russians are planning to go transatlantic with several divisions now.

Yet no one was questioning it. No one is proposing we stop supporting the Ukrainians. The Democrats? Many in the party were not so long ago skeptical of the national security state. It is a stretch to say they are now all Lindsay Grahams, but they are no Rand Pauls.

What is missing in all of this is any definition as to what national security is. As part of that non-inquiry, any suggestion that our overseas adventures might not be working brings hisses of the epithet "isolationism." Hit someone with that and you receive absolution from having to define anything.

What does the "I" word really mean? When used it is meant to convey an image in the mind of an America sealed off from the world, with a narrow-minded people. A strawman like that is negative, but does it have any meaning?

Someone seems to think so. On October 16, 2019, *Washington Post* columnist Josh Rogin tweeted: "George W Bush takes a direct shot at Trump: 'An isolationist United States is destabilizing around the world. We are becoming isolationist and that's dangerous for the sake of peace.'"

Other than the alternative media, there was little reaction to suggest that quoting the former president on peace was a bit rich. Whatever halting steps Trump took to move troops in Syria, they were hardly isolationist.

Neither were the comments he made while running for president, suggesting we get along with Russia and opining that what came after Assad in Syria might be worse, was considered an abject surrender and retreat from our mission to order the world.

George W. Bush's record was not one of success. No matter, because when he made his remarks the mainstream didn't note how the former president was not exactly the man to comment on "peace."

If anyone could give isolationism a good name unintentionally, it would be our forty-third president.

When we went into Iraq, we were hardly in isolation mode, but that was dumber than nation-building in Afghanistan. Even Bush supporters, other than a few "dead enders" (a term once used to describe insurgents in Iraq who wouldn't give) have fled from defending him.

Yet despite his failure he has been rehabilitated. Bush is embraced by Michelle Obama, who is loved by the media so that is a bit of an imprimatur. The former first lady refers to George as her "partner in crime." Another cultural icon, Ellen Degeneres, partied with the man at a football game.

Ellen, showing the man love, has been attacked in some circles, but the condemnation of isolationism has been shown little disfavor.

Contrast that with the man who abandoned the big "I" and set the twentieth century world for disaster. A man who got us into "the war to end all wars" decades before that would be technologically feasible. At Versailles, the European powers blew off his virtuous ideas and went off on a path to another war.

His grand "League of Nations" was rejected by the Senate. Oh, for the days when failure was rewarded with ignominy. Though not completely. Back then, there were academics and journalists who continued to back the cause and maybe some still do.

Wilson was, long after death, memorialized with an institute that does think tank things. Nothing can be found on the site claiming the mission is to follow in the successful footsteps of the eponymous hero, though it seems to be internationalist.

There is also a *Wilson Quarterly* that covers a wide range of topics with little reference to the man.

As misguided as the policy was, he is still considered to have an aura of greatness. Why?

According to the paper "War and Presidential Greatness" by economists David R. Henderson and Zachary Gouchenour:

> Historians and journalists commonly survey other historians on the relative "greatness" of American

presidents, and these rankings show remarkable consistency between surveys. In this paper we consider commonalities between highly ranked presidents and compare plausible determinants of greatness according to historians. We find that a strong predictor of greatness is the fraction of American lives lost in war during a president's tenure. We find this predictor to be robust and compare favorably to other predictors used in previous historical research. We discuss potential reasons for this correlation and conclude with a discussion of how historians' views might affect policy.

Academia does not cover itself in glory.

Woodrow made the cut. He would have done a lot less damage had he not killed any of our troops, and been as celebrated as Millard Fillmore. His rep may have suffered but the people whose lot he entered the crusade for might have been better off.

Wilson should be dragged out of obscurity to guide us in the current millennium. As the cliché has it, "if you can't be a good example, at least be a horrible warning."

True enough. As de Tocqueville said of the American politicians:

> *The pursuit of wealth generally diverts men of great talents and of great passions from the pursuit of power, and it very frequently happens that a man does not undertake to direct the fortune of the State until he has discovered his incompetence to conduct his own affairs. The vast number of very ordinary men who occupy public stations is quite as attributable to these causes as to the bad choice of the democracy. In the United States, I am not sure that the people would return the men of superior abilities who might solicit its support, but it is certain that men of this description do not come forward.*

People who loved Obama thought him godlike and the partisans of Trump are not shy in admiration as well. In the reverse, they accuse, depending on outlook, either Obama or Trump of unceasing imbecility.

However, if good ol' Alexis was correct, they are both merely men and one might grant a bit above the herd average, but maybe not the gods or devils as characterized.

In consideration of that, we should not want such men contemplating foreign wars as policy, and It does not have to be that way. There is little reason for our interventionist activity.

Jean-Jules Jusserand, the long-serving French Ambassador to the United States in the first quarter of the twentieth century, observed about our country, "On the north, she has a weak neighbor; on the south, another weak neighbor, on the east, fish, and on the west, more fish."

It is only our obsession to be the world's cop that causes us to range the globe projecting force that does nothing for us. There may be more than just a national obsession. There is the correlation of forces made up of the Military-Intelligence-Industrial-Congressional-Think Tank-Educational-Media Complex (The Grand Complex as mentioned in a prior chapter) that agitates, but at the end of the day it is all motion for the sake of motion.

Meanwhile, it just meanders on.

Iran is portrayed as the worst state to have ever possessed a government, yet we support the regime that is murdering Yemen.

We warn the world of the horror of an Iranian bomb that isn't, while just up the street two nuclear countries face each other. India and Pakistan may not be the most unstable places in the world, but they are not any more a sea of tranquility compared to Iran and the potential for horrible mischief far greater currently.

When the death of Osama bin Laden was announced, people took to the streets to celebrate. Many had not been born on September 11, yet they cheered the death of a man, but it cannot be considered a victory.

> *The previous ten years had been a cavalcade of American-made tragedy: the forever war in Afghanistan, catastrophic regime change in Iraq, indefinite detentions at Guantánamo Bay, extraordinary renditions, torture, targeted killings of civilians—even of American civilians—via drone strikes. Domestically, there was the Homeland Securitization of everything, which assigned a threat rating to every waking day (Red–Severe, Orange–High, Yellow–Elevated), and, from the Patriot Act on, the steady erosion of civil liberties, the very liberties we were allegedly fighting to protect. The cumulative damage—the malfeasance in aggregate—was staggering to contemplate and felt entirely irreversible, and yet we were still honking our horns and flashing our lights in jubilation.*

The words were written by Edward Snowden and come from his book *Permanent Record*. Not much has changed since, but in the Schiff hearings we learned that our national security is bound up with Ukraine, though no one addresses why your average American needs to be shackled together with a corrupt Eastern European country.

To even ask would bring on "I" word hysteria, and well it should if anyone was actually advocating such a policy.

It might be instructive to seek out the definition of *isolationism* as found in an online dictionary:

> *The policy or doctrine of isolating one's country from the affairs of other nations by declining to enter into alliances, foreign economic commitments, international agreements, etc., seeking to devote the entire efforts of*

one's country to its own advancement and remain at peace by avoiding foreign entanglements and responsibilities.

The way isolationism is used in the media and discussions of foreign policy is to tar someone as a fanatical advocate of a hermetically sealed-off America if they so much as suggest the possibility of not engaging everywhere. No one addresses the absurdity of it all if only because, as might have been once said in society drawing rooms, "It is just not done."

Contrast with the definition of *neutrality* from the same site: "The policy or advocacy of maintaining strict neutrality in foreign affairs."

The wisdom of maintaining a neutral, as opposed to isolationist, policy during World War I is so self-evident that no time need be wasted.

World War II needs more of a discussion. The discussion itself would not be necessary without Wilson's foolishness. The question is, Could a neutral policy have avoided U.S. involvement?

Certainly, if Japan was bound and determined to take us on, war was inevitable. And, if we were bound and determined to take on the world, war was inevitable. What is not arguable is that a neutralist policy was not honestly attempted.

Immediately after the Second World War, we did not pursue any policy of neutrality, let alone even partial disengagement. Having entangled ourselves on two continents, it would have been a process over time, but it was not even contemplated.

The Korean War, ending at the 38th Parallel, was officially a draw, but truly a loss. We were stuck there with no choice other than stay with our southern wards.

Vietnam would provide an opportunity, though we didn't realize it at the time. We spent more than a decade hoping the northerners would give up or collapse. They suffered a lot and were willing to suffer more. In the end, we made a pretend agreement. Whether people in government realized it was pretend is hard to say. Once we were gone, it was over and we were never going back.

We left and when the North Vietnamese Army was ready, they walked down to Saigon. We finally had what had eluded us elsewhere, a successful exit strategy. Postwar, we didn't bug them and they ignored us. We have diplomatic relations and trade with them now.

It is easier to argue that what eventuated—a united country instead of an eternal DMZ with all its attendant costs for us—was the best of all possible worlds than the opposite.

Zbig's brilliantly shrewd move to entangle the Soviets in Afghanistan helped the implosion of the USSR along. The event was a golden opportunity to neutralize and was missed.

Before it happened, those who were then liberals and pro peace (today, they claim a progressive banner and are for showing those Russkies what for) would wax poetic about a future "peace dividend." It would not happen.

As recounted elsewhere, Gorbachev was promised NATO would not move an inch to the east. As the regime failed, the West thought it had the Russians completely on the run. Industry was looted and problems multiplied and just about every country that could be found was inducted into NATO.

With the accession of North Macedonia, has anything really been achieved? Has the freedom and safety of the American people been enhanced? Probably not, but the American commitment to another state that could, someday, commit us to war has been added.

The prosperity of the Grand Complex has not been harmed by the growth of NATO.

In a *plus ça change* event, we are planning to send 1,800 troops to Saudi Arabia. As one of the motives for September 11, Osama claimed troops on sacred Saudi soil. Now, if our intel is good and police work is up to snuff, we should not need to worry, but how is American security enhanced by being there, or for that matter, anywhere in the Middle East?

No one answers that question. The ridiculous idea that Ukraine is vital to our national security has been repeated ad nauseum and yet why is never asked.

We can extend it all over the world. North Korea will enhance its weapons of mass destruction. Our being there did not stop them from getting the ones they have and will probably not deter them from improving.

President Trump did some negotiating with them and it has led to little. Who knows, if we left, the North Koreans might launch some big ones at Tokyo and Seoul, but probably not.

In the end, the whole enterprise serves the interest of the Grand Complex. The American people get nothing out of it.

When someone wants to advance some agenda, or obfuscate a policy, they will say we need a national "conversation" on, say, race or gender or bullying or whatever. It is usually a smokescreen, but no one suggests it about national security.

Maybe the answer is just too obvious.

There has been one aspect of our wars that has been left out: the cost. One of the criticisms of the war in Iraq was that Bush paid for it on the "credit card." Since then, Obama and Trump got paper routes and covered the ongoing conflicts with the tip money. Maybe not.

The figures that are mentioned are so large that they can have no meaning to the average man or woman. Maybe they don't have any meaning at all.

"The Costs of War Project" at Brown University's Watson Institute for International and Public Affairs has the tally at $6.4 trillion. Everett Dirksen was a piker with his comment, "A billion here, a billion there, and soon it adds up to real money."

But does it?

Shortly after I finished college in 1971, President Nixon closed "The Gold Window." He went to a room in the White House and closed an actual physical window. No, what he did was end dollar convertibility into gold. It was a big step and did it mean the end of the dollar?

Hard money folks might be shocked, as the dollar has gone from $35 for an ounce of gold to a bit north of $1,780500, but the economy still exists. Mom and dad are still getting Social Security and Medicare, and the military gets most of what it wants. Credit cards are magic.

How does this not all collapse? Darned if I know.

Vaguely remembered is a classmate's economic joke told to me many decades ago when I was pretending to be a college student.

It seems Congress, tired of the squabbling over policy that took too much time away from golf, wanted to get to the bottom of what the economy was all about. They impaneled a committee of members of both houses and called as many eminent economists as they could find to expound. This went on for days, and when the last man was about to finish, the chairman, an old southron with an aristocratic accent asked the well degreed man, "Suh, y'all have been testifyin' for days, and about all we get from you, is that there is a lotta disagreement on the economy. Can you tell us, is there anyone that y'all agree knows and understands the economy?"

The learned fellow took a long pause before answering: "Why, yes, there are two. One fellow with the Bank of England in London, and another man with Rothschild's in Paris."

A look of relief came over the old Senator's face. "Finally, we can get to the bottom of it all. What do they say?"

Again, the witness paused before answering: "They disagree."

Maybe, one of the august savants knows. Maybe, it's no great trick to keep all the balls in the air and war works for everyone, but the dead and maimed?

Yet, it goes against all intuition. Being raised in '50s New England by two parents with thrifty instincts in a working-class town, life was pleasant but hardly lush. No one could pinch a penny like my mom who made my sisters dresses and was a wonder with leftovers. Thus, amazement at the profligate spending on never ending wars is all that registers.

Can it go on forever? One must turn to an economist, Herbert Stein, who came up with the pithy, Stein's Law: "If something cannot go on forever, it will stop."

But, there is a predecessor of Stein's, the aforementioned Adam Smith, who had something to say about the question. A friend had written to Smith that the British loss at the Battle of Saratoga during the American Revolution signified the ruin of the nation. Adam Smith's oft-quoted reply, "There is a great deal of ruin in a nation" is true, but why would our nation want to test the upper limits of that.

To end, there is, it appears, one constant in American foreign military involvement: lying. One can look back to the Tonkin Gulf incident or the Weapons of Mass Destruction fraud.

It has come out now, that, on a grand scale, under three administrations, there has been, one could say, less than absolute fidelity to the truth in America's longest war.

On December 9, 2019, *The Washington Post* published "The Afghanistan Papers: A Secret History of the War," by investigative reporter Craig Whitlock. It opens with; "U.S. officials constantly said they were making progress. They were not, and they knew it, an exclusive Post investigation found."

"The Afghanistan Papers" At War With the Truth has generated comment, but so far, there is little denial. It is just part of the eternal recurrence of the truth being the first and ever casualty of war.

So, will we actually leave Afghanistan or leave some troops and contractors? Maybe Mr. Simon will do another one of his soulful Saturday monologues ten years hence telling us we can't go because transgender rights will not be safe in Taliban Afghanistan.

He need not worry too much. Inertia might keep them there for a long time, unless the interests of the Grand Complex appears to be in danger.

The zombie lives, sort of.

Addendum, August 29, 2021

History never stops.

The fall of Kabul has occurred and the mess is being reported on all forms of media.

This is the second collapse of an American foreign project the author has witnessed in his lifetime. The various outlets are giving the event no little coverage and even those that were sycophantic to Biden before his election, are asking hard questions.

Will questions be asked about whether or not we might withdraw from all the other places we are engaged as most do not look overly promising? Probably not.

There will be research papers on what went wrong and how to do it right, but that it was absolute failure is beyond denial.

The bombing of a tunnel and the loss of service members has complicated matters, but changes nothing. It is the obligation of the administration to get every American and anyone deserving out and then leave. The actions of ISIS-K or any other configuration change nothing in the end.

All the king's think tanks and all the king's undersecretaries can't put Kabul back together again.

Acknowledgments

For the most part, She Goes Abroad was done in the dark and I did not reach out to others. Nevertheless, there are those that I owe some gratitude to.

My son, Ciarán, was always there for encouragement, advice and help. My wife Robin, was also supportive.

First cousins, Christopher Gantz and Tim Murphy put up with me.

The owners and editors of the Sturbridge Times Magazine, Paul Carr and John Small, gave me a place to write and learn for many years. They indulged someone who occasionally was over the top.

There is my friend, mentor and verbal sparring partner, Dick Vaughan, who passed away not long before publication. I shall miss him dearly.

Also, Drew Anderson who organised the shows Dick and I did and also provided encouragement.

Barry Lyons edited She Goes Abroad, but as I made several last-minute changes, any errors are mine.

The late Peace advocate Ruth Harriet Jacobs encouraged me to write and I am still grateful.

About the Author

Richard Morchoe is the author of *She Goes Abroad Looking For Monsters to Destroy*. He is a baby boomer who enlisted in the army towards the end of the Vietnam War and spent his time in the American South.

Home as a civilian, he watched the televised demise of the South Vietnam state and saw it as an end of the world as we know it moment for the United States.

All the equipment and treasure spent to halt Communism was gone. The North took possession of the ordnance left behind. The money squandered amongst defense contractors and numerous other wasted accounts, had evaporated like melted snow.

Gone, all gone, but it could have been worse.

He was to re-evaluate that conclusion as time passed and he observed that we could have scored the same tie that we achieved in Korea. That would have been a debacle. Had the North agreed to a permanent cease-fire on the border, we would still have troops and planes and PXs and condom dispensing machines all over South Viet Nam. There would be brass on the border taking meetings ad infinitum with the North's Officers. We would be forever rebuilding the South. Swiss banks would be awash in skimmed cash from all the associated boondoggles.

Ah, but that was not the case. When the last of our boys left, we were gone. We had bled buckets and lost billions, but when we finally said au revoir, it was over. We even had a measure of revenge as Hanoi had its own Vietnam in Cambodia. All the dominos did not exactly domino.

In the end, it was one of the few places we got to leave. It was almost as if we left no forwarding address and they changed their phone number.

We could forget about the place, which is more than one can say about most of the other spots we're stuck in.

As Vietnam was obviously a defeat, the question became for him, were the other wars worth it. *She Goes Abroad* looks at that and comes to the conclusion that for the most part, the taxpayer and serviceman do not do well, but not all classes lose.

Richard Morchoe lives in exurban Massachusetts on a bit of land with a large garden and beehives. He was until recently the regular book reviewer and columnist at the now much missed Sturbridge Times Magazine that succumbed in the pandemic.

You can find him on Substack at The Long Hill Institute.

Bibliography

King Philip's War

Jennings, F. The Invasion of America: Indians, Colonialism and the Cant of Conquest. New York: Norton, 1975.

Schultz, Eric B. and Tougias, Michael J.: *The History and Legacy of America's Forgotten Conflict*. New York, The Countryman Press, 2000.

The American Revolution or One Becomes Two

Correspondence of Adam Smith, ed. E. C. Mossner and I. S. Ross, vol. VI of the Glasgow Edition of the Works and Correspondence of Adam Smith (Indianapolis: Liberty Fund, 1987). Appendix B: 'smith's Thoughts On the State of the Contest With America, February 1778'

The Quasi-War

Allen, Gardner Weld. *Our Naval War With France*, Boston, Houghton Mifflin Company, 1909.

The Barbary Wars

Lambert, F. The Barbary Wars: American Independence in the Atlantic World, New York, Hill and Wang, 2005.

Roberts, K. Lydia Bailey, Garden City, NY, The Country Life Press, 1947.

The War of 1812

Berton, Pierre (1981). "Ch. 13: Ghent, August–December, 1814". *Flames Across the Border: 1813–1814*. McClelland & Stewart. pp. 418–9.

Borneman, Walter R. *1812: The War That Forged a Nation.* New York: Harper Perennial, 2005

The Mexican War

Singletary, Otis A. *The Mexican War*, Chicago: The University of Chicago Press, 1960

Young, John Russell, *Around the World with General Grant*, Baltimore, MD: Johns Hopkins University Press, 2002

The Panama Canal

World War I

Ferguson, Niall, *The Pity Of War: Explaining World War I*, London, Allen Lane The Penguin Press, 1998.

Larson, Erik, *Dead Wake: The Last Crossing of the Lusitania*, New York, Crown Publishers, 2015.

Mosier, John, *The Myth of the Great War: A New Military History of World War I*, New York, HarperCollins Publishers, 2001.

Richard, Morchoe. "A quick look at Ferguson's book on WWI," *The Sturbridge Times Magazine*, September, 2014.

The Interwar Years

Office of the Historian, Foreign Service Institute, United States Department of State, *The London Naval Conference 1930*.

World War II

Liddell Hart, B.H., *Strategy: Second Revised Edition*, London, Faber & Faber Ltd. 1954.

Stinnett, Robert B., *Day of Deceit: The Truth About FDR and Pearl Harbor*, New York, The Free Press, December 7, 1999.

Taylor, A.J.P., *The Origins of The Second World War*, London, Hamish Hamilton, 1961.

Defense Media Network, Churchill's Deal With the Devil: The Anglo-Soviet Agreement of 1942, July 12, 2011, Dwight Jon Zimmerman.

Independent Institute, *How U.S. Economic Warfare Provoked Japan's Attack on Pearl Harbor*, May 1, 2006, Robert Higgs.

Korea

Consortium News, *How History Explains the Korean Crisis*, August 28. 2017 William R. Polk.

The 1950s

English, T.J., Havana Nocturne: *How the Mob Owned Cuba and Then Lost It to the Revolution*, New York, Harper, 2009.

Kinzer, Stephen, *The Brothers: John Foster Dulles, Allen Dulles, and Their Secret World War*, New York, Times Books, 2013.

Science & Society, *The 1953 Coup in Iran*, Vol. 65, No. 2, Summer 2001, Ervand Abrahamian.

The Vietnam War

Brinton, Crane, *The Anatomy of Revolution*, New York, Prentice-Hall, Inc., 1938.

Ferguson, Niall, *The Pity Of War: Explaining World War I*, London, Allen Lane The Penguin Press, 1998.

Post-Vietnam

Braithwaite, Rodric. *Afgantsy: The Russians in Afghanistan 1979-89* (Oxford University Press, 2013), p. 114

White Jr., John Bernell. "The strategic mind of Zbigniew Brzezinski: how a native Pole used Afghanistan to protect his homeland" Louisiana State University LSU Digital Commons LSU Master's Thesis Graduate School, 2012

The Reagan Revolution

Russell, G.; McWhirter, W.; Timothy Loughran; Stanely, Alessandra. "Nothing Will Stop This Revolution," *Time*, October 17, 1983. Retrieved 2009-03-30.

Massie, Suzanne. *Trust But Verify: Reagan, Russia and Me*, Maine Authors Publishing, 2013.

Coll, Steve. *Ghost Wars: The Secret History of the CIA, Afghanistan, and Bin Laden from the Soviet Invasion to September 10, 2001*. New York: The Penguin Press, 2004.

Matlock, Jack. *Reagan and Gorbachev: How the Cold War Ended*. New York: Random House, 2004.

The Elder Bush Presidency

Hornberger, Jacob G. *War for Peace in the Middle East*, The Future of Freedom Foundation, April 1, 1990.

"NATO Expansion: What Gorbachev Heard," National Security Archive, Washington, D.C. 2017.

Moreno, Elida. "Panama's Noriega: CIA spy turned drug-running dictator," Reuters, May 30, 2017.

The Clinton Administration

Antiwar.com, *Remember Kosovo?* February 1, 2016, Justin Raimondo.

Ramani, Samuel. "What North Korea Learned From the Kosovo War," *The Diplomat*, October 16, 2017.

Meyer, Carlton. "Why Does Camp Bondsteel Still Exist?", G2mil, 2011.

George W and The Beginning of The Eternal War

Walt, Stephen M. Walt. "The Broken Policy Promises of W. Bush, Clinton, and Obama," *Foreign Policy*, September 18, 2016.

King, Laura; Holley, David. "Afghanistan war nears 'tipping point,'" *Los Angeles Times*, December 9, 2006.

Davis, Daniel L. "Foreign, Policy Failure: America Has Not Learned from Its Wars," *The National Interest*, April 28, 2018.

TomDispatch.com, *Putting the "War" in the "War on Terror"Major*, November 26, 2017 Maj. Danny Sjursen.

The Second Iraq War

Daniszewski, John; Mohan, Geoffrey Mohan. "Looters Bring Baghdad New Havoc," *Los Angeles Times*, April 11, 2003.

Mastracci, Davide. "How the 'catastrophic' American decision to disband Saddam's military helped fuel the rise of ISIL," *National Post*,

Sic Semper Tyrannis, *Two new US bases in western Iraq*, December 27, 2018, Colonel W. Patrick Lang.

Sjursen, Daniel A. *Ghost Riders of Baghdad: Soldiers, Civilians, and the Myth of the Surge*. Lebanon, N.H.: ForeEdge, 2015.

Libya

Mizner, David. "Worse than Benghazi," *Jacobin*, July 17, 2015.

Shane, Scott; Becker, Jo. "A New Libya, With 'Very Little Time Left'," *New York Times*, February 27, 2016.

Norton, Ben. "Even critics understate how catastrophically bad the Hillary Clinton-led NATO bombing of Libya was," *Salon*, March 2, 2016.

Sic Semper Tyrannis, BLAST FROM THE PAST: Expanding on operation "Mermaid Dawn" in Libya April 10, 2015, Patrick Bahzad.

Syria

The American Conservative, "Make No Mistake: ISIS Needs The U.S. To Survive," January 18. 2019, Ritter, Scott.

AP News, *US has no evidence of Syrian use of sarin gas, Mattis says*, February 2, 2018, Burns, Robert

CBC News (Canadian Broadcasting Corporation), *U.S. admits funding Syrian opposition*, Apr 18, 2011.

CBS News, *Syria chemical weapons attack blame, but where's the evidenced on Assad?* August 30, 2013, Reals, Tucker

The Guardian, "US military to maintain open-ended presence in Syria, Tillerson says," January 17, 2018, Borger, Julian Kareem, Shaheen Wintour, Patrick

The Hill, "Graham: Syrian Kurds aligning with Assad would be 'major disaster'," Kheel, Rebecca, December 28, 2018.

Politico, "Obama's Red Line, Revisited: The offhand remark spurred a massive success in Syria. Why does the foreign policy establishment consider it a failure?, July 19, 2016, Chollet, Derek.

Sic Semper Tyrannis, "The generals rolled him, as they rolled Obama" August 22, 2017, Lang, Colonel W. Patrick.

Time, "Syria in Bush's Cross Hairs," Dec. 19, 2006, Zagorin, Adam.

The New Yorker, "Is the Administration's new policy benefitting our enemies in the war on terrorism?," February 26, 2007, Hersh, Seymour M..

The Washington Post, "Trump agrees to an indefinite military effort and new diplomatic push in Syria," September 6, 2018, DeYoung, Karen.

Iran

AgFax, "Soybean Market: Iran was Top U.S. Soybean Buyer in August, What Gives?" DTN, October 9, 2018, Todd Hultman

Al Jazeera, "Iran President Rouhani in Baghdad to 'expand ties with Iraq'," March 11, 2019

CNBC, "US likely to continue Iran sanctions waivers for Iraq, but neutering Tehran's influence is a long-term goal," December 5, 2018, Natasha Turak.

Consortium News, "Intel Vets Tell Trump Iran Is Not Top Terror Sponsor," December 21, 2017, Veteran Intelligence Professionals for Sanity (VIPS).

NPR (National Public Radio), "State Department Iran Specialist On Restoring Sanctions," November 9, 2018, Steve Inskeep.

Reuters, "Report contradicts Bush on Iran nuclear program," December 3, 2007, Matt Spetalnick.

The United States Department of Justice, "Two Individuals Sentenced in Connection with Work on Behalf of Iran," January 15, 2020, Office of Public Affairs.

Russia

Cohen, Stephen F., *War With Russia*, New York, Hot Books, 2019

Kovalik, Dan, *The Plot to Scapegoat Russia: How the CIA and the Deep State Have Conspired to Vilify Putin*, New York, Skyhorse Publishing, 2017.

Solzhenitsyn, Aleksandr I., *The Gulag Archipelago Three*, New York, Perennial Library, 1979.

Williams, Brian Glyn, Inferno in Chechnya: The Russian-Chechen Wars, the Al Qaeda Myth, and the Boston Marathon Bombings, Lebanon, N.H.: ForeEdge, 2015.

Al Jazeera, "NATO seeks to bolster Ukraine defenses amid 'Russian aggression'." March 6, 2019.

The Atlantic, "Russia Is Finished," May 2001, Jeffrey Tayler.

BBC News, "Russia's Putin: US agents gave direct help to Chechens," April 27, 2015, Sarah Rainsford.

Bloomberg Quint, U.S. Treasury Set to Borrow $1 Trillion for a Second Year to Finance the Deficit, January 29, 2109, Liz McCormick ,Saleha Mohsin, Alexandre Tanzi.

CounterPunch, "Chronology of the Ukrainian Coup," March 5, 2014, Renee Parsons.

Gallup, World-Low 9% of Ukrainians Confident in Government, March 21, 2019, Zach Bikus.

GlobalSecurity.org, First Chechnya War - 1994–1996.

MacAskill, E. "Ukraine crisis: bugged call reveals conspiracy theory about Kiev snipers," The Guardian, March 5, 2014.

Solomon, J. "Joe Biden's 2020 Ukrainian nightmare: A closed probe is revived," The Hill, April 1, 2019.

Johnston, M. "The Post-Soviet Union Russian Economy, Investopedia, June 25, 2019.

Hughes, J. "Chechnya : the causes of a protracted post-soviet conflict," LSE Research Online, 2001.

Cohen, Stephen F. "The Real Costs of Russiagate," The Nation, March 27, 2019.

Maté, A. "Where's the 'Collusion'?," The Real News Network (TRNN), December 23, 2017.

Pompeo, Michael R. "U.S. Foreign Policy in the New Age of Discovery", Keynote Address at CERAWeek: March 12, 2019.

Kofman, M. "The August War, Ten Years On: A Retrospective On The Russo-Georgian War," War on the Rocks, August 17, 2018.

China

Horton, M. "Is China Waiting Us Out?," *The American Conservative*, November/December 2018.

"China GDP Surpasses Japan, Capping Three-Decade Rise," Bloomberg News, August 16, 2010.

Freeman, Chas W. (USFS, Ret). "One Belt, One Road:" What's in It For Us?, chasfreeman.net, November 4, 2016.

Creveld, Martin Van, *A History of Strategy: From Sun Tzu to William S. Lind*, Kouvola, Finland, Castalia House, 2015.

Sweeney, J. Holsoe, J., Vulliamy, E. "NATO bombed Chinese deliberately," *The Guardian*, October 16, 1999.

Willmann, R. "3 criminal cases: Harvard professor Charles Lieber lies to DoD and NIH, plus two Chinese in science," *Sic Semper Tyrannis*, April 7, 2020.

Africom

Council on Foreign Relations, U.S. Africa Command (AFRICOM) Backgrounder, May 2, 2007, Stephanie Hanson.

Stars and Stripes, "AFRICOM commander calls for diplomatic push in Africa as US pulls troops from continent," March 7, 2019, John Vandiver.

Venezuela

FAIR (Fairness & Accuracy in Reporting), *Zero Percent of Elite Commentators Oppose Regime Change in Venezuela*, April 30, 2019, Teddy Ostrow.

Palast, George. "Don't believe everything you read in the papers about Venezuela," *The Guardian*, April 17, 2002.

Bellos A., Borger, J. "US 'gave the nod' to Venezuelan coup," *The Guardian*, April 17, 2002.

The Press and The Punditocracy

Blumenthal, Max, The Management of Savagery: How America's National Security State Fueled the Rise of Al Qaeda, ISIS, and Donald Trump, London/Brooklyn, Verso, 2019.

Cohen, Stephen F., War with Russia?: From Putin & Ukraine to Trump & Russiagate, New York, 2019.

Will, George. "Iraq War May Save Lives," ABC News March 16, 2003.

Beinart, Peter. "Even Iraq's Sinners Deserve to Be Heard," The Atlantic, June 18, 2014.

Morchoe, Richard. "Oh No! Bob Kaplan Says Now It's Moldova," Antiwar.com, July 19, 2014.

Boot, Max. "No Need to Repent for Support of Iraq War," Commentary, March of 2013,.

Masters, J (interviewer). "Was the Iraq War Worth It?," Council on Foreign Relation: Expert Roundup, December 15, 2011.

Henry, W. "When Andrew Sullivan Almost Seems Sane, You Know We're Crazy," The Federalist, May 14, 2018.

Blumenthal, Max. "Behind the Syrian Network for Human Rights: How an opposition front group became Western media's go-to monitor," The Grayzone, June 14, 2019.

Barnard, A. "Inside Syria's Secret Torture Prisons: How Bashar al-Assad Crushed Dissent," The New York Times, May 11, 2019.

Keller, Bill. "My Unfinished 9/11 Business," The New York Times, September 6, 2011.

Sierakowski, S. "Putin's Useful Idiots," The New York Times, April 29, 2014.

Brooks, David. "Voters, Your Foreign Policy Views Stinks!," The New York Times, July 14, 2019.

Fisher, M. "This quote about Putin's machismo from Angela Merkel is just devastating," Vox, May 20, 2015

Cohen, Richard. "The Lingo of Vietnam," The Washington Post, November 21, 2006.

Cohen, Richard. "A Winning Hand for Powell," The Washington Post, February 6, 2003.

Baldor, Lolita C. "'Hyperfit' women intrigue U.S. military," The Washington Times, July 21, 2019.

Wolfgang, B. "Military eyes 16-year-olds as ranks and candidates dwindle," The Washington Times, July 18, 2019.

Boot, Max. "The Case for American Empire," The Weekly Standard, October 15, 2001.

Newman, N. "Torture-Where's the outrage?," WHMP: The Civil Liberties Minute, May 14, 2019.

Force Structure

Snowden, Edward, Permanent Record, New York, Metropolitan Books, 2019.

Kelly, Mary Louise. Pulitzer Prize-winning author C.J. Chivers speaks with NPR's Mary Louise Kelly about his new book, The Fighters: Americans in Combat in Afghanistan and Iraq, All Things Considered (NPR), August 13, 2018.

Bacevich,, A. J. "One Percent Republic," The American Conservative, December/November 1913.

The Nation, "Generation Chickenhawk," July 11, 2005, Max Blumenthal.

Conclusion

De Tocqueville, Alexis, Democracy in America, Page 241.

Smith, Adam, An Inquiry into the Nature and Causes of the Wealth of Nations, Book 5, Chapter 3

All Things Considered (NPR), Pulitzer Prize-winning author C.J. Chivers speaks with NPR's Mary Louise Kelly about his new book, The Fighters: Americans in Combat in

Afghanistan and Iraq, August 13, 2018, Mary Louise Kelly with C.J. Chivers.

Antiwar.com, *Static From the Deep State*, February 8, 2019, Richard Morchoe.

<u>Independent Review,</u> *War and Presidential Greatness*, March 26, 2012, Gochenour, Zachary, Henderson, David.

Politico, "NSC official testifies Trump undermined national security with Ukraine pressure," October 28, 2019, Cheney, Kyle and Desiderio, Andrew.

The Washington Post, "At War With the truth: The Afghanistan Papers A secret history of the war," December 9, 2019, Craig Whitlock.

WATSON INSTITUTE FOR INTERNATIONAL AND PUBLIC AFFAIRS, Brown University, *Costs of War Project*.

Addendum, August 17, 2021

Horton, Scott, *Enough Already: Time to End the War on Terrorism*, Austin, TX, The Libertarian Institute, 2021

www.ingramcontent.com/pod-product-compliance
Lightning Source LLC
Chambersburg PA
CBHW072142100526
44589CB00015B/2056